America by the Numbers

☆ ☆ **America**

by the Numbers

*Facts and Figures from
the Weighty to the Way-Out*

Les Krantz

Houghton Mifflin Company   *Boston • New York*   1993

To my father, Manny Krantz (1910–1993)
Thanks for everything

———————

Copyright © 1993 by Les Krantz
All rights reserved

For information about permission to reproduce selections from
this book, write to Permissions, Houghton Mifflin Company,
215 Park Avenue South, New York, New York 10003.

Library of Congress Cataloging-in-Publication Data

Krantz, Les.
America by the numbers : facts and figures from the
weighty to the way-out / Les Krantz.
    p. cm.
  ISBN 0-395-65970-1 (paper)
   1. United States — Miscellanea.   I. Title.
E156.K73 1993   93-27307
973 — dc20   CIP

Printed in the United States of America

AGM 10 9 8 7 6 5 4 3 2 1

Contents

Preface   vi

Introduction   vii

Alphabetical Entries   1

American Highs   230

American Lows   231

Preface

Throughout this book, the latest available data were used. Because counting important things always takes time, events taking place in 1991, for example, are reported in 1992 or even 1993. In most cases, the data in this book concern events of 1991 or 1992. Wherever possible, 1993 "data to date" were used, or a reliable estimate was given and indicated as such. Sometimes data that involved dollar denominations from a previous year were updated and used. This was accomplished by using various established indexes such as the Consumer Price Index or the Department of Labor's Cost of Employment Index. In such cases, the data are identified as "adapted from." To make the statistics easier to use, they were often rounded. As a result, sometimes percentages will add up to 99% or 101%, when the actual total is 100%.

I owe much to those who made this book possible. Jim McCormick assisted me in developing the entries and contributed to the writing. Sharon Exley, my photo editor and friend, secured the illustrations. Mark Mravic came through for me, as always, polishing the text and providing material. Charley Custer also had a hand in polishing the manuscript. Luise Erdmann, my manuscript editor, really made the text sing where it needed it, and my editor, Liz Kubik, provided expert counsel, which was invaluable.

Introduction

This book is far more than just a statistical portrait of the nation. It is a compendium of what is perceived to be significant enough to be tracked by our government, our major corporations, professional organizations, opinion polls, and hundreds of other sources from which I have culled the data. With this in mind, I attempted to take a "snapshot" of the nation with a very wide lens. Accompanying the statistics are various commentaries, photographs, quotes, and anecdotal material, all of which paint the most up-to-date picture of our nation in print, at least for a little while.

Surely, the most revealing aspect of the data is that America's vital statistics are vastly different now than when most of us last consulted them. Even our most sacred institutions have undergone great change. Marriages among the young, for example, have declined from 80 to 60 percent; cohabitation has increased from 9 percent of couples in 1960 to 45 percent today. Suicide and AIDS are now the eighth and eleventh leading causes of death respectively. Americans spend $5 billion going to movies and $300 billion on gambling. Less than a generation ago the proportions were the opposite. When I was born, at the end of World War II, America was 90% white; today it is 75% white and by the year 2050, it is forecast, it will be 53% white.

A significant portion of the book deals with the fascinating but not so crucial things that take place in America. Did you know, for example, that among female celebrities, two in three are blondes (see "Blondes"); America's favorite chocolate, the Hershey bar, is 52% fat, and its favorite licorice, Good and Plenty, is fat free (see "Candy Calories"); 1 of 10 Americans has seen a flying saucer (see "UFOs"); and 5 in 10 Mafia dons are in jail (see "Crime Bosses").

America has its strengths and weaknesses, some of which are gleaned in this book, including some of my special selections found in the final pages, American Highs and American Lows.

Les Krantz

Actors

"I Would Like to Thank the Academy"

Those hallowed words are uttered by so few but dreamed of by so many. To be or not to be an actor is a decision that goes back to childhood. According to a Harris poll, 40% of American children think of an actor or actress as their hero, twice the number who regard athletes as their ideal.

There is certainly no profession in which it is harder to succeed in America. Although television, movies, and the stage offer tens of thousands of roles annually, it is most difficult to break into Hollywood. Each year about 250 major motion pictures are produced, with an average of 24 speaking parts in each one; almost exactly 100 times that number of actors compete for the roles. In the theater, television, and elsewhere, thousands of jobs are easier to get, but the pay is low. To make matters worse, in many of the less visible jobs, public recognition of the actors is not high.

Those intent on succeeding might want to note these statistics, compiled by the Screen Actors Guild and *The Jobs Rated Almanac:*

Incomes

Starting annual income	$3,310
Average income	$29,128
90th percentile income	$46,340
Top annual income, actor (Sylvester Stallone)	$20,000,000
Top annual income, actress (Julia Roberts)	$7,000,000

Roles Available

Male actors available	43,938
Male roles	31,991
Female actors available	32,564
Female roles	16,601

Michael Jordan is the most admired American among high school seniors. Photo, courtesy of the Chicago Bulls.

Admiration Societies
"I Want to Be Like Mike!"

Not only are they singing it, they are casting their ballots for him, too — Michael Jordan, the star of the three-time world champion Chicago Bulls basketball team. Jordan topped the list of the most admired individuals among college-bound students in a nationwide poll conducted by *Careers*

& Colleges magazine and the National Association of College Admissions Counselors.

The survey asked 3,500 high school seniors whom they most admired. Two athletes, two politicians, and two members of the TV show "Beverly Hills, 90210" made the list, along with a CBS news reporter and a billionaire. Below are the most admired, their field, and the percentage of votes they received among students of their gender.

Michael Jordan (basketball)	57%
Connie Chung (news anchor)	47%
Monica Seles (tennis player)	25%
Mario Cuomo (governor)	17%
Tori Spelling (actress)	15%
Patricia Schroeder (congresswoman)	13%
Bill Gates (entrepreneur)	14%
Luke Perry (actor)	12%

Adoptions
Fewer Infants Available

At any given time in the U.S., up to 2 million couples want to have children. Unfortunately, the difficulty in finding a child for those who must adopt has increased in the last two decades; the adoption rate peaked in 1970 at 89,200 and then started a decline, leveling off to around 50,000 in 1992.

One reason for the drop is that fewer babies are being born, thanks to later marriages, birth control, abortion, and publicly funded programs to control fertility. Foreign adoptions, too, have decreased since Korea curtailed the number it allowed in 1992 and Romania sharply restricted adoptions of its children the same year.

This list shows the number of adoptions in the U.S. during specific years, as compiled by the National Council for Adoptions.

Children Born in the U.S.

Year	Number
1951	33,000
1961	61,600
1970	89,200
1975	47,700
1982	50,720
1986	51,157
1992	50,000

Children Born Elsewhere

Year	Number
1982	5,707
1984	8,327
1986	9,946
1987	10,097
1991	9,008
1992	6,536

Home of Foreign Children Adopted in 1992 (Leading Countries)

Country	Number
Romania	2,552
Korea	1,787
Former Soviet Union	432
Guatemala	428
Colombia	403
Philippines	353

Adultery

Money may not buy true happiness, but it does seem to ensure a fair share of sexual activity, at least for married folks. Statistics reveal that marital infidelity is directly proportional to employment status and income. Wives who work outside the home have more affairs than wives who are homemakers. The more money husbands earn, the more likely they are to be unfaithful.

This list represents the proportions of married men who have affairs in different income brackets, according to data in a study by *American Couples.*

Under $5,000	16 in 100
$5,000 – $10,000	25 in 100
$10,000 – $20,000	33 in 100
$20,000 – $30,000	45 in 100
$30,000 – $40,000	55 in 100
$40,000 – $50,000	67 in 100
$60,000 or more	70 in 100

But it isn't just the affluent who have affairs. According to a 1991 book about American habits, *The Day America Told the Truth*, which included a sophisticated survey of more than 2,000 Americans, 31% have had an affair and 49% have considered it. Among those who did more than just think about it, the affairs took place under these circumstances:

Casual meeting/a bar	28%
Just happened/accident	12%
Growing friendship	10%
Introduced by friend	7%
Sexual attraction	7%
Pursued by eventual lover	7%
Midlife crisis	2%

. . . and with whom

Friend	24%
Coworker	23%
Old flame	21%
Stranger	20%
Friend of spouse	15%
Prostitute	9%
Boss	7%

Profile of "the Other Woman": According to the study cited above, she is a white woman in her forties, has bisexual tendencies, has teenage children, and is "an open book" about her most private experiences. "She has had four affairs during her marriage: with a friend of her husband, two neighbors, and a veterinarian," say the researchers.

Age Discrimination
Age Bias Complaints Soar

Call it downsizing, call it restructuring, or call it some other harmless-sounding euphemism, but American businesses continue to pare their work force in the economic downturn of the early 1990s. And though the job market is said to be difficult for new college graduates, older employers are taking their share of the hit.

According to the U.S. Equal Employment Opportunity Commission, money awarded in job-related bias suits through either court action or out of court settlements totaled $65 million in 1992 — the second highest total ever. A record portion of that total, $50.7 million, or 77%, came in settlements of age discrimination suits as employers attempted to reduce their payrolls by replacing higher-salaried experienced employees with juniors whom they could pay less.

The EEOC found 70,339 complaints filed overall, the second highest total since 1964, when the Civil Rights Act became law. That number was close to the all-time high set in 1988, when 70,749 complaints were filed. For the first time, the complaints included filings based on the new Americans with Disabilities Act — 774, or 1.1% of the complaints — even though the law did not go into effect until November 1992.

Older employees now join minorities as those who suffer discrimination in the workplace. Racial discrimination, in fact, continues be the most frequent reason for equal opportunity complaints, at 40% of all complaints; that, however, represents a decline of 3% from 1991.

Charges based on sexual bias rose 2.2% from 1991, to 29.8% of all complaints. The EEOC attributed the increase in this category to a higher number of sexual harassment cases filed.

Aging

"We as a society have not really addressed how to plan for an aging population." — *Diane Piktialis*, Work/ Family Directions

Tests on animals lead researchers to believe that all animals have an outer limit to the length of their lives: for mice it is 3 years; for horses, 30 years; chimpanzees can live to age 60. Although humans now know various life extension techniques — proper diet and exercise, to name two — under the best of circumstances human life is set at about 100 years. The reason continues to baffle gerontologists.

Since the beginning of the 20th century, Americans have increased their average life span by 50% — from 50 to 75 years. Today's life expectancy is 71.5 years for men and 78.7 for women. However, this miracle brings its set of problems: how to plan for aging and its inevitable complications. Surely the biggest ones are health problems and adjustments in lifestyle.

At present, seniors represent 12.6% of the population, up from 4% in 1900. With this enormous change in such a short time, increasing health care needs and the need for larger retirement incomes will become priorities with few solutions in sight. And the situation may get worse. By 2030, according to the American Association of Retired Persons, the life expectancy will be 72.5 years for men and 80.0 for women; by 2080 it will be 74.7 years for men, 81.3 for women. In a hundred years, seniors will account for about a quarter of the U.S. population — twice their present proportions.

This table on annual health care spending per person, listed by age, is adapted from figures supplied by the Census Bureau.

0–5	$1,389
6–7	$730
18–44	$1,242
45–64	$2,402
65+	$4,840

The table assumes that older individuals will not require confinement in nursing homes, which cost about $25,000 to $30,000 annually per person. Who will pay the bill remains the biggest question. Keeping seniors healthy enough to stay out of nursing homes is one answer, as well as a goal of most geriatric researchers.

AIDS Awareness Among Teens

Not only adults, gays, and narcotics users are afraid of becoming AIDS victims; so are teens, who have some answers about what can be done about the problem, according to a broad survey undertaken by one of them, Jeffrey Brodsky, 18, of Manchester, N.H.

His new polling service, National Scholastic Surveys, questioned 2,100 high school seniors in 56 schools in 37 states, providing a window on the general student attitude toward one of the most dreaded epidemics of the century.

Here are some of the significant findings of the poll:

• According to 55% of the students, teachers with AIDS should be identified; 88% say they should be allowed to continue teaching.

- Students with AIDs should be allowed to remain in school, say 88%.
- Public figures should state publicly if they are HIV-positive, say 51%.
- Condoms should be passed out in schools, 81%.
- The availability of condoms does not encourage sex, 78%.
- Although 28% of the students carry a condom on dates, only 20% of those who are sexually active use them.

AIDS Threatens Minorities
Opinions and Reality Don't Jibe

"It's denial. We deal with the fact that we have sex. We say we don't have abortions, but we do. We say we don't have bisexual and intravenous drug-using partners, but we do. It's all denial." — *Eleanor Hinton, director of programs for the Council of Negro Women.*

Some 6 of every 10 women of color in the U.S., statistically the fastest-growing segment of the HIV-infected population, believe that they will not contract AIDS, according to a 1991–92 report by Women of Color Reproductive Health Poll. It also revealed that 84% of black women and 83% of Hispanic women say they have little chance or none of getting the disease. The survey, sponsored by the Consortium Media Center and the National Council of Negro Women for the Women of Color Reproductive Health Poll, questioned 1,157 black, Asian, Hispanic, and Native American women aged 18 and older in 1991.

According to the Census Bureau, 13,873 black women had contracted AIDS as of June 1992; 5,505 Hispanics were infected, 123 Asians, and 57 Native Americans.

This list notes the proportions of the populations of the three largest racial groups in the U.S. who are infected, according to the book *What the Odds Are.*

Whites	1 in 1,873
Blacks	1 in 552
Hispanics	1 in 583

What does this mean for minorities? Blacks and Hispanics are three times more likely than whites to be infected.

Air Bags

Their Time Has Finally Come

General Motors' introduction of the automobile air bag in the 1970s was met with little enthusiasm in the industry and with seeming indifference by the driving public. It was too cumbersome, too ugly, and too expensive, even though it had proved to save lives: overall automobile safety improves by 18% in vehicles with air bags.

How times have changed. The air bag has become de rigueur in the 1990s, and with good reason. Drivers now want them, so much so that the law will require air bags as standard features on all new cars in the near future. In the meantime, air bags, along with antilock brakes, have become strong selling points as standard features and popular optional items. A 1992 survey conducted for *Woman's Day* by the consulting firm Yankelovich Clancy Shulman found that 24% of women car buyers put safety first when considering an automobile purchase, while 23% made value their top priority. The response from automakers: driver's side air bags are now widely available as standard equipment or as an option, and it's rare that a midsize or full-size sedan doesn't have one. Now the passenger-side air bag is a new selling point, as automakers compete in the increasingly tough market for new car sales.

GM studies, however, remind the driver that lap and shoulder belts are not on the way out. These traditional seatbelt configurations reduce accident fatalities by 42%, and the belts combined with air bags reduce fatalities by 46%. GM's statistics show that the average driver will use an air bag once in 175 years — i.e., most drivers will never use one. Safety belts, air bags, and energy-absorbing steering wheels come into play in fewer than 1% of driving emergencies.

Here are some additional facts about air bags, from the National Highway Traffic Administration:

- All 1998 passenger cars and all 1999 light trucks will have air bags and safety belts for the driver and right front passenger, as required by law.
- Air bags provide the best protection in head-on crashes.
- An air bag inflates faster than it takes to blink an eye.

Airline Ailments

Chronology: Estimated number of annual air passengers and most advanced aircraft at the time

1783	2 (fire balloon)
1800	100 (gas balloon)
1906	1,000 (biplane)
1913	20,000 (monoplane)
1938	4 million ("Clipper")
1952	100 million ("Comet")
1960	200 million (jet prop)
1970	400 million (turbojet)
1990	700 million (supersonic jet)

Pan Am flew away for good in 1991, when it filed for bankruptcy.

Maybe the swallows happily fly into San Juan Capistrano on time; unlike the swallows, airplanes flying into La Guardia Airport must compete for landing time with other air traffic around the holidays. Since the demise of People's Express, the airline industry has lacked an identifiable archfiend, but disgruntled travelers abound.

What's everyone grumbling about? Only 1 in every 4,000 passengers gets bumped due to overbooking, which translates into just a paltry 125,000 travelers per year. Upon arrival, 99.55% get their luggage at the baggage claim; the other minute percentage (2.8 million passengers) is out of luck. About 80% of the flights are on time.

Breakdown of Complaints: Each year 7,000 passengers complain to the U.S. Department of Transportation about some aspect of airline service. Here are the proportions of consumer complaints, according to the *Air Travel Consumer Report:*

Flight difficulties	1 in 2
Baggage	1 in 5
Refunds	1 in 5
Ticketing problems	1 in 13
Overbooking	1 in 14
Smoking	1 in 35
Fares	1 in 42

Advertising	1 in 134
Credit	1 in 420
Tour problems	1 in 485

Who's at Fault? No one knows for sure, but a careful tally is made by the Department of Transportion of the airlines getting the flak. This list cites the number of complaints per 100,000 passengers during March 1993.

Southwest	0.30
Delta	0.61
Northwest	0.74
United	1.04
America West	1.23
USAir	1.24
American	1.43
Continental	1.84
TWA	2.60

Airline Arrivals

More Than One Quarter Late

A report by the U.S. Department of Transportation in March 1993 revealed that complaints against the nation's air carriers are up 28.5% from the previous month and up 11.5% from more than a year ago. Chief among the complaints is that flights fail to arrive on schedule. This report showed that 73.5% of flights by the 10 largest carriers arrived on time (within 15 minutes). Compared to March 1992, 9% fewer get to the gate when they are supposed to. During 1991, 9% fewer arrived on time.

Below are the carriers' records for flights that arrived on time, according to the report.

Alaska	91.6%
Southwest	87.6%
American West	82.8%
Northwest	77.5%
TWA	74.1%
American	73.9%
USAir	71.8%
Continental	69.5%
United	69.2%
Delta	67.3%

Cities on Schedule: This list cites the airports with the best and worst records for on-time arrivals and the percentage of flights that arrive on time, according to the Department of Transportation:

The Best	
Detroit Metro	92.4%
Memphis	92.4%
Phoenix	91.7%

Raleigh/Durham	91.7%
Las Vegas	90.6%

The Worst

Boston	79.5%
Los Angeles	81.5%
Newark	82.2%
San Francisco	82.9%
Dallas/Fort Worth	83.3%

Airline Routes

Busiest of Them All

Where are all those people going who flood the airports? The facts are that the most traveled routes involve passage to or from the Big Apple — 6 of the 10 busiest airline routes have New York City as the point of arrival or departure.

This list shows the most heavily traveled airline routes and the number of passengers who fly them annually, according to the *Travel Industry World Yearbook*.

Domestic Departures

New York–Los Angeles	2,998,000
New York–Boston	2,948,000
New York–Washington	2,877,000
New York–Miami	2,590,000
Los Angeles–San Francisco	2,423,000
New York–Chicago	2,383,000
Dallas–Houston	2,306,000
Honolulu–Kahului (Maui)	2,055,000
New York–San Francisco	2,042,000
New York–Orlando	2,004,000

Foreign Departures

Mexico	2,696,000
United Kingdom	2,273,000
West Germany	1,209,000
Bahamas	979,000
Japan	973,000
France	845,000
Dominican Republic	655,000
Jamaica	578,000
Italy	458,000
Netherlands Antilles	408,000

Air Safety

It's not too difficult to spot first-time fliers. They are the ones who hang on every word of the flight attendant's preflight instructions. They are the ones who swallow hard when use of the oxygen mask and the flotation cushion is demonstrated. They are the ones you hear hyperventilating each time the aircraft bounces or makes a noise.

Though the odds of your being killed on your next airplane trip are 1 in 4.6 million, there may be reason to be alarmed. Unlike other carriers, airplanes have a high number of passengers who die when the vehicle is in a major accident. When an airliner is involved in a crash, the chances are 2 in 3 that someone on board will die, which compares to 1 in 258 in an automobile.

Fortunately, the U.S. Department of Transportation has good news for nervous fliers: the number of accidents that occur in general aviation has gone down significantly in the last twenty years. Here is its tally of aircraft accidents between 1970 and 1990, the latest annual statistic available.

1970	4,712
1975	3,995
1980	3,590
1985	2,737
1989	2,201
1990	2,138

There are even more encouraging figures. Only about 1 of each 100 air accidents involves commercial passenger carriers. The majority of crashes affect private aircraft, the military, and air freight carriers.

Alzheimer's Disease
Disease Without a Cure

One of the greatest fears of aging is the fear of dementia, through either stroke, Alzheimer's disease, or other nervous system disorders. The most mysterious and the chief cause of senile dementia is Alzheimer's, for which there is no known cure. But a vast amount of research on the disease has been done since 1980, when it began to capture the attention of the medical world. Today, according to the Alzheimer's Association, 4 million Americans suffer from Alzheimer's, and 100,000 die from it each year. The number of Alzheimer's sufferers in the U.S. is expected to rise to 14 million by the year 2040.

First diagnosed by a German neurologist in 1907, Alzheimer's affects 5% of the U.S. population over age 65 in its severe form, 10% in its mild and moderate forms. Those 85 and older are at greatest risk from the disease. But Alzheimer's is not solely a disease of the elderly; it has been diagnosed in patients as young as their mid-40s.

Once the disease takes effect, symptoms of confusion, memory loss, and emotional dullness can be so severe that sufferers are dangerous to themselves and require constant supervision. Patients are frequently confined to nursing homes, at an estimated cost of $36,000 a year. Even more debilitating than the cost of medical care may be the untold emotional hardship on the families of sufferers.

This list represents the percentage that suffer from Alzheimer's disease at various ages, according to the Alzheimer's Association and the National Institute on Aging.

65-year-olds	6%
75-year-olds	20%
85-year-olds	47%

Given figures this high and the increasing life expectancy in the U.S., money is speedily being infused into research. The next list represents federal research funding for Alzheimer's.

1989	$134 million
1990	$150 million
1991	$247 million
1992	$282 million
1993 (est.)	$294 million

Animal Experiments
Animal Rights and Wrongs

Prodded by animal welfare groups, Avon has stopped using animals for consumer product safety testing. Revlon has followed suit, as have Amway, Mary Kay, Fabergé, and Benetton's cosmetics division.

Because of pressure from animal rights groups, many companies no longer publicize figures for their use of animals; however, at one time the Department of Agriculture kept track of animal testing. The last report available, from 1988, listed 140,471 dogs, 42,271 cats, 51,641 primates, 431,457 guinea pigs, 331,945 hamsters, 459,254 rabbits, 178,249 "wild animals," and 1.6 million rats and mice. In 1986, the congressional Office of Technology Assessment reported that "estimates of animals used in the United States each year (for experimental purposes) range from 10 million to more than 100 million." The office admitted that its estimates might be unreliable, but it suggested that 17 million to 22 million animals per year are used for research.

Man's Best Friend: Our closest animal soulmates, dogs, and our nearest biological cousins, primates, have a privileged status. The only federal law concerning animal experimentation is the Animal Welfare Act, which bars giving dogs continual electric shocks, which produce a state of helplessness, and giving monkeys drugs that keep them happy or oblivious of pain.

The law does not deal with experimental procedures, nor does it affect mice, rats, birds, and farm animals.

The following figures, compiled by the Investor Responsibility Research Center, represent the number of experiments on animals in one year and the companies that performed them.

American Cyanamid	55,460
Rorer Group	39,984
Bayer	39,983
American Home Products	38,033
ICI Americas	34,065
Smith Kline Beecham	33,011
Merck	28,499
Johnson & Johnson	22,541
Schering Plough	20,162

Answering Machines

Today's new answering machines have remote control devices, voice recognition, and a calendar and clock; the next innovation may be a voice-activated kiss. Ten years ago answering machines were a rarity, and people were frequently unsure how to respond to them. Now, more than 50 million machines answer the nation's phones (46% of all households).

These figures show the growth in sales of answering machines, according to *Electronic Industries*.

1983	2.2 million
1984	3.0 million
1985	4.2 million
1986	6.5 million
1987	8.8 million
1988	11.1 million
1989	12.5 million
1990	13.8 million
1991	14.5 million

Arts Funding
Americans Give Green Light

Ever since Senator Jesse Helms attacked the National Endowment for the Arts for funding Robert Mapplethorpe's homoerotic photograph exhibition, the government has wheedled and whined about supporting the arts. Most Americans, however, support federal funding for the arts, an opinion shared by large majorities of all demographic segments of the population.

A Louis Harris poll called "Americans and the Arts" reported that 60% of Americans — mostly those in the East and South — call for more federal funding, and 52% believe it should support individual artists directly. An overwhelming portion, 80%, believe that "for the arts to come forth with their best and most creative efforts, the arts need to operate with a minimum of government control." About 69% back a $5 individual tax increase to fund the arts; 64% favor a hike of $10.

Athletes' Salaries

Roll Over, Babe Ruth

Poor Babe! He earned scarcely more than President Hoover: the chief executive's salary in 1930 was $75,000; Babe got a paltry $80,000, about as much as the *average* ballplayer earns in two weeks today.

Though professional athletes were always well paid in the big three sports — baseball, basketball, and football, few made more than $100,000 annually until the 1970s. Today, a professional athlete, even an average one, is often a millionaire. In major league baseball, for example, salaries have escalated 17.83% annually in the last ten years. In 1983, the average player earned $143,756; today, an average salary is more than $1 million. This list represents average salaries in 1982 and 1991.

	1982	1991
Baseball	$241,497	$1,012,000
Basketball	$235,000	$1,041,667
Football	$95,925	$414,920

The average baseball salary in 1992 is up 275% since 1983. In basketball, in which average salaries are now $1.2 million, the increase is 365%, and in football average earnings are now close to $500,000, up 271% in ten years. Salaries today account for 50% to 70% of the costs of doing business in sports.

Where does it come from? The fans will claim ticket gouging, but in fact, new or vastly increased sources of revenue have brought in the dollars to make the insanely high salaries possible: corporate sponsors, skyboxes, concession deals, and the licensing of souvenir merchandise. The real cash cow, however, has been television rights. A typical NFL television contract now goes in the *billion*-dollar range, twice as much as it did ten years ago. Baseball and basketball are also commanding similar fees.

New Partners in Cri . . ., er, Time: A revolutionary new deal is happening in baseball. Beginning in 1994 and for six years, NBC, ABC, and Major League Baseball will be partners in selling commercial time on their broadcasts. The deal may sound good, but it's good for broadcasters rather than teams. It is projected that in the first few years, MLB will collect about half as much as it did under its sweetheart deal with CBS. A noted sports economist, Gerald Scully of the University of Texas, commented, "It is clear that the golden age of revenue growth is over, at least for the time being." Today the age of risk will replace the guaranteed upfront revenue.

Automobile Colors

Most people in the Western world see more automobiles daily than any other object. The most popular color should be therefore obvious to everybody, right? The fact that most people don't have a clue about what it is says something about the changed status of cars, for at one time a car was a family's most prized and pampered possession.

Automobile colors are almost always a sign of the times. During the Great Depression, black was the most popular color. Green, the color of renewal, was in vogue after World War II. In the sixties and seventies, white dominated. Today's colors are cool and have a high-tech look, with various shades of blue dominating.

This list shows the most popular colors in 1991 for full- and midsize cars, according to *Automotive News*.

Light blue	10.08%
Silver	9.36%
Dark blue	8.72%
Bright red	5.79%
Black	5.57%
Medium blue	3.80%

Dark red	2.99%
Light brown	2.16%
Beige	1.45%
Purple brown	0.97%

Hot, Hot, Hot! When it comes to luxury cars, however, no cool colors will do. Red is hot — the top color. And flamboyance is back for those who want to show off. After years of decline, Cadillac has returned as the top seller in luxury cars, complete with extra length and fender skirts, outselling Mercedes-Benz and BMW by 3 to 1.

Automobile Thefts

A 50–50 Chance

Each year more than 600,000 automobile owners head for their cars to find them gone. If it hasn't happened to you yet, it's an even chance that it will in your lifetime.

Having an ignition key and no place to put it is the second most likely way an American will be the victim of crime. First place goes to larceny-theft — and guess where it happens most often? (Hint: it has four wheels and it's not a shopping cart or a stagecoach.) When it happens, the average cost to you is $110 — $10 for the sunglasses you left on the seat and $100 to fix the window the thief smashed.

But what do the smart criminals want to steal? This list, compiled by the Highway Loss Data Institute, names the models (in order of preference) that car thieves prefer for the model years 1991–92, proving that thieves have as good taste as any well-heeled auto buyer.

Infiniti Q45
Volkswagen Jetta
Chevrolet Camaro
  convertible
Acura Legend 4-door
Lincoln Mark VII
Toyota Supra
Ford Mustang
Cadillac Brougham
BMW 525/535
BMW 318/325 4-door

Will you ever get it back? According to *What the Odds Are*, the probability is 2 in 3, the best recovery odds of any type of stolen merchandise.

Baby Busters

No one imagined that any generation could have more impact on the size of the American population than the soldiers returning from World War II. Their offspring, as well as the children of the rest of their generation — now called the Baby Boomers — have outdone their parents by giving birth to 80 million new Americans between 1961 and 1981 — the "Baby Busters."

Today's Busters will be a unique generation in American history. They will be the first since the Civil War who will be unable to match the standard of living of their parents. They are also the most diverse generation of Americans yet. Though their parents were born into a nation that was close to 90% white, the Busters will live in a nation that is 70% white. They will share their country's bounty, not only with more blacks and American-born Hispanics, but also with the new immigrants of the 1980s and 1990s: Mexicans, Filipinos, Koreans, Cubans, Vietnamese, Indians, Pakistanis, and others from Asia, Africa, and Ireland.

The most dramatic feature of the Busters will be their having grown up in a nation that has demoted children to last place. Their parents, products of the "Me" generation, raised them in a climate of different priorities than those of past generations. Divorce, day care, and corporate transfers, just a few of the trends that flourished, will change how this new generation carries on American values.

The most significant change will surely be the pressures they will face in solving the nation's debt crisis. They are likely to spend their entire lives dealing with the federal deficit. This has already caused friction between the Busters and the oldest generation of Americans, who, unlike earlier generations, are enjoying more financial security. During the initial phase of this new generation, the poverty rate has more than doubled among households headed by persons under 30 years old. The economic writer Robert Kuttner has referred to their plight as "generation disease." Among the maladies: College tuitions have risen so high that many people can no longer afford higher education. Those who manage to attend college are often faced with low-paying jobs or none at all upon graduation.

The Busters will be the survival generation, that is, the generation that must put out fires they did not start. As the heat rises, there is likely to be a growing conflict with the older generations, who are enjoying the remnants of their excesses of the fifties, sixties, and seventies, decades in which promises were made to Americans which will have to be kept by the Busters. Two side effects that many expect will be ethnic rivalries and a declining economy.

Bad Guys

The Criminal Gender Enigma

Of the slightly more than 11 million Americans arrested annually, 9 million (82%) are men and 2 million (18%) are women. Just what is it that makes the criminal populace overwhelmingly male? Considering that crime costs the American public $300 billion annually, an explanation might prove cost effective. Every imaginable academic discipline, from economics to psychoanalysis, offers answers. Recently, a related question has been raised: Should both sexes pay equally for the sins of criminals when they are so overwhelmingly males?

The June Stephenson Solution: Hitting men where they are deeply vulnerable — in their wallets — is the choice of the psychologist June Stephenson, who advocates a radical idea: make men pay for the costs of crime in the U.S. In her book *Men Are Not Cost-Effective*, Stephenson argues that since males commit the vast majority of crimes in this country, women should be given a special exemption on their income tax forms to relieve them of having to share the costs that men incur by their crimes. Suggesting a direct "man tax" on men, she suggests $100 a year.

Their blood rising, men have been quick to attack Stephenson's idea. The economist Raaj Sah of the University of Chicago called the argument "absurd" and said no rational theory of jurisprudence supports such an approach. But Stephenson is willing to give a guy a break. If it is determined that biological fate is the cause of male criminality, she admits that penalizing men for fulfilling their deep biological urges would be unfair. On the other hand, maybe she won't be so forgiving. According to Stephenson, one man phoned her publisher and said he was coming to kill the author. The FBI traced the call and arrested the suspect — a man. Just one more statistic to support her argument?

These figures represent the proportions of males vs. females who are arrested for various offenses in the U.S., according to the Department of Justice.

	Male	Female
Illegally possessing a weapon	93%	7%
Burglary	91%	9%
Robbery	91%	9%
Murder, manslaughter	90%	10%
Drunken driving	87%	13%
Arson	87%	13%
Aggravated assault	86%	14%

Bank Failures

Far Better or Worse?

In 1992, 122 FDIC-backed banks failed, 2 fewer than in 1991 and the lowest figure since 1985, when 120 failed, costing the FDIC $1 billion. The price of failure has risen since '85, though. The failed banks in 1992 carried assets around $40 billion, a figure second only to the record $63 billion in the closure of 124 banks in 1991. Altogether, since 1980, more than 1,000 U.S. banks have closed, but the number per year has declined since 1988.

The December Surprise: In early 1992, the federal government forecast that as many as 200 U.S. banks would fail before the end of the year. The prediction was made because of the passage of new federal rules mandating a minimum 2% equity capital, to take effect on December 19. Many said a large number of banks would be unable to comply, hence a "December surprise" was predicted, when the banks would announce insolvency because of insufficient equity. December 19 came and went, and FDIC officials and members of the news media who had spread across the financial battlefield hunting for bodies found none. While interest rates were dropping, no banks had fallen since December 18. Like all waves of crisis, that one receded, and depositors went back to the business of saving money or investing it in bank offerings.

This list shows the number of commercial banks closed yearly since 1985 and what it cost to bail them out, in billions, according to the FDIC.

Year	Banks	Assets	Bailout Cost
1985	120	$8.7	$1.0
1986	138	$7.0	$1.7
1987	184	$6.8	$2.1
1988	221	$35.7	$6.6
1989	207	$29.0	$6.3
1990	169	$15.7	$3.4
1991	124	$63.0	$7.4
1992	122	$46.0	$4.6

Bank Heists

Johnny Carson: *"Why do you rob banks, Willie?"* **Willie Sutton** *(convicted bank robber): "Cause that's where the money is."*

In spite of tighter security, surveillance cameras, and "bandit barriers" of bulletproof glass, people still try to rob banks. In recent years, between 7,000 and 8,000 U.S. banks have been robbed each year. Most robberies occur on Friday afternoons and are over-the-counter crimes, meaning, according to the FBI, "Hand over the cash cases." An average holdup nets about $2,000.

In 1991, 8 of the 15 largest U.S. cities — and some smaller cities as well — reported a record number of bank heists. Los Angeles had 810, tops in the nation, breaking the record of 742 set in 1983. Thefts more than doubled in Atlanta, from 109 the previous year to 247. Chicago went from 59 to 95. The Minneapolis–St. Paul area logged 73, breaking its 1981 record of 59.

"We've got an increasing drug problem and we're finding that a primary consideration in almost all our robberies," said Carmen Piccirillo of the FBI bank robbery unit. Three out of five arrested bank robbery suspects have tested positive for drugs. Bob Long, another FBI agent, cites another reason: "When you go through so-called hard times, it seems that crime may take an increase, but there aren't any statistics to back that up." Another reason offered has been the growth in branch banking, which has spread banks to isolated areas with poor security.

Banks may be easier pickings for robbers today, but the penalties are severe if they are caught, and 3 out of 4 are. Those convicted face up to 25 years in prison, a few years less if they were unarmed. Long points out that bank robbers "aren't the most intelligent people."

Though there is no readily identifiable reason, most bank robberies take place in large coastal cities. Here are the cities with the most bank robberies in 1991, a year that saw many records set, and the percentage of change from the previous year.

Los Angeles	810	+177%
New York City	464	−53%
Miami	345	14%
San Diego	317	−5%
Seattle	311	+56%
Atlanta	247	+138%
Boston	207	−78%
Philadelphia	158	+61%
San Francisco	158	−106%
Cleveland	106	+27%
Chicago	95	+36%
Detroit	93	+59%

Baseball — Home Runs
Who Hit the Longest Ball of All?

Though it is well known that Babe Ruth, with his 714 career homers, was the home run king until Hank Aaron compiled the all-time record of 755, the biggest unknown in baseball is who hit the longest ball of all. Possible candidates read like the *Who's Who* of home run kings:

Top 10, Career Home Runs
Hank Aaron   755

Detroit's Rob Deer gets ready to slug one out of Tiger Stadium, the launching pad of some of the longest hits in baseball.

Babe Ruth	714
Willie Mays	660
Frank Robinson	586
HarmonKillebrew	573
Reggie Jackson	563
Mike Schmidt	548
Mickey Mantle	536
Jimmie Foxx	534
Willie McCovey	521

Veteran baseball watchers will almost invariably give the honor of the longest ball to "the King of Swat," the Babe, but no one knows for sure what the longest home run is. IBM is now measuring all the home runs hit out of major league parks. At midseason 1993, the longest home runs measured have been as follows:

Player/Team	Feet
Dean Palmer/Texas	477
Ken Griffey, Jr./Seattle	471
Archi Cianfrocco/ Montreal	470
Andres Galarraga/ Colorado	464
Rob Deer/Detroit	439

Of all the ball parks, Tiger Stadium seems to be the launching pad for the longest home runs, with 5 of the 10 longest hits. The average length of a home run has been 384.7 feet since IBM began its tale of the tape.

Baseball Beefs

Hot Dog Prices Are Hard to Swallow

Fans may be cheering in the stands, but they are also crying in their beer. According to 42% of 305 volunteer *USA Today* "team members" — a group the newspaper formed to check out the general state of ball games — food is the biggest gripe and the priciest feature at the parks. Despite the beef, the ballpark dog has a noble history.

It was in 1850 that the butchers' guild introduced the spicy smoked pork sausage that would eventually capitivate the American kid. It was introduced as "dachshund sausage." Harry Stevens, a vendor at the Giants' Polo Grounds in New York City, stuck one on a bun in 1906 and sold it in the bleachers as "a red-hot dachshund sausage." The rest is history. Today, 16.5 billion "dogs" are turned out every year, and baseball parks are still one of America's favorite places in which to buy them at any price. The Big Apple is the top dog when it comes to a hefty price: a hot dog costs $3 at Yankee Stadium. Baltimore sells them for $2.75. The average around the league is $1.81. Cincinnati and Philadelphia fans have a bargain — $1.

Other complaints about prices and the percentage that was irked about them were as follows:

Tickets	31%
Souvenirs	14%

Parking	12%
Nothing	1%

And Who's to Blame? For a change, it's not the umpire or the team's manager. The volunteer team members blamed the parties below in the following percentages:

Owners	51%
Players	35%
Fans	7%
Concessionaires	7%

But What Are They Doing about It? The volunteers reported that their plans for future games are as follows:

Will attend more	28%
Will attend fewer	15%
Will attend about the same number	41%
Will not attend	16%

Basketball

Up from the Dead

In 1980, NBA game attendance dropped amid negative publicity about cocaine scandals, high player salaries, and other public relations problems. While many television viewers looked elsewhere, 18 of the NBA's 23 teams lost money; 4 teetered on the edge of bankruptcy. In a decade-long turnaround that began in 1983, NBA revenues increased from $140 million to $1.1 billion in 1992, when an average game was attended by 17,000 spectators.

No doubt the clean image of the game's superstars — Kareem Abdul-Jabbar, Magic Johnson, Larry Bird, and Michael Jordan — contributed to rebuilding the game's popularity.

Television broadcast revenues grew to $750 million by 1992, a 25% increase from 1988. Today's 27 NBA teams have a market value ranging from $32 million to $85 million each; the highest is the Orlando Magic, which fetched the latter amount in 1990. The next expansion teams, scheduled for 1995–96, are expected to go for $100 million. Of the major sports — baseball, basketball, football, and hockey — basketball was the only one to turn a profit in 1992 for its host broadcaster, NBC. This enabled the NBA owners to negotiate a $750 million, four-year contract with NBC for 1993 while baseball's owners were weighing an annual $144 million pact.

Each year the NBA compiles a list of "defined gross revenues" that are shared with the players. Below are listed those revenues in 1992 (in millions), according to the National Basketball Players Association.

Tickets	$352.1
Network TV	$142.3
Cable TV	$65.7
Local cable TV	$58.0
Local TV	$55.2
Local radio	$25.3
International TV	$13.2
Exhibition games	$12.9
Other	$0.8

Other 1992 NBA revenues (in millions), which are not shared with the players, are:

Skyboxes	$150
Expansion fees	$100
Merchandise licensing	$75
"Signage"	$50

The Bird Man (Larry Bird, shooting) and others like him brought basketball back from the depths. Photo, Sarah Hood; courtesy Mass. Office of Travel & Tourism.

Bedroom Activities

Sex and sleep may be the all-time favorite activities in the bedroom, but what comes next? Eating? Entertaining? Surprisingly, slightly more than 1 in 6 people eat in the boudoir, and almost an equal number entertain there. But what else do most people do?

According to a recent survey of 1,020 men, conducted by LDB Interior Textiles, the most popular activities and the percentage that engages in them are as follows:

Read	62%
Talk on the telephone	58%
Listen to music	51%
Watch television	42%
Exercise	26%
Work	22%
Eat	18%
Entertain	18%

Beer Barrels

Sales Up, Hopes Down

The barons of brewing are crying in their beer as they look at a future that is quite bubbly, but the bubbles are flat, at least in beer. Aging baby boomers and the health-conscious youth market increasingly turn toward diet soda and sparkling water as their liquid refreshments of choice; legislators plead for higher taxes on alcoholic beverages as a way of generating revenue; a public outraged at drunken driving cries for stricter penalties for violators; and minority groups and women express anger at being targeted by the alcohol industry. All of which adds up to a bear market for brewers. For only the second time in a decade, annual domestic beer sales saw a gain, a paltry one of 0.3%, up from 189.8 million barrels in 1991 to 190.4 million in '92.

By and large, beer drinkers are buying American; imported beers filled a negligible share of the market, 8.2 million barrels. A report in *Beverage Industry* magazine in January 1993, by John C. Maxwell, Jr., of Wheat, First Securities, found only Anheuser-Busch increasing sales, by 1 million barrels, to 87 million in 1992. Its flagship Budweiser label remained the dominant domestic brand, although its sales slipped 3%, to 45.9 million barrels from 47.4 million in 1991. The top gainer was Miller Genuine Draft, up 19%, to 8.9 million barrels. Miller High Life dropped 14%, to 8.9 million barrels.

This list shows barrelage (in millions) and the market share percentage of the five top domestic beer brands, according to *Beverage Industry*.

Budweiser	45.9	24.1%
Miller Lite	18	9.7%
Bud Light	13.5	7.1%

Coors Lite	12.8	6.5%
Busch	10.2	5.3%

Beer Bellies: Beer sells better in some places than others. The southern states have relatively low beer consumption rates — 6 of the 10 lowest-consuming states are below the Maxon-Dixon Line (no doubt a result of many counties in the "Bible Belt" prohibit the sale of alcoholic beverages).

The following states have the highest and lowest annual consumption of beer per adult, according to the book *The Best and Worst of Everything.*

Highest Consumption (in Gallons)

New Hampshire	52.4
Nevada	48.5
Wisconsin	46.7
Hawaii	45.0
Montana	43.3

Lowest Consumption (in Gallons)

Utah	21.6
Alabama	24.6
Arkansas	24.9
Oklahoma	25.6
Connecticut	26.6

Behavioral Risks
The 3 Ns: Smokin', Drinkin', and Eatin'

The Good News: Smoking continues to decline. **The Bad News:** Americans are getting fatter.

Smoking rates hover around 23%, down from 27% five years ago, according to the government's Behavioral Risk Factor Surveillance Survey. The percentage of Americans who are

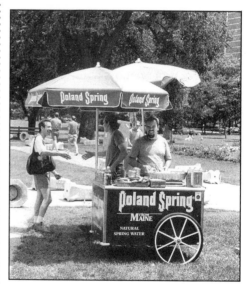

Mineral waters are catching the fancy of the young and cutting into beer sales.

overweight is around 23%, up 2% from 1987.

Disparities in smoking were found across the country. The heaviest concentration of smokers is in Kentucky and Michigan, where 29% of adults smoke; the lowest is in Utah, with 17%.

Overweight individuals ranged from 16% in Colorado to 27% in the District of Columbia, which also ranked highest, at 73%, for those leading a "sedentary lifestyle," defined as having fewer than three 20-minute exercise sessions weekly; Colorado was the lowest, with 45%.

The survey also found that:

- A large proportion of Americans, 29%, do not engage in physical activity in their leisure time. The state in which the most citizens are physically active is Montana, 82% of the population. The worst area is Washington, D.C., where 52% do not pursue physical activity.
- As much as 15% of Americans engage in binge drinking, defined as 5 or more drinks on one occasion in a given month.

Big Game

A bighorn sheep's head, a bearskin rug, antlers above the fireplace, were prized trophies at one time. Today, populations of big game are strictly protected in the last ranges they inhabit. The following lists note the numbers of some of the animals once stalked by hunters, according to the Public Land Statistics, Department of the Interior.

Bighorn Sheep: The list below gives state populations for bighorn sheep on federal land and includes Rocky Mountain, Dall, California, and Desert bighorn sheep. Smaller populations can be found in most other western states.

California	3,205
Alaska	3,200
Arizona	3,095
Oregon	1,600
Colorado	1,559
Wyoming	1,214
Utah	1,065
Montana	1,000
New Mexico	80

Shoot all the bighorn sheep you please, but do it with a camera. Hunting them and other big game is strictly forbidden on federal land. Photos, courtesy of Wyoming Division of Tourism.

Where the Deer and the Antelope Play: In addition to its 370,000 deer and antelope, Wyoming is the home of the country's largest herd of buffalo, in Yellowstone National Park. The larg-est populations on other federal lands are:

State	Antelope	Deer
Wyoming	172,852	196,938
Montana	49,933	127,700
Oregon	15,780	204,300
Utah	12,550	190,000
Colorado	12,510	199,307
California	6,210	101,000
New Mexico	4,900	58,000
Arizona	1,147	35,140

Bear Population: The following figures for bear populations in the U.S. refer to the total numbers of bears on public federal lands and include black, grizzly, and brown bears. California, which used to count so many bears in its domain that it put the animal on its state flag, now holds fewer than 400 bears on its federal lands. Alaska, on the other hand, America's last great wilderness, still has a fairly healthy bear population. The bear is all but gone from the wild in the East, except in specially protected areas of the Appalachians.

Alaska	8,700
Oregon	1,980
Colorado	1,243
Montana	650

Utah	503
Wyoming	433
California	385
Arizona	80
Eastern states	22

Black-owned Firms

In the Black

Some predicted that the nineties would mean doom for many U.S. companies, but to date, black-owned businesses have fared better than many of the corporate giants, according to *Black Enterprise* magazine.

Revenue at the top 100 black businesses jumped 10.4% in 1991, to $7.9 billion, while revenue for the nation's top industrial corporations fell 1.8%.

Earl Graves, the publisher of *BE*, said that recession times means merely tightening the belt another notch. Black businesses have always lived in a "be ready" mode for bad economic times, he added. The report indicated that black businesses held down costs wherever possible; for example, while the revenues of the top 100 businesses rose significantly in 1991, employment rose a mere 3.9%, to 32,590 workers.

The top 10 black-owned companies in the magazine's report, with their revenues (in millions), are:

TLC Beatrice International	$1,542.0
Johnson Publishing	$261.4
Philadelphia Coca-Cola Bottling	$256.0
H. J. Russell	$143.6
Barden Communications	$91.2
Garden State Cable TV	$88.0
Soft Sheen Products	$87.9
RMS Technologies	$79.9
Stop Shop and Save	$66.0
Bing Group	$64.9

Black Ph.D.'s

"When you're dealing with such small numbers, [moderate] percent changes are important." — *Deborah Carter, American Council of Education*

A significant percentage gain in black Ph.D.'s has been registered, mostly at black colleges, according to figures from the National Research Council. Its report showed a 13% in-largest number of black Ph.D.'s, 1,047, came in 1982.

Education experts attributed the increase to college recruiting programs begun in the 1970s, because traditionally black students take eight or nine years to get a doctorate. Frank Matthews, the publisher of *Black Issues in Higher Education*, noted that twelve black colleges graduate the most blacks, though three predominantly white schools are among the top twenty. He said, "Black colleges are still producing and carrying a disproportional share of the load."

Blondes

Though only some 15% of all American men and women are naturally blonde, according to a Clairol survey, 18% of the women artificially color their hair to various blonde tones. Roughly speaking, that means 1 in 3 American women are blondes.

Why blonde? Americans have had a love affair with flaxen hair since Mae West appeared on the silver screen in the thirties. Blonde Betty Grable dominated the forties; Marilyn Monroe, the fifties. By the sixties, so many female stars had caught on to

Earl G. Graves, publisher, Black Enterprises magazine, keeps tabs on the achievements of top blacks and black-owned companies.

crease from 1989 to 1991, when 933 blacks earned the degree, 4% over the 1990 figure of 897, which represented a 9% increase over the 821 black Ph.D.'s in 1989. In 1992, 18 out of every 1,000 white college students earned doctorates compared to 8 out of 1,000 black college students. The

America's preference for the golden hue that the majority of women in the spotlight were blondes.

A 1991 CBS News story reported that 73% of all *Playboy* centerfolds were blondes, 70% of all magazine cover models, 65% of all Miss Americas, and 64% of all female TV news personalities.

Whether blondes have more fun, no one knows, but according to the book

Dolly Parton, one of America's favorite blondes, has her own amusement park, Dollywood, in Pigeon Forge, Tenn.

The Best and Worst of Everything, they definitely have more publicity. Madonna, who until June 1991 adorned herself with blonde locks, received 42% more press coverage from 1986 to 1991 than the number-two female headliner, Jane Fonda (an "off-blonde"), followed by Marilyn Monroe (long-deceased blonde), Cher (a brunette, at one time a redhead), and Meryl Streep (blonde, of course).

Blue Jeans

"The secratt of them Pents is the Rivits that I put in those Pockets." — *Jacob Davis, July 8, 1872, in a letter to Levi Strauss proposing to split the patent rights*

Carson City, Nev. (ca. 1870): Jacob Davis, a Jewish tailor from Latvia, knew a dissatisfied client could be serious business, maybe even deadly serious. His disgruntled customer, a silver prospector called "Alkali Ike," was daily ripping his pants from stuffing them with too many ore samples. To solve the problem, the cautious tailor sewed rivets in Ike's pants, and the idea caught on around town. "My nabors are getting yealouse of these success," the haberdasher wrote to the wholesaler who sold pants to him, a

Mr. Levi Strauss. Soon, Strauss put up the $68 needed to secure a patent, and an about-to-be-famous partnership began.

Those fancy pants are still admired today and are the uniform of the comfort culture from Manhattan to Moscow, where a good pair of faded jeans can sell for more than $100. With the U.S. being the world's point of denim departure, an astounding two of the three largest U.S. apparel makers are rooted in the manufacture of casual pants. Below are the sales figures (in billions) for 1990, compiled in *Superbrand*'s report on the top sellers.

Levi's, Dockers	$3.5
Hanes, L'Eggs	$3.0
Lee, Wrangler	$2.5
Liz Claiborne	$1.5
Fruit of the Loom	$1.0

A Million Jeans Ago: In 1981, 502 million pairs of jeans were sold, but by 1985 sales had dropped to 416 million, and today they have dropped to below 400 million pairs. The April 5, 1992, *Chicago Tribune Magazine* reported: "The initial appeal of jeans, as a 'raw' garment 'cooked' by use, plunged like Narcissus into its own reflection. Ralph Lauren's touting his Polo jeans

The world's first blue jeans, Levi's 501 (ca. 1882), are just as faded and worn as today's model. Photo, courtesy Levi Strauss & Co.

as genuine '30s dungarees was a tip-off: His product was aimed at people pretending to be preppies pretending to be cowboys."

Bluntness

Pardon Me, But . . .

Ever tell somebody he has parsley stuck in his teeth and it's ruining his smile? Or tell a woman she has a run in her pantyhose? Or, worst of all, that a person has bad breath and it's bowling you over? If you're squeamish about being too candid, you're not alone.

There's something about confrontations over picky matters that foreshadow larger confrontations that could happen as a result. Perhaps that's why people avoid them. Or is it because they live in glass houses, and they fear giving others an easy excuse to smash them? Maritz Marketing Research for Oral-B Laboratories has tried to tabulate this perhaps not so trivial phenomenon, showing the percentage of men and women who are unabashedly willing to tell it like it is.

Situation	Men	Women
Smudge on face	89%	77%
Food stuck between teeth	61%	53%
Dandruff	22%	14%

Boating Accidents

Licensing Might Help Prevent Them

With high-speed boats growing in number in the U.S., the National Transportation Safety Board is urgently recommending that states consider licensing recreational boaters to curb the reckless ones. It won't be an easy task, with naysayers insisting that education is the better way to solve the problem.

In Florida, the state with the highest number of boating accidents, the number of power boats capable of 50 mph has grown from 100,000 to 500,000 in just ten years, and some of them can top 100 mph. The safety board says that in a survey of 18 states, 37% of boat operators involved in fatal accidents probably had consumed alcohol and 85% who drowned were not wearing life jackets. Licensing laws would cut those numbers drastically, the board says.

This list shows the states with the most boating accidents and the number of other mishaps in 1991, according to the board.

Florida	1,019
California	750

Michigan	357
New York	257
New Jersey	241
Texas	227
Missouri	214
Wisconsin	208
Washington	188
Ohio	168

Bombs

Until March 1993, not very many Americans worried about the likelihood of falling victim to a terrorist's bomb. Perhaps the bombing of the World Trade Center in New York City awoke us to our vulnerability. According to the FBI, bombings are up significantly in the last two years, as can be seen in the data for 1991 and 1992.

	1991	1992
Incidents	2,491	2,989
Deaths	26	27
Injuries	246	349

Though these figures represent a 20% increase, bombings are relatively rare, especially those causing injury or death. Even in states with the highest bombing rates, the odds of being a victim are relatively slim, according to a recent report by the FBI. This list represents those odds in the states with the highest rates.

Colorado	1 in 93,000
Florida	1 in 126,000
Washington	1 in 128,000
California	1 in 129,000
Illinois	1 in 165,000
Virginia	1 in 176,000
Ohio	1 in 202,000
Michigan	1 in 249,000
Texas	1 in 268,000
New York	1 in 366,000

Book Buying
"Superstores" Emerge

With the number of bookstores soaring by 73% in the last decade, to 17,320, and sales more than doubling, to $8 billion annually, the major bookselling chains are getting the message that independents have known all along: people like to buy books in stores with a homey feeling.

The chains' answer is an industry turnaround. Instead of 2,500-square-foot stores pushing best sellers on busy shoppers, they're opening giant stores of up to 30,000 square feet that carry up to 150,000 titles and serve "ambiance" as well. Piped-in music, espresso bars, and overstuffed chairs provide a homey touch as well as a library feeling for those who just wish to browse.

Leonard Riggio, the chairman of Barnes & Noble, says his firm has learned that people will spend 40% more in a superstore; Robert Haft, the founder of Crown Books, estimates 25%. Given that both chains offer big discounts on many books, that translates to customers purchasing more books for less money. Driving the new message to the cash register, where it belongs, Barnes & Noble has opened 17 superstores around the nation, Crown 16, and Bookstop 44; latecomer Waldenbooks opened the first of 20 planned big stores, under the name Basset, in Stamford, Conn., in 1992.

Other significant book facts include the following, according to *Newsweek* magazine:

- 81% of the nation's adults read at least one book in the last year; 58% gave or received books at Christmas.

- Reading is the favorite leisure activity of 25% of adults; 19% prefer watching TV.
- Consumers spent $7.9 billion on books in 1991 and $4.9 billion on going to the movies.
- The fastest-growing segment of the industry, children's books, more than doubled in sales between 1985 and 1991.

Breast Cancer
Saving Breasts Varies by Region

About 1 in every 9 American women, 13 million in all, will suffer from breast cancer. Although surgery is not always the prescribed treatment, it is the most common, but the practice varies widely throughout the nation. Women in some areas are five times more likely to have their breasts saved through conservation surgery than those elsewhere.

In 1985, a consensus of cancer experts said that breast-conserving procedures such as the removal of either a breast cyst or tumor (a lumpectomy) should be considered as alternatives to the removal of all or part of the breast (a mastectomy). After a year, acceptance of those recommendations varied widely around the nation. The rates of breast-saving surgery varied from 21% in Massachusetts to 4% in Kentucky, and women treated in large urban teaching hospitals had fewer mastectomies. Dr. Ann Butler Nattinger, of the Medical College of Wisconsin in Milwaukee, isn't sure that this discrepancy still exists, but her group is studying the data from 1990 to find out.

This list outlines the rates of breast-saving operations by region, according to a Medicare study of patients aged 65–79, which was released in 1992.

- Middle Atlantic (N.J., N.Y., Pa.) — 20% of 6,334
- New England (Conn., Mass., N.H., R.I.) — 17% of 2,288
- Pacific (Alaska, Calif., Hawaii, Oreg., Wash.) — 13% of 5,000
- East North Central (Ill., Ind., Mich., Ohio, Wis.) — 11% of 6,436
- South Atlantic (Del., D.C., Fla., Ga., Md., N.C., S.C., Va., W. Va.) — 10% of 6,457
- Mountain (Ariz., Idaho, Mont., Nev., N. Mex., Utah, Wyo.) — 10% of 1,636
- West North Central (Iowa, Kans., Minn., Mo., Nebr., N.Dak., S.Dak.) — 8% of 3,225
- West South Central (Ark., La., Okla., Tex.) — 7% of 3,252
- East South Central (Ala., Ky., Miss., Tenn.) — 6% of 2,245

Burglaries
Boon to Home Security Systems

The number of residential burglaries annually in the U.S. has increased steadily, from 1.5 million in 1982 to 2.1 million in 1993, meaning that about 1 in every 20 homes in the U.S. is burglarized every year. According to FBI statistics, intruders take an average of $1,018 in property from each burglary; the highest total came in 1991, when burglars got an average of $1,201 in valuables from every haul.

An Ounce of Prevention: An increasing number of home owners keep guns to protect themselves from a invasion. A study conducted in Seattle, however, indicated that a gun in the home is forty times more likely to kill a family member or friend than a crim-

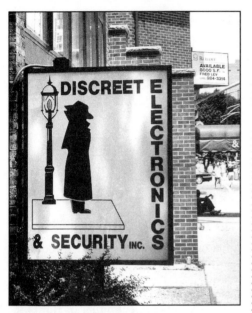

Burglaries by the millions have created the billion-dollar home security industry, made up primarily of small businesses like this one in Chicago.

$15 to $30 a month in monitoring fees for systems connected with a central station. Deluxe models can run as high as $4,000.

Police say that sturdy doors, deadbolt locks, secure windows, outdoor lighting, dogs, and neighborhood watch groups are often effective in discouraging prowlers. Joe Mele, a loss prevention expert at the National Crime Prevention Institute at the University of Louisville and a police consultant in crime prevention, said studies prove that having a home security system in itself is a strong deterrent to burglars. "I think anyone who has any sort of collection, whether baseball cards or stamps or dolls or paperweights, ought to have an alarm," he said.

inal. A security system, a far safer route, is the choice of 1 million Americans annually. In 1992, they spent $1 billion on them. Ironically, the average cost of a system, about $1,000, is close to the average loss in a burglary. The most basic home security systems cost about $500 to install and about

Cabbies of New York
A United Nations of Taxi Drivers

The language barrier is proving more effective in raising a barrier between cabbie and passenger than the once ubiquitous bulletproof window. Pakistani, Haitian, Arabic, Spanish, and African languages spoken from the front seat are hardly conducive to exchanges of anything but money.

A demographic study by New York's Taxi and Limousine Commission shows that 43% of those applying for a new job came from the Indian subcontinent; eight years ago, only 10% of those who applied were from that region. In 1984, about 1 of every 4 prospective New York drivers was born in the U.S.; now it's only 1 in 10. The others come from 84 countries.

This table on the national origin of applicants for New York City taxi licenses has been adapted from data supplied by the Taxi and Limousine Commission.

National Origin	1984	1991
South Asia	10.0%	42.8%
Africa	4.2%	25.8%
United States	25.8%	10.5%
Caribbean	26.8%	7.6%
Middle East	6.3%	7.0%
Former Soviet Union	3.1%	6.8%
Rest of Europe	8.2%	5.6%
South America	7.6%	3.8%
Asia	7.5%	2.8%
Central America	0.7%	1.9%

$50,000 Gross: Most new drivers find work at one of 29 taxi fleets, according to the Metropolitan Taxicab Board of Trade. They work 12-hour shifts, have expenses of $77 to $91 a shift, and bring in about $200 on an average day.

Caesarean Births
Slight Decline Not Enough

Doctors haven't gotten the message: most of the caesarean sections they perform are not needed; the surgery can endanger the lives of both mother and infant and add to the cost of childbirth. That is the conclusion of a study by the Public Citizens' Health Research Group, founded by Ralph Nader. The study disclosed that the rate of caesarean births in 1990 was 22.7%, down a mere .3%, from 1989, when it was 23%. The extra cost of the operations was a staggering $1.3 billion.

In 1970, when caesareans were used chiefly in emergencies, the rate was 5.5% of all births; it reached a high of 24.7% in 1988. The "optimal" national caesarean rate is 12%, according to a scale devised by Dr. Edward Quillian, dean of the School of Medicine at the University of California. Calling the 1990 decline still not enough, the group blasted doctors who perform unnecessary sections. They cited the reasons as fear of a lawsuit if something goes wrong, the convenience of scheduling labor for both doctor and patient, and the increased revenue the procedure brings both doctors and hospitals — almost twice as much as a vaginal birth does.

Candy Calories

American GIs won friends for the nation all over Europe and Asia by passing out candy bars to children. But that was in the forties, fifties, and sixties. In the nineties even kids, not only grownups, know that most packaged candies have enough fat to turn them all into heart attacks waiting to happen by the time they grow up.

Some American candies, however, are worse than others. Researchers at Tufts University's Diet & Nutrition Center examined the nutritional content of some of America's favorite treats. Here are some of their findings — both the good and the bad:

Fat Stuff
- Mr. Goodbar: 1.65 ounces, 240 calories, 15 grams fat (56% fat calories)
- Reese's peanut butter cup: 1.6 ounces, 250 calories, 15 grams fat (54% fat calories)
- Hershey's milk chocolate: 1.55 ounces, 240 calories, 14 grams fat (52% fat calories)
- Almond Joy: 1.76 ounces, 250 calories, 14 grams fat (50% fat calories)
- Kit Kat: 1.5 ounces, 230 calories, 12 grams fat (47% fat calories)
- M&M's peanut: 1.74 ounces, 250 calories, 13 grams fat (47% fat calories)

Won't Kill You
- Good & Plenty: 1.8 ounces, 191 calories, 0 grams fat (0% fat calorie)
- Life Savers: 0.9 ounces, 88 calories, 0 grams fat (4% fat calories)
- Sugar Daddy: 2 ounces, 218 calories, 1 gram fat (4% fat calories)
- York Peppermint Pattie: 1.5 ounces, 180 calories, 4 grams fat (21% fat calories)

- Tootsie Roll: 2.25 ounces, 252 calories, 6 grams fat (21% fat calories)
- Junior Mints: 1.6 ounces, 192 calories, 5 grams fat (23% fat calories)

Capital Punishment

America has been accused of having a killing pace. For those convicted of capital crimes, indeed it does, and the pace is quickening. Though the nation had a hiatus in executions for almost a decade, in 1993 a dubious anniversary took place: the 200th execution since the death penalty was reinstated.

Until the U.S. government temporarily outlawed capital punishment in 1972, the number of prisoners executed declined steadily. Following are the numbers of condemned prisoners put to death during various periods in modern American history.

1930s	1,667
1940s	1,284
1950s	717
1960–67	191
1968–76	0
1977–93*	200

*as of May 4

Who Are We Kidding . . . or Killing? About 90% of those condemned to death are still awaiting execution, and it is doubtful that many of these 2,600 now on death row will actually lose their lives. The death penalty has been adopted in 36 states, but only 21 states have actually carried out the sentences. Texas has executed the most, 57 prisoners. During the period from 1930 to 1967, 45.4% of those executed were white and 53.5% were black. From 1930 to 1990, 45.9% were white and 53.0% black, according to the Department of Justice.

Those who advocate capital punishment as a way to save taxpayers' money should look at the real costs of carrying out sentences. According to the Associated Press, each execution costs between $3 million and $10 million, whereas a life sentence costs $1 million. With 25,000 homicides annually, the death penalty is expensive.

Celebrities Postmortem

Who's Still Alive in Our Consciousness?

Paula Abdul is in love with Cary Grant; you can tell by the look of love she gives him in the soft drink commercial they starred in — six years after his death. New technology has made it possible to "team" on film and CD today's stars and yesterday's late ones, including such favorites as Humphrey Bogart, James Cagney, and Nat King Cole.

In order to find out who of the deceased celebrities is "most alive," the editors of *The Best and Worst of Everything* searched for stories in 86 major U.S. magazines between 1986 and 1991. Listed below are the late stars who received the most attention and the number of articles about them.

Elvis Presley	362
John Wayne	168
Laurence Olivier	157
Marilyn Monroe	156
John Lennon	126
Charlie Chaplin	103
Fred Astaire	97
Cary Grant	81
Orson Welles	79
Humphrey Bogart	70

Four of the top ten celebrities — Olivier, Lennon, Chaplin, and Grant — were British. Other top scorers included James Dean (69), who trails Bogie by only 1 point, Gary Cooper (67), and, a surprise, Frank Capra (52), the director of the Christmas classic *It's a Wonderful Life*. Capra outscored such highly regarded figures as Alfred Hitchcock and John Ford.

Cellular Phones

When AT&T invented cellular phones in 1947, it envisioned them principally as car phones for business use. Little did they anticipate that the cellular phone would turn the car into a veritable office on wheels for salespersons and that the portable phone would pervade everyday life, with corporate types chattering away on flip phones at ball games, on the beach, and on city sidewalks. There are even reports that some parents buy cellular phones for their children out on a date and that disabled persons' lives have been saved by the phones.

The Underestimate of the Century? In the 1980s, surveys for AT&T projected the potential market for cellular phones at 900,000 by the year 2000. The giant communications corporation, not interested, abandoned several of its cellular lines. Those surveys grossly underestimated the phones' potential. By 1991, there were 10 million cellular phones in use in the U.S. By decade's end there could be manyfold more. In a move that made headlines nationwide, AT&T offered McCaw Cellular Communications, the principal manufacturer of the instruments, $3.8 billion for a mere 33% of its business.

In 1993, most cellular phones are sold to nonbusiness customers. The industry has created 100,000 new jobs; prices are down, from the $700 range of a decade ago to the $200 range; quality is up; and demand keeps soaring. The U.S. market is the world's largest, with 10 million cellular phone subscribers who pay 50 to 75 cents per minute for each call. Now American companies are battling with their foreign competitors to build cellular systems in the vast, untapped markets of Eastern Europe, South America, and India. Can the day be far off when everyone on the planet will be connected via the microwave transmitters of the cellular phone network?

The sales of cellular phones have been as follows, according to data collected by the Electronic Industries Association and the Computer and Business Equipment Manufacturers Association.

1986	280,000
1987	300,000
1988	500,000
1989	870,000
1990	2,100,000
1991	3,100,000

Census Bureau
Counting Heads in the Stratosphere

In addition to cries of the need for Census Bureau reform because of undercounting — mostly of minorities — an additional chorus of dismay has mounted against the expense of the count. In 1990, the census cost $2.6 billion, or $25 a head, a 25% increase over the 1980 count, said the General Accounting Office.

Census officials put part of the blame on the public. The 1990 rate of return of census questionnaires was 74%, compared to 81% in 1980. The low return forced the bureau to hire 300,000 "enumerators" to follow up on the 34 million questionnaires not returned, which cost $317 million. Complicating matters further, the composition of the U.S. family has changed — from 78% of households headed by married couples in 1980 to 56% in 1990 — and the 44% of this group which responded were unlikely to give information about their former spouses.

The bureau took the blame for some of its problems. Because it failed to identify vacant housing units before sending out the questionnaires, 8.6 million mailings were sent "nowhere" and 4.8 million to addresses that were not housing units. The GAO offered some ideas that could improve the next census: streamline the questionnaires, ask the Postal Service to help identify bad addresses, sample a portion of nonresponding households to learn what the problems are — and prepare for more trouble in 2000.

Chicken Stuff

America's chicken producers are no longer small shoestring farmers who cram their birds into coops.

Today the chicken business is a multi-billion dollar industry and is considered by agribusiness to be one of the great success stories of farming, with 102 million broilers slaughtered each week by large corporations that rear them in well lighted sheds which are hundreds of feet long.

Frank Perdue's Nipple Drinkers: Chicken tycoon Frank Perdue, fourth largest broiler producer in the U.S., likes to pamper his chickens. His birds are housed in 150-yard-long buildings each containing about 20,000 birds. Next to tending his chickens, Perdue likes to talk about his "nipple feeder," a device that allows even the most henpecked of the batch to get as much liquid as the ruler of the roost. It had to be a "boy genius," Perdue maintains, who dreamed up the invention. Happier, well-fed chickens are good for Frank's business—6.8 million of his birds wind up as someone's chicken dinner each week.

Perdue's chicken company is among the eight corporations which account for 50 percent of the 5.3 billion birds killed annually, according to the industry trade journal *Broiler Industry*. Studies have shown that each bird knows its place among a flock of 90, but above that they fight frequently. But not to fret—the proverbial pecking order is part of growing up as a chicken and "chickens have learned to live with it," according to Chris Whaley, public relations director of Perdue Farms.

Child Smokers
Kids Like Old Joe

It may come as a shock to the growing number of trendy adults who have thrown away their cigarettes, but smoking among teens, beginning with ninth-graders, hasn't declined for a decade; about 3,000 young people start the habit each day. This disturbing news was revealed by U.S. Surgeon General Dr. Antonia Novello, who adds the fact uncovered by the Centers for Disease Control that Camels was the preferred brand for 30% of the ninth-graders who smoke — five times the market share of Camels among adult smokers. Dr. Novello blames Camels' Old Joe campaign, which began in 1988.

Before Old Joe began, only 2% of young people smoked Camels. Now Old Joe is as familiar to American youngsters as Mickey Mouse. Nevertheless, according to the CDC, Marlboro is far and away the most popular brand-name cigarette among ninth-grade smokers, 43% of whom use it. Next in rank after Camels is Newport, with 20%, and Winston, with 3.3%. The three brands together account for almost 95% of the total youth market. Novello's answer: Shout out the truth about cigarettes and demand industry accountability.

Child Support
Deadbeat Dads in Trouble

How tough is it to make dads pay child support? Plenty tough, according to a U.S. Census Bureau report, which indicates that nationwide, almost half of the women deserving child support payments receive less than their due: 24.8% of the women receive none, and 23.8% receive only partial payments. Moreover, the annual support payments expected average $3,292, but those actually received average $2,252. The women owed that money are not living in the lap of luxury. The average income of women who receive child support payments is $16,171; for those who do not get their money, the average income is $13,761. Neither figure is much above the national poverty level — $13,359 for a family of four, the absolute minimum level necessary to live on.

Armed with those figures, Governor William Weld of Massachusetts is setting out to create the toughest child support enforcement laws in the country. He is spearheading a package of new laws against deadbeat dads which he estimates could save the state $67 million a year by getting 7,000 families off the welfare rolls within three years. The package is almost certain to serve as a model for other states. Among the bill's features:

- Hospitals must encourage fathers to acknowledge paternity by signing sworn statements of fatherhood.
- Willful failure to make support payments could be punished by up to five years in prison.
- Driver's licenses and trade and professional licenses could be revoked for failure to comply with the child support laws.
- The state could legally attach workers' compensation payments, unemployment benefits, and lottery winnings.
- Employer and labor union files and telephone and utility company records could be searched to track down deadbeats.

Christmas Gifts
If You're Going to Play Super Mario Brothers, at Least Wear a Nice Shirt

A Harris poll taken in 1992 suggests that parents are fighting back against Nintendo brainwashing, judging from the kinds of gifts they're giving their kids. Though the kids may clamor for electronic hypnosis, their parents would rather have them well clothed and well read.

When the poll asked 1,190 parents what they had in mind for the kids, clothing was the most popular selection of 77% of the respondents. Non-electronic games and puzzles scarcely beat out books, 70% going for the fun gifts and 69% for books. Dolls were on the shopping list for 48% of the parents, 2 percentage points above the mundane gift certificate or the gift that always fits, cash. Stuffed animals, at 41%, were popular, as was sports equipment, at 40%. In contrast, electronic games, the current rage, were considered by only 29%, the lowest percentage among the top choices mentioned.

What are the most popular gifts for Mom and Dad or for a lover or friend? Clothing again, along with money and perfume or cologne.

True Believers: The average respondent in the poll think kids stop believing in Santa Claus around age 8. Nearly half thought of the holiday as a time for family gatherings rather than religious communion. Turkey is still considered the appropriate Christmas dinner — it's served by 50% of American households; 38% feast on ham.

Cigarette Prices
Penny a Puff

Time was when cigarettes cost about 1 cent each. Now they are about 12.5 cents each, about a penny a puff for most brand-name cigarettes — an increase of 1,250% since 1961. What may be most remarkable is that the "narcotic power" of cigarettes has been drastically reduced by the trend toward low tar and nicotine, yet they still cost more.

In 1961, according to the Tobacco Merchants Association of the United States, a favorite brand package of smokes cost 27 cents; ten years later it rose to 40 cents, in 1981 to 70 cents, and in 1991 it skyrocketed almost 150%, to $1.82. In 1993, many merchants are charging $2.50 a pack, and the end is not in sight.

Cigarettes

"The makers of Camels are naturally proud of the fact that, out of 113,597 doctors who were asked recently to name the cigarette they preferred to smoke, more doctors named Camel than any other brand." — Life *magazine ad, July 8, 1946*

The tradition of magazines selling cigarettes to their readers continues today. More than $500 million is spent in the U.S. annually on cigarette advertising. And does it ever work! A carton of Marlboros is the most common purchase in the supermarket. In fact, about 50 million Americans smoke cigarettes daily, and they spend about $50 million each and every day. Every day, 1.5 billion cigarettes are purchased. That adds up to half a trillion annually, which looks like this — 500,000,000,000 — and measured end to end adds up to 26 million miles of cigarettes a year.

Passing It Along: You choose not to smoke? Like it or not, almost everybody is inhaling tobacco smoke through the phenomenon of "passive smoking." Studies show that the risk of cancer is doubled in nonsmokers who are married to smokers who consume 20 or more cigarettes a day. The American Cancer Society estimates that more than 6,000 nonsmokers die each year in the U.S. due to the inhalation of others' cigarette smoke.

Antonia Novello, the U.S. surgeon general, warned the nation: 3,000 youths start smoking every day.

Class Rings

With monstrous college loans to pay off and the prospect of no job after graduation, class rings are no longer standard fare on the fingers of recent college graduates. Like college tuitions, class ring costs have risen manyfold. A 14-karat-gold class ring that sold for $35 in 1949 will cost today's students between $300 and $400, and ringmakers are finding that only 3 out of 10 are buying rings at graduation.

Alumni with jobs buy 35% of all class rings, keeping the class ring market alive. Jostens, Inc., one of the nation's largest makers of class rings, reported in 1992 that 11.5% of its customers had been out of school for three or more years. For example, a direct mail promotion by the University of Illinois Alumni Association for a "fine class ring" brought 500 responses. Lou Liay, director of the association, said there had been a steep downturn in senior class sales in the 1960s and a revival of interest in the late '70s and the '80s.

Jostens spokesman said the 75% of the rings they sell annually through telemarketing are for alumni. Colleges and universities make a percentage on the sales of rings through their bookstores. Ring makers say they may or may not pay a percentage on sales made through direct mail and telemarketing, depending on whether their school insignia are copyrighted.

Are They Really Alums? Since proof of graduation is not required, no one knows how many bogus alumni buy a class ring. Mike Garvey, a spokesman for Notre Dame, wondered how strict

Some buy their school rings, others earn them, such as one of these NCAA final-four basketball rings. Photo courtesy of Jostens.

his school was on the question, so he asked at the campus bookstore. "If I wanted to buy a ring," he said, "they would not sell it to me until they verified that I had gone here and graduated." A Notre Dame alumnus himself, Garvey doesn't have a class ring.

Collection Plates

Catholics Study Parishioners' Donations

The tough economy has been hard on just about everybody, including the Catholic church, which has been forced to close churches and schools for lack of funds. In a first-of-its-kind survey of 330,000 Catholics conducted for the Life Cycle Center of Catholic University in Washington, D.C., church leaders learned to their dismay that in 1991, 60% of Catholic households gave the church an average of less than a dollar a week. The study found that although many parishes asked their parishioners to contribute 5% of their annual income, the average donation was closer to 1.2% ($262 per year) — the lowest percentage of any faith, according to another survey, conducted by General Social Surveys from 1987 to 1989.

This study also revealed that Mormons gave the most, 6.2% of their income, or $1,713 a year; Baptists gave 2.9%, or $734 a year; and Lutherans 1.3%, or $349 a year.

Of the total Sunday collections, 19% of Catholics gave an average of $950 a year, 19% gave $294, and the remaining 62% gave just $42. Churches with 10,000 or more members had household donations of $237 a year; in churhes with 5,000–10,000 members, the average annual donation was $245. Those with 1,000–1,500 members, households gave an average of $336.

Single people and divorced or separated Catholics were the least generous, singles giving $175 a year, and divorced or separated Catholics, $148. In contrast, married households gave $313, and widowed Catholics an average of $261.

The new study, the first to ask data from parishes instead of individual Catholics, surveyed only those parishes with computerized accounting systems. Of 714 parishes contacted, 278 responded.

College Grads

Prediction: By the year 2000, 1 in 3 college graduates will hold a job that does not require a college degree. — *Bureau of Labor Statistics, 1988*

Reality: One third of 1991 and 1992 college graduates hold jobs that do not require a college degree. — *Michigan State University's Collegiate Employment Research Institute, 1993*

It's almost unanimous — the 1.1 million college graduates of 1993 face the toughest job market since the GIs returned home from World War II, and there does not appear to be any relief in sight. According to most universities in the nation, the number of companies that come to recruit new graduates has dropped by 60% since the late 1980s. In 1986, the nation's largest employers visited an average of 42 schools. According to the College Placement Council, the average is now down to 23. The nation's biggest, General Motors, did no college recruiting in 1993 for the second year in a row, nor did Kodak. Hewlett-Packard, which formerly hired as many as 2,000 grads, will hire approximately 350. Itel reports receiving as many as 20,000 résumés from graduates annually.

In 1990, the average salary for all college graduates was about $45,000 versus $25,000 for those without a degree. Those just graduating, however, are setting their sights lower, taking jobs that pay $6 to $7 per hour and often less, for their bachelor's degrees are not as marketable as they had hoped in today's job market.

The liberal arts major may have the worst job prospects of all. According to Patrick Scheetz, the assistant director of career development and placement at Michigan State, the unemployment rate for liberal arts grads will be 20% to 30% compared to 6% to 10% for technical grads. At Cornell, for example, even the best computer science graduates are getting two or three job offers compared to five or six a few years ago.

The Temporary Solution: Many graduates are choosing jobs obtained though temporary employment agencies. One of the biggest, Manpower, reports that about a third of its work force is made up of recent college graduates. The previous year it was 22%. Another agency, Temps and Co. of Washington, D.C., reports that half of its 1,500 workers have college degrees and are earning between $5 and $6 an hour.

Other ways college grads are coping, according to *USA Today*, are as follows:

- Some have moved back with their parents.
- Graduate school enrollments are up.

- The Peace Corps is getting a new wave of graduates.
- Volunteer jobs, which offer no pay, are popular.
- Underemployment — taking jobs with low pay — is on the rise.
- Part-time employment is considered better than no job at all.

Congressional Costs

$5.2 Million a Head

No one knew it in 1970, but American taxpayers had a bargain: the U.S. Congress. Back then it cost a mere $343 million to operate. Today it costs $2.8 billion, more than double the 280% rise in prices over the period.

The House of Representatives, with 435 members, and the Senate, with 100, is the most expensive legislature to run in the world, costing ten times that of its Canadian counterpart, which has 346 members.

The Foley Plan: House Speaker Thomas Foley (D-Washington) has a plan. His suggestion that legislators pay for *something* has some merit, but there's a flaw in the idea. Foley is endorsing a new fee, $520 a year for each legislator to use the office of the attending physician. Sounds fair, but this will generate a paltry $278,200, 15% of the cost of the service and about .001% (that's one thousandth of 1%) of the cost of running Congress.

To put the high cost of Congress another way, each member gets, in addition to a salary, $5 million of costs picked up, ranging from office space, perks, and postage to other items. And the salaries? Bargains indeed — $129,500 annually for House members

Next to the White House, the overhead at the U.S. Capitol is the highest per capita in the federal government.

and $168,202 for senators, more than what 98% of Americans earn.

Congressional Mail
100 Million Pieces Coming

Imagine running for Congress against an incumbent who is deluging the district with taxpayer-financed mailings to voters while you are ringing doorbells. That's what happens when legislators head into an election year.

After spending $14.3 million in the first half of the last election year, House and Senate members hit the post office with $30.4 million in campaign literature in the last six months of the year, according to James Davidson, the chairman of the National Taxpayers Union. House members alone spent $10.5 million in the last three weeks of the campaign, sending out 85 million pieces of mail.

The congressional free-mail budget for election year 1992 was $80 million, nearly twice the previous year's $45 million figure. In 1991, the group found, free-mail spending for 185 House members exceeded $108,506 each, the average total campaign budget of their challengers in the 1990 House election.

As an additional temptation to incumbents, the law allows House members to dip into their office budgets for additional mailing costs — as much as $25,000 per member.

Contraception

Some 41% of American women practice some form of birth control. Among American couples, approximately one third practice some form of contraception.

The Guttmacher Institute, an organization that polls sexual behavior, reported in 1990 that a growing number of Americans voluntarily sterilize themselves — fully one quarter of adults. In 1992, another survey commissioned by *Family Planning Perspectives*, called "Contraceptive Practices in the United States," reported that nearly 40% of couples have used sterilization; among them, 70% opt for female sterilization and 30% rely on vasectomies.

The increased incidence of sterilization among women can be attributed in some part to the aging of the female population — in the period from 1982 to 1988, the number of women aged 15 to 24 dropped by 1.5 million and those from 25 to 44 (the ones more likely to opt for nonreversible birth control methods) rose by nearly 5.4 million. The decline of the IUD, with its many dangers, also contributes to the higher number of women relying on sterilization.

The use of the pill, which declined in the late 1970s because of health concerns, has also become more popular, due to its convenience and high rate of effectiveness. The condom, being the most effective method in guarding against sexually transmitted diseases (save abstinence), has increased in use rapidly among teenagers and single women, but the pill remains the method of choice for the younger set.

This list cites the most common forms of contraception and the proportions of Americans who use them, according to the survey.

Pill	34%
Condom	26%
Sterilization	25%
Diaphragm	6%
Abstinence	2%
Withdrawal	2%
Other	2%
IUD	2%
Foam	1%

Convertibles
On the Road Again

A passport to youth for older drivers, to romance for younger ones, convertibles are back again, and for drivers of any age they're a springboard to dreams.

Convertibles have always had an aura, part of which is the announcement that spring has sprung when they appear on the road. With the oil embargo of 1973, the top went up on the fun cars as automakers focused on more economical cars to meet higher gasoline prices and lower emissions, according to auto analyst Ray Windecker.

The record year for convertible sales was 1963, when 542,000 were sold; the low point came in 1982, when 43,200 hit the road, half a percentage point of the car market. Not until Lee Iacocca began producing them again at Chrysler in 1982 did they return to favor. Ford jumped in with its line the next year, and sales began to climb. In 1992, 178,800 convertibles of all makes were sold, and the figures are still climbing.

Topping the Car Market: This sample of some of the hottest convertibles was compiled and commented on by Dan Jedlica of the *Chicago Tribune*.

- **Alfa Romeo Spider** ($21,764–$24,870). Still "fun," but with an awkward driving position.
- **Chevrolet Cavalier** ($15,675–$18,305). Z24 version superior, but base model still a good deal.
- **Chevrolet Corvette** ($41,195). One of the world's best performance convertibles, but sales are slow.
- **Dodge Shadow** ($14,028). A low-priced U.S. convertible, solidly built and weathertight.
- **Honda Civic del Sol** ($13,350–$15,150). Fast and nimble with little cockpit wind buffeting.
- **Mazda Miata** ($15,300). Still going strong. More fun to drive than most.
- **Mercedes-Benz 300CE Cabriolet** ($76,000). Quiet even with the top down.
- **Pontiac Sunbird** ($15,403). Sassy styling with a strong heater for cool evenings.
- **Saab 900S** ($32,160–$37,060). Soft tops among the best made, sure-footed and fun to drive.

It's the snazziest thing on wheels: a 'Vette with the top down.

Corporate Name Changes
A Corporate Identity Crisis?

A rose by any other name would still smell sweet, but will the garbage managed by Waste Management Corp. smell any better now that the company is called simply WMX? In May 1993, Waste Management joined the national trend toward new names for old businesses as companies merge, expand their scope, or simply seek better public recognition.

But what's in a name change for the economic health of the country? Plenty, according to the corporate identity consulting firm Anspach Grossman Portugal in New York, which says the trend augurs well for the nation's economic future: for advertising agencies hired to publicize the new name, for graphic design firms that develop new logos, and especially for the printing companies that must crank out reams of new stationery and business cards.

The pattern began in the recession of 1982 and took off through the rest of the decade, when the merger and acquisition craze went through the roof. The trend peaked in 1988, when a record 1,864 companies gained new identities. In 1992, 1,285 companies changed names — a 20% jump from 1991. Of these, 899, or 70%, involved mergers, acquisitions, or reorganizations.

Who's in Kansas, What's on Second? If you think Abbott and Costello can be confusing with their name-game routine, consider this Kansas power company. Joel Portugal, a partner in Anspach Grossman Portugal, said that Kansas Power & Light of Topeka changed its name to Western Resources because the new name was "an environmentally aware moniker more appropriate for the '90s and beyond."

Thomas Sloan, the director of corporate communications for Western Resources, said the change was made to reflect the broader scope of the company's business. Stock analysts made another guess: Kansas Power & Light of Topeka was often confused with Kansas City Power & Light in Missouri and with Kansas Gas and Electric, which Kansas Power & Light of Topeka bought before changing its name.

The number of corporate name changes since 1988, according to Anspach Grossman Portugal, are:

1988	1,864
1989	1,600
1990	1,321
1991	1,069
1992	1,285

Cosmetic Surgery

More than 41 million Americans rebuilt their face or reshaped their body by the miracle of cosmetic surgery — a number of procedures tempered only by one's ability to suffer discomfort and pay bills. Here are the most popular operations, according to the American Association of Plastic and Reconstructive Surgeons, and the proportions of Americans undergoing them.

Aesthetic surgery (any kind)	1 in 5.7
Hair transplant (men)	1 in 547
Facelift (both genders)	1 in 50
Facelift (women)	1 in 29
Facelift (men)	1 in 245
Nose job (both genders)	1 in 37
Nose job (women)	1 in 31
Nose job (men)	1 in 78
Breast lift (women)	1 in 101
Breast augmentation (women)	1 in 19

Counterfeit Bills

Iran Faking U.S. Currency

The U.S. Department of the Treasury has traditionally been close-lipped about the amount of counterfeiting that goes on. The reason is a good one: if there were an official estimate of fake U.S. currency, it would almost certainly devalue the American dollar, thereby causing inflation at home and abroad. The Treasury will, however, tell us about known enemies of the integrity of official U.S. currency, and there are many to expose.

Iranians and Syrians are busy flooding Europe, Asia, Africa, and the cash-starved nations of the former Soviet Union with phony U.S. money. Worse, they use presses built in the U.S., chemists trained in the U.S., and counterfeiting expertise obtained from the U.S. during the rule of the shah of Iran.

In denominations of $100, they plan to print bills worth up to $12 billion a year to erase Iran's foreign currency shortfall, according to evidence gathered by the congressional Task Force on Terrorism and Unconventional Warfare and passed on to the Secret Service and the Treasury Department in 1993. "The implications for the dollar's role as the international medium of exchange could be serious," said Congressman Bill McCollum of Florida in one of the understatements of the year.

The task force report said that Iran and Syria began the titanic gamble in 1989 and by 1993 had perfected it on paper that's nearly identical to the real thing. Vaughn Forrest, the task force's chief of staff, said his information came from reliable sources in both countries; he added that boxes of up to $500,000 of the phony money have been reported.

Court Cases
State Courts Choking to Death

A crisis is coming in the courts unless changes are made. The number of civil and criminal cases being filed is growing six times faster than the U.S. population. There are now approximately 100 million cases on file in the state courts alone, close to one for every household in the nation. Federal bankruptcy cases are adding another 2 million cases annually to the already clogged court system.

The reasons are varied. Some blame the increased caseload on the increase in the number of legal practitioners. According to *The Jobs Rated Almanac*, there were 500,000 lawyers in the U.S. in 1985. Today there are 800,000. The number of paralegals — assistants who can perform many legal procedures that lawyers themselves are too busy to handle — has grown from 76,000 to about 140,000 during the same period. Other factors have been the increased prosecution of drug offenders, hard economic times, and accelerated civil cases involving contracts and property disputes, as reported by the National Center for State Courts.

Caseloads are staggering and getting worse. This list represents the increase in cases by percent and the number of cases on file from 1984 to 1990, according to the center.

Civil cases	18.4 million	+30%
Criminal cases	13 million	+33%
Juvenile cases	1.5 million	+28%
Traffic and minor cases	67 million	+125%

Today Americans are spending about $90 billion on litigation and insurance, much of it on lawyers. Trying to make sense of all this, John Banzhaf, a law professor at George Washington University, said that state courts face a caseload crisis unless something is done, including "dragging our courts into the 21st century" through the increased use of computers.

Credit Cards

Have any Interest?

With more than 6,000 banks issuing VISA and MasterCard cards in the U.S., consumers have plenty of alternatives in picking credit cards. Making an intelligent choice can save big bucks in interest and annual fees.

According to Bankcard Holders of America, a consumer group, bank card spending has soared like the national debt and is reaching an estimated $300 billion annually, about six times what it was in 1980. Average interest charges hovered at around 19% on unpaid balances, because there are few low-interest cards to bring down the average (the industry standard is 19.8%). That may explain why every mailbox in the country is flooded with "pre-approved" invitations from large banks — and small banks acting as agents for big ones — offering yet another card to pay off the balance on one's present and at a lower rate (the bait!), hence shifting the debt to a rival bank.

Competition among the proliferating issuers has nudged some banks to reduce their interest rates. Some 9 million Citibank cardholders enjoyed that experience in the spring of 1993, when the bank lowered its interest rate to 15.4% (from 19.8%) for its best customers. This translates to the bank's having 27 million cards — 70% of its total — carrying rates below the 19.8% standard.

Seductive little helpmates that they are, credit cards are usually taken out with the users planning to revolve charges or pay them off at their own pace, but they often wind up with thousands of dollars billed to the card, and many cannot pay off the principal, even in installments. Like the federal government, most cardholders pay only the interest charges. Banks, however, usually require a token installment toward the balance every month. As a result, smart consumers scan newspapers and business magazines to find the cards with the lowest interest rates.

In 1992, some states' usury laws — regulations to limit the amount of interest or fees that banks can charge on credit cards — allowed rates as high as 36% annually (Wyoming), and the national average in May 1993 was still a whopping 18.24%. But cardholders who do not pay off the principal each month can find variable rates of as low as 8%, according to Bank Rate Monitor.

The list on the following page shows the increase in credit card spending (in millions), adapted from data from the Federal Reserve Board, Bankcard Holders of America, and credit card companies.

	Bank Cards	All Cards
1980	$54	$206
1983	$80	$240
1986	$142	$335
1989	$216	$529
1990	$250	$563
1991	$260	$659
1992 (est.)	$300	$770

It's Not the Purchase but the Interest: Are you paying 30% interest on your 15%–18% interest bank card? Very likely you are, charges Bankcard Holders of America. It estimates a total cost of $8.5 billion to consumers for the "maze of secret billing tactics and fees" and says that it constitutes "loansharking of the worst kind."

In one study, "What You Don't Know Can Cost You," written after examining 35 issuers that serve 60% of the credit card market, the group hit particularly hard at what it called "phantom grace periods," which offer the holder 25 days to pay a bill before interest charges take effect. Actually, the study says, if the user makes only a partial payment on that bill, the grace period is usually eliminated on all new purchases until the former bill is paid in full. The group also

- condemned fees, which average $2.50, charged on top of interest for cash advances.
- criticized "nuisance" fees, which average $11 for exceeding a card's credit limit and $8 for a late payment.
- warned that some banks charge interest from day one of a purchase instead of on the date the purchase was posted to the holder's account.

"Hogwash," said the American Bankers Association. None of the criticism is valid since all the practices mentioned are fully disclosed (in small print) in the literature soliciting business and on the applications themselves.

Crime Bosses
The Richest Men in the Pen

The adage "crime doesn't pay" is often disputed. Those who think it does should look beyond the $1,500 suit John Gotti used to wear. He recently traded it in for a prison suit. His archrival, Paul Castellano, wasn't so lucky. Although he is dead, he is arguably one of the richest men in the cemetery.

In 1986, *Fortune* magazine ran a list of the top 50 Mafia bosses, the "Fortune 50." According to the magazine, they are among the wealthiest men in America. But do they get away with their crimes?

In 1986, 29 of the infamous 50 were in jail (fewer than half were free) and 6 mobsters (1 in 8) were out on bail. One of the biggest bosses of all, however, evaded jail, then and until the day he died in 1992: He was Tony "Big Tuna" Accardo, reputed triggerman for the Capone gang in the 1930s and the boss of Chicago by the 1950s.

This list represents the disposition of these men seven years later.

In prison	1 in 2
Retired	1 in 5

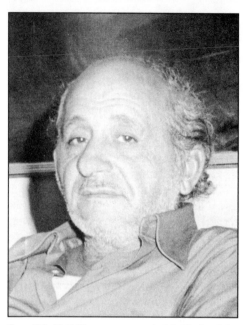

Sam "MoMo" Giancana was shot in the back in his basement. Photo, courtesy Chicago Crime Commission.

Still pursuing crime	1 in 6
Dead	1 in 8
Out on bail	1 in 16
On the lam	1 in 50

Crime

Midsize Cities Now Hit Hard

Omaha saw a startling 192% increase in murders in 1991, according to FBI figures. Virginia Beach, Va., Indianapolis, Ind. and Portland, Oreg., have seen their rates go up more than 60% as criminals sprout increasingly in the grassroots parts of the nation.

"Crime is beginning to peak in cities like New York and Los Angeles," observed the sociologist James O'Kane, of Drew University, mostly because economic and other pressures are sending people likely to commit crimes — young males — to other areas of the country for their easily obtained drugs and guns. An increase in violent crimes was noted most in the South, which saw an 8% growth, while the rate rose 7% in the West, 6% in the Midwest, and dropped 1% in the Northwest. Reports of murder nationwide soared 7% in 1991 as total crimes climbed 3%, violent crimes 5%, and property crimes 2%, undoubtedly providing writers with no end of new material for TV docudramas.

This table shows the percentages of increase and decrease of violent crime in the hardest hit cities of various sizes, according to the FBI Uniform Crime Report for 1991.

	Murder	Rape	Robbery
Over 1 million	+4%	–6%	+6%
500,000–1 million	+3%	0%	–2%
250,000–499,000	+17%	+1%	+10%
100,000–249,000	+12%	+3%	+12%
50,000–99,000	+22%	+65%	+12%
10,000–49,000	+1%	+11%	+9%
Under 10,000	–3%	+5%	+12%
National average	+7%	+3%	+8%

The cities that experienced at least a 50% increase in murders are:

Omaha, Nebr.	192%
Virginia Beach, Va.	69%
Indianapolis, Ind.	64%
Portland, Oreg.	61%
Columbus, Ohio	55%
Sacramento, Calif.	54%
San Jose, Calif.	51%
Albuquerque, N.M.	50%
Fort Worth, Tex.	50%

Dating

Not What It Used to Be

There is no doubt that the AIDS epidemic has changed the way single people meet. Bars and discos are no longer where America's 72 million singles go to find prospective dates. In the nineties, some 6 in 10 singles report that they meet their dates in "traditional" ways — through friends, family, social events, and work.

This list from *Singles, the New Americans* represents how single men and women meet dates and the relevant percentages.

	Men	Women
Friends	30%	36%
Social gatherings	22%	18%
Bars and discos	24%	18%
Singles functions	14%	18%
Work	10%	9%
Newspaper ads	1%	1%

What Attracts Women: American women are attracted by the upper torso and, most of all, by the most conspicuous physical characteristics rather than the sexual anatomy of the male. The following list from *Sex, A User's Manual* represents what women find most attractive in a man.

Face	55%
Hair	8%
Shoulders	7%
Chest	6%
Hands	4%

Women also like men in the following order: for their achievements, status, and intelligence.

What Attracts Men: Though men are attracted by a pretty face, legs are high on their list. This list, from the book just cited, represents what men find most attractive in women.

Face	27%
Legs	24%
Bust	18%
Hair	5%
Buttocks	4%

Unlike women, men did not report a strong attraction to women's achievements or intelligence. They respond to physical appearance, the power to arouse them, and affection.

Death and Its Causes

Each year 2.1 million Americans' leases on life expire — about .9%

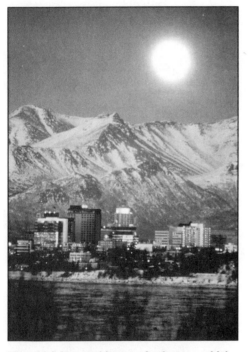

The midnight sun shines on Anchorage, which has the lowest death rate in the nation. Photo, courtesy Alaska Division of Tourism.

of those who were alive in the previous year.

Many of the lists in this volume represent the top 10 of various phenomena; however, this list shows the 11 leading causes of death by percent to demonstrate how AIDS (now in the eleventh position) has climbed from the forty-fourth leading cause of death in 1980.

Heart disease	35.8%
Cancer	22.4%
Stroke	7.2%
Accident	4.3%
Pulmonary disease	3.3%
Pneumonia/influenza	3.3%
Diabetes	1.7%
Suicide	1.4%
Liver ailments	1.2%
Atherosclerosis	1.2%
AIDS	1.1%

Source: National Safety Council

Liveliest Cities: Death rates and causes vary enormously from city to city because they are more a matter of demographics than of geography. One of the most frightening reports came out in mid-1993: AIDS is the biggest killer of males between the ages of 18 and 44 in New York, Los Angeles, San

Francisco, and more than 70 other locales. In St. Petersburg, Fla., 1.8% of the population dies of AIDS annually; in St. Louis, 1.4%; in Anch-orage, only .31%; and in Arlington, Tex., a Dallas suburb, .41%.

Assuming individuals live to age 65, here is a calculation of the number of years lost annually due to the deaths of those under age 65, according to the Centers for Disease Control and Prevention.

Accidents	2.1 million
Cancer	1.9 million
Suicide/	
homicide	1.6 million
Heart disease	1.4 million
AIDS	0.8 million

Debts Among Young Families

Overspending Adds Up

Maybe the federal government taught young couples this lesson: spend beyond your income and just pay the interest. For they have too many seductive choices that they cannot resist — cars; clothes; appliances to buy; as well as entertainment.

According to the *Family Economics Review*, this is the scenario being followed by the average young couple with children in the U.S. Their typical after-tax annual income, which must cover sales and excise taxes, charitable contributions, license plates, insurance payments, and the like, is $19,783. By the end of the year, however, this couple has spent $21,401.

Defense Cuts

Job Losses Staggering

The target date for the completion of President Clinton's plan to cut $80 billion from the defense budget is 1998, and to reach that goal, more than 2 million military and related

The world's largest office building is the 3.7-million-square-foot Pentagon.

jobs will disappear. Cries of anguish are resounding across the land, not only from the soon-to-be-laid-off, but from mayors, governors, and congressional representatives who will see jobs eliminated in their region — not to mention the Defense Department itself.

This list represents the areas in which defense cuts will be made and the number of jobs in each that will be lost, according to the Bureau of Labor Statistics.

Manufacturing	594,000
Services	286,000
Trade	139,000
Transportation	62,000

Government officials are trying to soften the blow by maintaining that most communities in which military bases have been closed were able to replace the lost jobs "within a few years."

Depression in Elders
Something's-Not-Quite-Right Syndrome

"I mostly stay at home. I can't go out too much because I have to save my money, and even when I do, I just get tired and, even worse, everybody I see — at the movies, at the mall, everywhere — they're so much younger and having so much more fun." — *Anonymous senior citizen*

Sadness and disappointment are normal on-and-off experiences that no one escapes. Among the elderly they can cause permanent debilitation; of the more than 65 million seniors in the U.S., 12% suffer from it, with 3% considered pathologically depressed, according to the National Institute for Aging. It went on to note that estimates for depression range as high as 25% for residents in nursing homes, who may feel alone, unhappy, and unstimulated.

The American Association for Aging adds that the suicide rate for people 65 and older is 50% higher than for the general population, making them the group most at risk. Depression is found to be more common in older women than in men and is the mental complaint most often reported by women in physicians' offices and in outpatient clinics.

Disabled Persons
Blacks Do Not Receive Their Fair Share

Under its broadest program for disabled workers, the Social Security disability programs dispense $43.2 billion annually. In addition to the usual payouts for those who cannot work, the federal government pays disability insurance — more than $2 billion monthly — to 3.2 million individuals, including 1.3 million children. The average amount received is $610 monthly for disability. For the last thirty years, blacks have not received a proportionate share.

According to a 1993 study done by the General Accounting Office for 1988, the latest year analyzed, whites had an 8% better chance of receiving aid after an initial rejection for disability insurance and a 4% advantage under the Supplemental Security Income program, the two largest federal programs for people with severe disabilities.

If you're black and disabled and have been turned down for help by a Social Security disability program, your chances of winning an appeal from an administrative law judge are not good.

The greatest racial disparities in the appeals process were found in Chicago, where blacks had a 10% to 17% disadvantage, and in New York, where they had an average 15% disadvantage. Senator William Cohen (R-Maine) said that at least 1 judge in 10 had denied claims by blacks 25% more often than those by whites and that 1 judge in 3 had a 15% difference. He also cited a judge who had a 50% disparity. Blacks as a group, however, were found to receive more benefits than whites from the two programs, which pay $3.6 billion a month to 4.8 million Americans.

Earthquakes
Waiting for the Big One

The San Francisco earthquake of October 17, 1989, which killed 67 persons, was not as deadly as the city's 1906 quake, which claimed 503 lives. Still, it gave San Franciscans the shakes and reminded them about "the big one," which is still to come along the infamous San Andreas Fault. The U.S. Geological Survey gives it a 40% chance of arriving sometime before 2018; it is predicted that it will cause

14,000 deaths and serious injury to 55,000 persons.

Californians have good reason to be scared. The 10 biggest earthquakes of this century have occurred in their state, and aftershocks — who can count them? This list notes the biggest quakes of the century to date, according to their magnitude on the Richter scale, and the resulting number of deaths, as compiled by the U.S. Geological Survey.

	Magnitude	Deaths
Anchorage (3/27/64)	8.4	131
San Francisco Bay area (4/18/06)	8.3	503
Kern County (7/20/52)	7.7	12
Joshua Tree (6/28/92)	7.6	1
Off the California coast (4/17/91)	7.3	0
San Francisco Bay area (10/17/89)	7.1	67
Cape Mendocino (4/25/92)	6.9	0
San Fernando Valley (2/9/71)	6.4	5
Long Beach (3/10/33)	6.3	117
Joshua (4/23/92)	6.3	0

What's Coming Up? Geologists label their predictions as follows: short, medium, and long time scales. The last is based on a pattern established by past quakes which is used to make predictions over a 500-year period, generally considered reliable. Here are some short-time-scale predictions in the U.S. culled from the 1993 edition of the *Handbook of Current Science & Technology*; they indicate the location and the number of years from now the quake is predicted.

Parkfield, Calif.	due in 1993
East Coast	20 years
San Francisco	27 years
Palm Springs, Calif.	30 years
Utah	43 years

Education Shortchanged?

"[American colleges] are secondary schools, as the rest of the world defines college — the highest-cost secondary schools in the world." — *Marc Tucker, president of the National Center on Education and the Economy*

There are about 14 million undergraduate students enrolled in America's 3,500 two- and four-year colleges, pursuing a vital part of the American dream.

Undergrads Take Second Place to Research: Half of those who enter college never graduate, and for those who do, the educational experience resembles Henry Ford's assembly line more than Plato's Academy. A Gallup poll in 1991 found that 73% of the public rated a college education of vital importance, but according to critics, many U.S. universities in the early nineties have shifted their emphasis away from undergraduate teaching and toward expansion and research. In the face of budget cuts, many have all but abandoned the mission of educating the undergraduate.

Class size is one of the problems in America's educational system. Many schools shunt undergraduates into lectures of up to 1,000 students, often taught by graduate teaching assistants or "visiting professors," who work for little money and no job security.

The list below represents lecture class sizes for various courses at selected state universities, according to the *Chicago Tribune*.

Michigan State (economics)	464
Minnesota (psychology)	568
Wisconsin (engineering)	600
Texas (psychology)	605
Michigan (psychology)	605
Colorado (marketing)	618
Illinois at Urbana (political science)	1,156

Larger classes, of course, mean less time for valuable personal attention from tenured faculty. In 1993, close to 60% of graduates are taking more than four years to earn a degree, up from the 46% of the mid-seventies.

The American Association of University Professors reported that close to 40% of the faculty surveyed were visiting lecturers, an increase from 32% in 1980. This trend was most prevalent at community colleges, where 52% of faculty were visitors. At schools granting doctorates, the figure was 26.4%; at liberal arts colleges, 32%.

Eggs
A Good Egg Is Hard to Find

Nothing breaks easier than an egg, but American egg producers know how to keep the damage down and production up. Each year they supply the nation with about 68 billion eggs, almost all of which are perfect when the chickens lay them, but all that changes once the human hand enters the equation. As a result, you can expect to find one broken egg in every 24 cartons that leave the farm. By the time they get to the supermarket, 1 in 10 cartons will have a broken egg.

Dropping Eggs: America is consuming fewer eggs, and egg production has been dropping precipitously in the last ten years, presumably because Americans are increasingly aware of the high cholesterol in egg yolks. The list below, compiled by the Department of Agriculture, represents the per capita consumption of eggs in the U.S. between 1970 and 1990.

1970	309
1975	276
1980	271
1985	255
1986	254
1987	254
1988	246
1989	236
1990	233

How They're Eaten: According to the American Egg Board, the average person will eat approximately 250 eggs per year prepared in the following ways:

Scrambled	34%
Fried	31%
Boiled	23%
In omelettes	4%
Other	5%
Poached	3%

800 Numbers

Since AT&T first developed the "800 number" service in 1967, the 800 market has grown to include 700,000 U.S. businesses that receive 13 billion 800-number calls a year, or about 52 for every person in the country. Now the $7.8-billion-a-year market is open to all comers.

When the deregulation of "800 number" toll-free phone lines went into effect in May 1993, AT&T held a 74% share of the market over its rivals MCI (17%) and Sprint (7%). With the new "portability" of the number, which allows customers of one company to switch to another without losing their current phone number, Sprint, MCI, and the smaller companies that make up the other 2% of the market began scrambling for a big bite of AT&T's pie, and AT&T began fighting back in what was anticipated as the biggest marketing war of 1993.

MCI claims that before portability went into effect, it had already attracted 2,000 customers. Sprint hopes to double its annual 800-number revenue, from $750 million in 1992 to $1.5 billion in 1994.

Competition was already working its magic even before deregulation, creating better service. MCI and AT&T reduced the time it took to restore faulty service from 2 hours in 1989 to 5 minutes in 1993, and AT&T is offering activation or deactivation of 800 numbers within 24 hours of an order.

Endangered Species

"Today I feel as important as a snail darter." — *Exclamation of anonymous graduate (class of '88) upon accepting her diploma*

The Snail Darter Fiasco: In the 1980s, when environmentalists showed concern for a near-extinct minnow-like fish because its last brood was confined to a pool near a dam under construction, critics of the movement were pushed to action. Millions of dollars were at stake while construction on the TVA dam was idled as environ-

Next on the endangered species list? The rare jackalope, native to Wyoming, is often denounced as a hoax. Photo, courtesy Wyoming Division of Tourism.

mentalists clashed with citizens crying for an end to what they perceived as fanaticism. The story made national headlines as the snail darter became a rallying point for those opposed to support for a *fish* while millions of Americans had problems yet to be addressed by the federal government. The feds compromised almost two years later by moving the remaining several thousand darter fish at a purported cost in the $100 million range.

When the U.S. published its first list of endangered species — plants, mammals, fish, and microorganisms — in 1967, there were 78 species on the roll. Since then, the fateful list has grown to include more than 2,000 species either threatened or endangered. Such classifications by the U.S. Fish and Wildlife Service, in accordance with the Endangered Species Act of 1973 and its renewal in 1988, protect species threatened with extinction in the wild. Although the occasional success story does make headlines, the General Accounting Office reported that 16% of endangered or threatened species in the U.S. were making a comeback while the status of 33% was deteriorating.

For instance, grizzly bears, once the proud masters of the West, now number only 800–1,200 in the continental U.S., where they live in protected refuges such as Yellowstone National Park. The Florida panther is endangered by the continued desecration and destruction of the Everglades. The Key deer exists only on one small island in the Florida Keys; residents keep a running count of the number killed by motorists on busy U.S. 1.

This table cites the 10 rarest mammals in America and their estimated populations.

Florida panther	30–50
Vancouver Island marmot	100
Sanborn's long-nosed bat	135
Mount Graham red squirrel	215
Right whale	240–600
Key deer	300
Wood bison	320
Morro Bay kangaroo rat	340
Sonoran pronghorn	400–550
Ozark big-eared bat	750

Source: World Wildlife Federation

The estimated annual cost of saving various endangered species follows, adapted from figures of the U.S. Fish and Wildlife Services.

Bald eagle	$3.1 million
Grizzly and brown bears	$2.9 million
Red-cockaded woodpecker	$2.8 million
American peregrine falcon	$2.7 million
Gray wolf	$2.7 million
Whooping crane	$1.4 million
Southern sea otter	$1.3 million
West Indian manatee	$1.2 million

Tunamoc globe-berry	$1.2 million
Black-footed ferret	$1.0 million

Endorsements

Athletes' Salaries Pale by Comparison

Poor Michael Jackson! He received only $10 million from Pepsi to dance all over the television and tell everyone, in verse, how much he loves to take a swig. He had to work a whole year to earn his other $100 million. The message is clear: entertainers who want to cash in on endorsements as profitably as athletes should work on their jump shots or their putting.

Most celebrities earn $1 million or more for endorsing products, but it's the athletes who earn the megabucks for pushing merchandise. To make matters even more unfair for the entertainers who dominate the movies and television, the masters of the courts and fields don't even have to work much during the off-season, thanks to the size of their paychecks for endorsing everything from Chevys to coffee machines.

This list shows the top athletes who endorse products and their estimated annual income from these promotions, according to *USA Today*.

Michael Jordan (basketball)	$32 million
Arnold Palmer (golf)	$11 million
Shaquille O'Neal (basketball)	$10 million
Andre Agassi (tennis)	$9 million
Jack Nicklaus (golf)	$9 million
Joe Montana (football)	$8 million

Entertainment Incomes

If there is one field in which success embraces a cross section of America, it is surely show business. The top three earners in the industry are black, number four is Jewish, number five is the son of an Austrian policeman, and the others represent almost every large ethnic group in America.

This list shows the earnings of popular entertainers in 1992, according to *Forbes* magazine.

Oprah Winfrey	$46 million
Bill Cosby	$40 million
Prince	$35 million
Steven Spielberg	$30 million
Arnold Schwarze- negger	$28 million
Guns 'n Roses	$28 million
Michael Jackson	$26 million
Garth Brooks	$24 million
Madonna	$24 million
Dustin Hoffman	$23 million
Kevin Costner	$21 million

And Now the Bad News: According to *The Jobs Rated Almanac*, actors, dancers, and singers have the lowest starting salaries of all the jobs cited in the book. This list indicates what aspiring entertainers may expect to earn if they don't become stars.

	Starting	Average	Top*
Actors	$3,300	$29,000	$46,000
Dancers	$3,300	$23,000	$30,000
Singers	$6,800	$26,000	$69,000

*The book defines top income as an average of those in the 90th percentile of the earnings scale in a given profession.

Entitlements
Eleven-fold Growth, Going on Twelve

Federal entitlement programs have grown every year since 1965, when Congress began adding legislation to existing social insurance programs for different groups of citizens, from toddlers to the retired. To date, a total of $1.382 *trillion* has been paid, up from $118 billion in 1965 — an increase of 1,148%.

Drops in the Bucket: Once you get in the trillion range, what's a few $100 million here or there? In 1993, the proliferation of mandated spending prompted Health and Human Services Secretary Donna Shalala to ask Congress for a supplemental sum of more than $300 million to add to the 1993 budget, mostly to assist millions of disabled Americans covered by social insurance programs. Bill Hughes, the acting chairman of the House Select Committee on Aging, points out, "The General Accounting Office reports that there is a backlog of 1.1 million cases of continuing disability reviews. Last year only 70,000 cases were reviewed." He added that the lack of continuing disability reviews was costing the Social Security Administration $1.4 billion every year.

The list below shows the growth of major entitlements (in billions), according to the congressional Office of Management and Budget:

	1965	1992	Change
Family support	$2.8	$16.0	+471%
Federal retirement	$2.9	$49.0	+2,482%
Food and nutrition	$0.3	$29.0	+9,566%
Medicaid	$0.3	$67.8	+22,500%
Medicare*	$5.8	$116.2	+1,903%
Social Security	$17.1	$285.1	+1,567%
Supplemental security**	$4.3	18.0	+319%
Unemployment	$2.3	$7.0	+1,509%
Veterans' benefits	$4.3	$16.0	+272%

* (1970)
** (1975)

Environmental Consciousness

Who Should Pay for the Cleanup?

It sounds like a list of what could go wrong: the buildup of waste materials, the depletion of natural resources, industrial pollution, acid rain, the destruction of the ozone layer, harmful chemicals in food and drink, radon pollution in the home, global warming. And just about all of them have happened to one degree or another.

Almost everybody who peeks outside knows that the atmosphere, the earth, and water are in a state of emergency. Almost everybody in industry and many in politics deny it.

Parade magazine, which is highly sympathetic to environmental issues, plunged in and surveyed "the people" on how to pay for the cleanup, polling 2,500 persons nationwide between 18 and 65 years old. They gave a variety of answers. Nearly 80% think we "are killing ourselves by what we are doing to the environment"; 55% believe the problems today are worse than they were in 1990. In addition, 92% think the government bears a stronger responsibility for the cleanup than it has shown to date.

When people were asked to name the number one problem with the environment, they cited the following issues.

Waste materials	21%
Overpopulation	21%

Depletion of natural resources	16%
Destruction of the ozone layer	15%
Acid rain	14%

And Who Should Foot the Bill? Some 41% of the respondents think the general public should bear the cost and responsibility for cleaning up the nightmare; 34% suggested industry, and 22%, the government.

The survey also found that 92% said we should be doing more. The following suggestions were made by the indicated percentage of respondents.

- More regulations on the disposal of industrial waste — 83%
- More recycling programs in neighborhoods — 81%
- More efforts finding alternative sources of energy — 78%
- More education so that individuals can help — 76%
- More regulations against industrial waste — 73%

Ethnicity

In 1990, the U.S. Census takers went to 1 in 6 households asking, among other questions, of what ancestry Americans consider themselves. German Americans are the nation's largest ethnic group. And while there have never been more than 4 million people living in Ireland, almost 39 million Americans proclaim themselves to be "Irish."

This list represents ancestries of Americans with more than a million members, according to the Census Bureau.

German	57.9 million
Irish	38.7 million
English	32.7 million
African American	23.8 million
Italian	14.7 million
American	12.4 million
Mexican	11.6 million
French	10.3 million
Polish	9.4 million
Dutch	6.2 million
Scotch-Irish	5.6 million
Scottish	5.4 million
Swedish	4.7 million
Norwegian	3.9 million
Russian	3 million
French Canadian	2.2 million
Welsh	2 million
Spanish	2 million
Puerto Rican	2 million
Slovak	1.9 million

White	1.8 million
Danish	1.6 million
Hungarian	1.6 million
Chinese	1.5 million
Filipino	1.5 million
Czech	1.3 million
Portuguese	1.2 million
British	1.1 million
Hispanic	1.1 million
Greek	1.1 million
Swiss	1 million
Japanese	1 million

Not listed is any reference to "Jewish," since Judaism is officially designated as a religion. There are about 6 million Jews in the U.S., most of whom — about 80% — trace their ancestry to Central and Eastern Europe, chiefly Germany, Poland, and Russia. The largest populations of American Jews live on the East Coast and in California.

California has the largest concentration of northern and western European groups: German, Irish, English, French, and Dutch. It also has the largest group of Mexicans. Minnesota ranks first for Norwegians, Massachusetts for French Canadians, Pennsylvania for Slovaks, and Ohio for Hungarians.

Farmers

1945: Average Farm Net Worth: $12,502
1991: Average Farm Net Worth: $326,215

Over the last hundred years, the percentage of the population living on farms has plummeted from 23.2% in 1940 to 2.5% in 1991, giving rise to the misconception that the family farm is dying. The vast majority — 90.7% — of America's 2.14 million

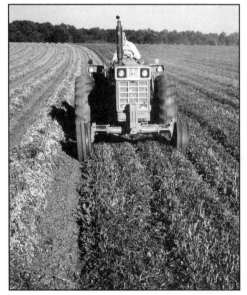

America has 1 billion acres of farmland. Photo, courtesy Georgia Bureau of Industry and Trade.

farms, which average 467 acres each, still belong to families, some 6 million farmers. Giant corporations own only 3.2% and foreign corporations or individuals, 1.1%, according to the Department of Agriculture.

This list represents the top five types of farm by specialties:

Beef cattle	34.3%
Cash grain	22.0%
Dairy	6.6%
Field crops	6.1%
Hogs	5.4%

Hayseeds? In 1940, 3.4% of American farmers had been to college and 10.2% had graduated from high school. By 1990, 36.9% had been to college and 81.8% were high school graduates. "Farmers aren't rubes or hicks," said Calvin Beale, a senior demographer for the Department of Agriculture. "Farming is big business [more than $1 trillion in annual output]. People who don't want to be big can't make a living [at farming] without other income." The result is that many family farms are so large that they've incorporated, squeezing out the giants instead of the other way around.

The Census Bureau and the Department of Agriculture report the following farm facts:

- Blacks have largely abandoned the agrarian life (1.1% of today's total versus 13% in 1900).
- Women are displaying more interest in farming, with 131,641 (6.3% of the total) farming in 1987, up from 112,799 in 1978.
- There are only a few Hispanics (.8%) and Asians (.3%) on farms.
- Texas is the state with the most farms, 186,000.
- The average age of farmers is 52, up from 48 in 1940.
- The average farm family had 3.20 persons in 1989, 4.25 in 1940, 5.20 in 1890.
- The number of people fed by each farm worker was 89 in 1989, 10.7 in 1940, 5.8 in 1890.
- The percentage of crops exported was 25% in 1990, 3% in 1940, 19% in 1890.

Fax Machines

When fax machines were invented in the 1960s, it took an average of 6 minutes to send a document. When technological improvements brought the time down to seconds, fax machine sales soared — from 580,000 in 1987 to 11 million in 1992.

Jay Kaye, the author of *Light Your House with Potatoes*, a book about "totally off-the-wall solutions to life's little problems," reports a unique use of the fax machine, one that involves an Oklahoma convict who found jail to be relentlessly boring.

The Case of Jean Paul Barret: In Oklahoma, Jean Paul Barret was taken from the state prison to the Pima County Jail to await a hearing. Barret had a smart friend who apparently knew all about a new technique to finagle a way out of jail in the age of instant communication and document transfer. Barret's jailers received a fax ordering the inmate's release — the usual way they get orders to release prisoners, some 60 a day. Apparently Barret's friend got hold of an actual court document, and with a little typewriter white-out and some new names and dates, he faxed the forged release papers. It is therefore no longer true that bars and barbed wire may keep the criminals in jail, for telephone wires can get them out faster than a good lawyer.

Fax machines are changing the life of those outside jail, too; in fact, they are an addiction that is changing the face of office life. Today, Fortune 500 companies send an average of 49 documents a day, up from 40 a year ago. In 1992, their faxes averaged 4.6 pages; in 1993, 5.3 pages, mostly purchase orders and reports, as noted by a survey taken by Pitney Bowes, the office solution giant.

A Gallup poll found that 75% of the Fortune 500 fax senders didn't know how much it cost. It's cheap enough, though, averaging 15 to 18 cents a minute for a machine requiring 30 seconds to send a page.

Federal Budget

"A hundred million here, a billion there, adds up to real money." — *Everett Dirksen*

When Ronald Reagan campaigned for office in 1980 the national debt was $900 billion. By the time he left office in 1989, the national debt was very close to $3 *trillion* and today it is $4.2 trillion. If every American family shared equally the burden of paying off the national debt, each household would have to contribute about $40,000.

In fiscal 1994, President Clinton plans to spend $1.5 trillion, give or take a few tens of billions, depending on what he can push through the legislature. The Clinton budget shows the deficit declining from $302 billion to $264 billion next year and to a low of $212 billion in 1996. That projection, of course, is based on "on budget items." "Off budget" items are Social Security payments (now, and perhaps temporarily, running a surplus) and the cost to run the river of red ink called the U.S. Postal Service.

The list below represents where federal government funds come from, according to the U.S. Treasury Department.

Individual income tax	37%
Social insurance receipts*	31%
Borrowing	17%
Corporate income tax	8%
Excise taxes	3%
Other	4%

Social Security, Medicaid and other deductions from workers salaries.

... and where it goes

Individual benefits	46%
Defense	18%
State, local grants	15%
Interest on debt	14%
Other	7%

Changing Priorities: Despite the rhetoric of politicians, few things change how money is spent. Only two spending areas are being "significantly changed" — expenditures on defense (cuts of 4.9%) and Health and Human Services (an increase of less than 1%). Following are the biggest gainers and losers (in billions), if Clinton passes his proposed 1994 budget.

Biggest Losers

	Spending	Loss
Military	$264.3	-$13.1
Labor	$37.5	-$9.2
Agriculture	$63.0	-$3.9
Federal Emergency Management Agency	$1.8	-$1.3
Justice	$10.3	-$0.3
Interior	$7.2	-$0.03

Biggest Gainers

	Spending	Gain
Health and Human Services	$640.1	+$48.0
Treasury	$318.9	+$17.2
Housing and Urban Development	$28.9	+$2.9
Transportation	$39.1	+$2.6
Veterans Affairs	$37.7	+$1.5
Office of Personnel Management	$38.7	+$2.3
NASA	$14.7	+$1.5
Judicial branch	$3.1	+$0.6
Legislative branch	$3.1	+$0.03

Feminist Issues
Not Much Solidarity

A 1992 survey conducted by the MS. Foundation for Women and the Center for Policy Awareness shows that women have a broad range of views on some very important issues, feminism among them.

A New Label Needed: At one time, many a woman would proudly proclaim herself "a feminist." Today, many women who support women's issues don't like the label. Some 66% of the women surveyed said they would be likely to join a group seeking increased professional and educational opportunities, equal pay, and equal rights for women. When the question was rephrased to include the words "feminist group" seeking the same things, only half the respondents said they would be likely to join such a group.

When the women named the most important problem they faced today, only the issue of balancing work and family reached double digits, with 14%. No other subject got more than 7%.

What would improve family life? Below are the women's answers and the percentage who gave them.

More flexible hours	25%
Higher-paying job	19%
More help at home	12%
More reliable day care	5%
Nothing	13%

Firearms
Stick 'em Up!

Snipers, holdups, street murders, armed gangs of teens, family murders — the grimmest statistic is that there are an estimated 30 million handguns in America, many times the number owned by the U.S. military. In 1990, more than 3.7 million firearms of all types were sold; in 1965, the year of the Watts riots in Los Angeles, 2.4 million were sold. Rifle sales decreased 4% and shotgun sales fell 16% — good news for wildlife — while human life was wearing bulletproof vests and uttering cries of anguish and pleas for sterner vigilance and harsh laws against handguns.

This list represents the percentages of three types of firearms sold in 1965 and 1990, compiled by the National Association of Federally Licensed Firearms Dealers.

	1965	1990
Handguns	28%	48%
Rifles	34%	30%
Shotguns	38%	22%

Food "faves"

Pass the Pizza, Please

Each year, Americans spend about $8 billion on snack food, much of it fried, high in fat, covered with gooey cheese, and absolutely delicious! So much so that it is often the staple when Mom and Dad are not there to curb the voracious appetites that are part of youth.

What are the favorites of our nutritionally misspent youth? According to a Gallup poll, they are the following, with the percentages of those who eat them regularly:

Pizza	82%
Chicken nuggets	51%
Hot dogs	45%
Cheeseburgers	42%
Macaroni and cheese	42%
Hamburgers	38%
Spaghetti and meatballs	37%
Fried chicken	37%
Tacos	32%
Grilled cheese sandwiches	22%

In Good Taste: Even though doctors may object to our eating too many hot dogs and french fries, there are at least a few things we've come to accept and even relish. On an average day:

- 16 million people eat at McDonald's.
- Teenage girls spend $4.86 on food.
- 2,739,726 Dunkin' Donuts are served.

- 17 million Tootsie Rolls are produced.
- 100 million M&Ms are sold.
- 24,657,534 hot dogs are sold.
- 524 million Coca-Colas are served.

Source: On an Average Day, *by Tom Heymann*

In Bad Taste: Every taco, every chocolate bar, every hot dog, and every other piece of food we consume brings some consequences. As Tom Heymann notes, on an average day:

- $289 million is spent on doctors.
- $92 million is spent on dentists.
- 2 million people suffer heartburn.
- 41 million men are on a diet.
- 60 million women are on a diet.

Foot Ailments
Sufferers Never Walk Alone

Each year, more than 80 million Americans have problems with the body's most specialized feature, feet. Each foot has 26 bones and is laced with ligaments, muscles, nerves, and blood vessels. About 3% of Americans — more than 7 million people — suffer from bunions, the most excruciat-

ing and disfiguring foot problem, and pay from $2,000 to $5,000 for operations to remove them, according to recent surveys.

Here is a list of the most common foot ailments in the U.S. and their occurrence per 1,000 of the population, according to Dr. Charles Kissel, APMA Public Opinion Research.

Corns/calluses	70
Heel pain	41
Ingrown toenails	39
Bunions	28
Athlete's foot	27
Blisters	27

Football Professionals
The Rocky Road to the Pros

Almost every young man who has ever picked up a pigskin would like to make it to the pros. The road is not an easy one; nevertheless, every year more than 300 men are drafted into the National Football League.

The Climb: Only about 1 of every 25 high school players will play on

Will he make it to the pros? The odds are about 1,000 to 1 for a high school football player.

NCAA teams in college. Of them, only about 1 in 30 will get drafted into the pros. Each year, 10,000 college players are eligible for the draft; 336 are selected. If a player is drafted, there is about an even chance he will make the team. Those who are drafted in the first round are almost certain to get in. The odds of getting on a team diminish with each round, and by the time the last round is drawn, the odds are 3 to 1 against a player's actually getting a place on the team after summer camp, when the draftees compete against current team members. Free-agent rookies have almost no chance at all, about 1 in 500.

College players who come from the major NCAA conferences have the greatest chance of making a pro team. This list names the conferences with the most players drafted in the NFL in 1993, as compiled by the Pacific 10 conference.

Big Eight	16
Big Ten	20
ACC	27
SEC	30
Pac 10	31

The Super Bowl: According to *What the Odds Are*, getting to play in one is a long shot. Mark Mravic, the sports editor of the book, describes what it takes: "Given an average NFL career of 6 years, the straight odds of making it to a Super Bowl are a little less than even, giving a high school player odds of 2,350 to 1 against playing in a Super Bowl. (Of course, the odds are a lot better if he's drafted by a good team rather than a bad one.) The odds of being the starting quarterback are another 45 to 1 against him, hence it is a 100,000 to 1 shot for a high school player; of being the winning quarterback, 200 to 1. And since odds of a Super Bowl being won in the last two minutes are 8.5 to 1 against; it's about a 2,000,000 to 1 shot that a high school hero will end up leading his team to a last-minute win in the Super Bowl." Mravic's advice to a high school player determined to play in one? "Keep practicing!"

Foreign Students
Asians Help Set Record

Along with a record 62% of U.S. high school graduates who enrolled in colleges and universities in 1991 — up from 60% the previous year — came a record number of foreign students, 407,500, a 5.3% increase over the previous year.

Of the top 10 countries sending students to America, 9 were in Asia and accounted for 56% of the total, according to the Institute of International Education. China led the way for the third year in a row, followed, in order, by Japan, Taiwan, India, South Korea, Canada, Malaysia, Hong Kong, Indonesia, and Pakistan.

The most popular foreign student major for the second year in a row was business. Engineering had been most popular for the previous forty years.

Foreign Takeovers
Japan Moves Up to No. 2

Somewhat more than 7% of the gross national product in the U.S. is produced by former U.S. companies that are now owned by foreigners. The most acquisitive nation is an old friend, Great Britain, but Japan is hot on its tail. In 1992, Japan placed second among the five top countries that are purchasing businesses in the U.S., putting it just behind the United Kingdom. The "Big Five" account for $407,577 billion in total foreign investment in U.S. property.

This list compares the Big Five's total investment in the U.S., in billions of dollars, between 1970 and

1991, as compiled by the Department of Commerce, Bureau of Economic Analysis.

	1970	1991
United Kingdom	$4.1	$106.1
Canada	$3.1	$30.0
Netherlands	$2.1	$63.8
Switzerland	$1.5	$17.6
Germany	$0.68	$28.2
Japan	$0.229	$86.7

Since 1970, Japan's purchases in the U.S. have totaled $86.8 billion, Britain's, $106.1 billion. Since 1985, however, Japan has moved into high gear, spending $171 billion of its new money and making splashy headlines by buying some of America's most treasured landmarks. Among them are:

- 1988: BankAmerica Corp. (part ownership), $200 million
- 1988: Breckenridge Resort (Colorado), $65 million
- 1988: Talbots clothing chain, $325 million
- 1989: Rockefeller Center, Radio City Music Hall, and the Time-Life Building (controlling interest), $846 million
- 1989: Selkirk Ranch (Montana), $13 million
- 1990: MCA, $6.13 billion
- 1992: Seattle Mariners baseball team (part ownership), $100 million

Foreign Visitors

Since the fall of the American dollar in 1972, when President Nixon took it off the gold standard, the prices of American goods and services have increasingly become a bargain for foreigners. In the 1960s, Americans traveling abroad marveled at the low prices. Today, it's foreigners in America who are snatching up goods at a much lower price than they would pay at home.

This phenomenon has made the U.S. a mecca for foreign travelers, and each year more than 20 million people visit our country. According to the Immigration and Naturalization Service, in 1992 the majority came from these top 10 nations in the following numbers:

Japan	3.95 million
United Kingdom	2.98 million
Germany	1.71 million
Mexico	1.53 million

France	.86 million
Italy	.64 million
Brazil	.49 million
China	.48 million
Australia	.47 million
Netherlands	.39 million

Why? Foreigners have many reasons to visit America, the first and foremost of which is to enjoy a vacation. This list shows the reasons of those who come, and their numbers, according to the INS.

Tourism	16.40 million
Business	2.80 million
Student/ family	.41 million
Exchange programs	.23 million
Temp work/ family	.21 million
Officials/ media	.20 million
Other	.63 million

Franchises

More Than 500,000 Sold

It became trendy in the early 1960s, grew to more than a $100-billion phe-nomenon by 1970, and by the 1980s became a mania. Today, more than one third of all retail dollars are spent at franchise operations, 9 of 10 people eat regularly at fast-food franchises, and more than 300,000 people sleep at a Holiday Inn each night. More than 500,000 franchises do business in America, accounting for $800 billion in annual sales. About 8 million people earn their living from franchises.

Today, lots of people with savings want to buy a successful franchise. It's a crowded playing field for franchisers who want to sell a new outlet, with some 2,000 to 3,000 companies hawking their wares from city to city like the old purveyors of medicines.

Foreigners Moving In: Into this maelstrom of moneymaking activities are now coming merchandisers from countries as far off as South Africa and Australia. One such company, Timbalyte International Franchisees of Cape Town, is hoping to franchise the quaint idea of coffins in kit form, which it is marketing for those interested in cremation. Heretofore, Canada has been the biggest foreign franchiser in the U.S.; as Susan Whyte, the director of marketing for

Successful franchising started primarily with chicken and burger outlets, but today even fragrant soap and toiletries are marketed at franchises such as Canada's latest export, SoapBerry's.

SoapBerry Shop in Toronto, says, "As a foreign country, we're the least foreign." SoapBerry has opened 5 units in the U.S. to sell its environmentally safe skin care products and projects 10 more in 1993.

The franchisers entering the country today are as diverse as the people who came to Ellis Island two generations ago. Into the crowded rental car field has come an Australian firm with the concept of short-term car and pickup rentals — even two-hour hires. Its goal for the U.S. is 25,000 franchises. Fisk School, of São Paulo, Brazil, has opened 420 schools in Brazil that teach English as a second language; it hopes to cash in on its expertise in the U.S.

Bruce Barnes, a Canadian, has purchased the northeastern U.S. rights to Le Club Français Ltd., of Hampshire, England, which helps children from 3 to 11 years old learn foreign languages through playing, singing, and acting, at $7.50 for a one-hour lesson. "It's very clubbish," he says.

Freshwater Fish
Contamination from Maine to California

Freshwater fish were the subject of cautionary notices in 1992, when the Environmental Protection Agency reported that 46 of 388 locations studied nationwide held dangerously contaminated fish. The EPA reported that it found DDT, banned in the U.S. as a cancer-causing agent twenty years ago, in nearly all the sites tested. PCBs represented the highest cancer risk, although the substance has been out of production since 1977. PCBs showed up in 91% of all samples tested.

Mirex, an insecticide used to control fire ants in the South, was the biggest problem. The deadly chemical, which was banned in 1975, was reported found in Lake Ontario, at Olcott, N.Y., where it was manufactured. To make matters worse, mercury was found in 92% of all fish sampled. Some of the people most at risk from the contaminated fish are Native Americans, for many of whom fish is a dietary staple. But it goes beyond that. Says Maxine Caldwell of the Assembly of First Nations: "It's not just hunting, fishing, and trapping. For First Nation people, it's a way of life."

Experts say that waterways become contaminated from leaky waste dumps, industrial discharges of toxins, and runoff from farms using toxic fertilizers. Where are fish lovers turning? To the oceans, it seems. According to the National Fisheries Institute, in 1991 tuna was the favorite seafood consumed in the U.S., at 3.60 pounds per capita. Shrimp was next, at 2.40 pounds per capita, followed by cod, 1.12, Alaska pollock, .99, and salmon, .97.

The list below notes those waterways and sites containing the most contaminants and the fish species affected by them, according to the EPA.

Most DDT
- Alamo River (Calipatria, Calif.) — Flathead catfish
- Blanco Drain (Salinas, Calif.) — Largemouth bass
- Delaware River (Torresdale, Pa.) — Channel catfish
- Mississippi River (Memphis) — Channel catfish/Bigmouth bass
- Waukegan Harbor (Waukegan, Ill.) —Lake trout

Most PCBs
- Hudson River (Fort Miller, N.Y.) — Largemouth bass
- Lake Ontario (Olcott, N.Y.) — Chinook salmon
- Little Valley Creek (Paoli, Pa.) — Brown trout
- Milwaukee River (Milwaukee) — Northern pike

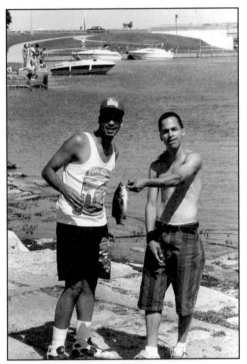

Should they eat it? Freshwater fish are good sport but potentially dangerous fare for dinner.

- Waukegan Harbor (Waukegan, Ill.) — Lake trout

Most Chlordane

- Delaware River (Torresdale, Pa.) — Channel catfish

- Lake Ontario (Olcott, N.Y.) — Chinook salmon
- Mississippi River (Memphis) — Channel catfish/Bigmouth bass
- Mississippi River (Quincy, Ill.) — Carp
- Waukegan Harbor (Waukegan, Ill.) — Lake trout

Most Mirex

- Lake Ontario (Olcott, N.Y.) — Chinook salmon
- Lake Ontario (Rochester, N.Y.) — Brown trout
- Mississippi River (East St. Louis, Ill.) — Catfish
- Niagara River Delta (Porter, N.Y.) — Smallmouth bass
- Oswego Harbor (Oswego, N.Y.) — Smallmouth bass

Frozen Assets
Five Nations, $2 Billion

A 1993 FBI report summed up the problem: "Members of certain international terrorist groups have infrastructures in the United States, and some provide financial support to their counterparts overseas. This financial support has been developed by various methods such as fund-raisers, money laundering via front companies, and counterfeiting."

What's being done about it may be one of the government's most ineffectual policies: it has frozen $2.1 billion of assets in the U.S. of five of the key nations accused of sponsoring international terrorism. A breakdown of these assets is:

Iraq	$1.1 billion
Libya	$903 million
Cuba	$111 million
Iran	$22 million
North Korea	$2.8 million

*Primarily real estate that was blocked since the hostage crisis in Tehran in 1979–81

Syria, which the State Department has designated as a "state sponsor of terrorism," may be the next country to have its assets seized. While no official involvement has been alleged, Syria provides a safe haven for terrorist groups, and their American assets have been carefully counted by the Treasury Office of Foreign Assets Control: $249 million, none of which has yet been blocked.

The Treasury is examining its new list of 39 terrorist groups to determine if further action against the nations that harbor them is in order. It is believed that Iran is the most dangerous, with more than 20 acts attributable to groups within its borders in 1992.

The nations that are most closely watched for hidden involvement are Cuba and North Korea. The former, however, has sharply curtailed its financial assistance to leftist Latin American nations, more perhaps because of fiscal pressures than ideology. North Korea continues to harbor the hijackers of a Japanese airliner and is a potential candidate to have its U.S. assets frozen if another incident takes place which is in any way attributed to them.

Gambling
Wanna Bet?

". . . Loan sharks, prostitutes, and drug dealers will be attracted to the casino locations. We're going to need 1,000 more officers." —William Nolan, president of Chicago's Fraternal Order of Police, commenting on the city's proposed gambling ordinance

They are gambling on riverboats, on Indian reservations, at the track, off the track, at church fund-raisers, and even at the grocery store where lottery tickets are sold.

Gambling is legal in one form or another in 48 of the 50 states, and Americans spend $300 billion on this recreation, about as much as the Department of Defense annually spends. The mania began in the 1980s, when state lotteries became popular as a way of raising money without raising taxes, a phenomenon supported by all but a few state and U.S. legislators. Thirty-four states now have them, twice as many as did ten years ago.

Poor Donald Trump: "How can I compete with them [Native Americans]?" says the Donald. He went on to tell the nation during a 1993 television interview that the casinos owned by Na-

Forty-eight states offer some form of gambling, but Vegas's Strip is still the Mecca of high rollers, complete with star-studded entertainment. Photo, courtesy Las Vegas News Bureau.

tive Americans in Connecticut are bringing down his gambling enterprises. His fabulously appointed Trump Castle, which is purported to have a daily overhead of $1 million, is in trouble. "I have to pay taxes," he said, reminding us that Native Americans don't. For all intents and purposes, Indian reservations are sovereign nations when it comes to taxation: its residents don't have to pay taxes on gambling revenues, nor are they required to abide by state gambling prohibitions. When the first casino opened in 1989 on a South

Dakota reservation, it earned $300 million the first year. Today, 175 tribes operate casinos on 200 reservations. And Donald Trump still has just one . . . and a hefty tax bill as well.

This list ranks, from most popular to least, ways in which Americans wager their money, according to *Gaming and Wagering Business Magazine.*

Lotteries
Casinos
Pari-mutuel betting
Charitable games
Bingo
Card rooms
Sports bookmaking

Garbage
What We Throw Away

No nation in history has produced the volume of garbage that America has. We burn it, ship it cross-country on barges, bury it, recycle it, even catalogue it to analyze our way of life. Here is a profile of what we throw away:

Paper products	37%
Yard waste	18%
Metal	10%
Glass	10%
Food waste	7%
Plastic	6%
Other	6%
Wood	4%

Profile of a Garbage Collector: "When you go to a cocktail party," the auditioning talk show host asked the sanitation worker, "what do you tell people you do for a living?" (If the audition went well, the host on trial would get his own show.) He nervously awaited the reply. "I don't go to too many cocktail parties," the garbage collector said. Of course, thought the embarrassed host; he had asked a stupid question. "But I guess," the garbage collector continued, "I'd tell 'em I make $40,000 a year — and that's not including overtime." Not only do garbage collectors make above-average incomes, in some municipal districts they have a coveted job. According to *The Jobs Rated Almanac,* the garbage collectors in a top-paying city earn an average of $30,486 annually. With one of the most secure jobs in the public sector, they are off work by 3:30 P.M. According to the book's scoring method, the job of a garbage collector ranks 231 out of a possible 250, 10 notches below the most coveted job of

Why is this garbage man smiling? He has good reason, indeed.

all, president of the United States, which ranks 241.

Garbage collectors have plenty to do. The average American throws away almost 1,300 pounds of garbage annually, about 100,000 pounds over a lifetime, which includes almost 15,000 pounds of food. In addition, the average American disposes of 10,370 aluminum cans, 67 tires, 487 pens, and 609 razors.

What happens to America's possessions once their owner officially designates them as garbage? Here is a breakdown:

	lbs.
Sent to landfills	76,548
Recycled	10,525
Converted to energy	5,741
Incinerated	2,871

Government Paychecks
Substandard at Best

The average pay of a president or CEO of a major U.S. corporation is more than $1 million, and many "second-tier" executives earn in the six-figure range. Those occupying comparable government jobs earn far less.

The salaries for the nation's 10 highest-paying government jobs, according to the Federal Information Center, are:

President	$200,000
Vice president	$160,600
Chief justice	$160,600
Associate justice	$153,600
Cabinet secretary	$138,900

Assistant secretary	$125,100	
Member of Congress	$129,500	
U.S. District Court judge	$125,100	
Deputy assistant secretary	$115,300	
Bureau chief	$108,300	

Grocery Shopping

The New Criteria

Not taste, not price, not convenience, but *nutrition* is the chief consideration of supermarket shoppers when buying everything from cake mixes to a can of soup. So says a survey conducted by the Grocery Manufacturers of America, a trade association representing 85% of the food and nonfood grocery products sold in the U.S.

According to the survey, the first and second consumer priorities were as follows:

	First	Second
Nutrition	44%	65%
Price	19%	26%
Taste	17%	20%
Product safety	9%	11%
Ease of preparation	5%	8%

Environmentally responsible packaging	3%	11%

And the label? Some 71% read the nutritional information all or most of the time, and 76% read the list of ingredients. The changes in packaged food products considered the most important in the last few years are reduced salt, fat, and cholesterol, according to 58% of the shoppers. The safety of the products satisfied 72% of them, but they were split on the value of additives, preservative residues, and toxic chemicals.

Hate Crimes

In its first report ever on the subject of hate crimes, the FBI confirmed what everybody knows: this country still has a serious race relations problem. In a survey of 2,771 law enforcement agencies out of the 16,000 nationwide that report to it on murders, aggravated assaults, and robberies, the FBI found 4,558 hate crimes in the U.S. in one year. More than half of them — 2,963 in all — stemmed from racial bias. The racial violence was twice as likely to be directed toward blacks as toward whites. Fully 35.5% of all the hate crimes were directed toward blacks because of their race, 18.7% toward whites because they were white.

But intolerance doesn't stop there. Of the remaining hate crimes, religious belief served as the reason in 27.4% of the crimes. Ethnic bias was next, at 9.5%, and sexual orientation, mostly directed against homosexuals, accounted for 8.9%.

"Weapons" of Choice: Unlike other crimes, in which guns or knives are used, hate crimes are often perpetrated with psychological weapons. Intimidation was the most common weapon used; in 1,614 incidents, or 33.9%, it was the preferred means of torment. Vandalism was next, with 1,301 incidents, 27.4% of the total. Simple assault occurred 796 times and aggravated assault, 773 times. In 12 instances, the violence resulted in the victims' death. Seven forcible hate-rapes were reported. The Hate Crime Statistics Acts of 1990 required the FBI to compile the figures but did not require all law enforcement agencies to participate.

Health Costs
It's Cheaper to Die

Anyone who has borne the financial burden of a terminally ill relative or friend can confirm that the final expense, the funeral, is minuscule compared to the medical costs. In 1993, Americans are expected to spend a mind-boggling $900 billion on health care and $8 billion on funeral expenses.

The cost of health care has quadrupled since 1980, whereas the cost for all other goods and services has increased an average of 65%. Those who keep an eye on medical costs refer to the rate at which prices rise above general inflation as "excess medical inflation," and it is not a pretty picture. Medical inflation is growing at an annual rate of 6%, and it was up to 9.7% in 1991.

General inflation has also contributed to the increased cost of health care; in 1991, it was 4.2%. Another factor has been a 1% growth in the nation's population. Other items and services have added 3.5%; they include advances in medical technology and the aging of the population, which means that there are more people to be treated.

Complicating the situation, Americans are more health conscious than ever and are seeking medical services at an increasing rate. In 1985, the average American saw a doctor 5 times a year. By 1991, the figure grew to 6 times. According to the National Center for Health Statistics, between 1980 and 1991 coronary bypass operations for men increased almost threefold, from 108,000 to 296,000. Ultrasounds for women rose from 114,000 to 652,000, and CAT scans rose from 306,000 to more than 1.4 million, a better than fourfold increase.

According to the Bureau of Labor Statistics, Health Care Financing Administration, here is where Americans will spend their health care dollars in 1993:

Hospitals	$359 billion
Physicians	$167 billion
Nursing homes	$74 billion
Drugs	$71 billion
Administration/ insurance	$48 billion
Other services	$45 billion
Dental services	$41 billion
Public health	$24 billion
Other personal health care	$20 billion
Research and development	$16 billion
Vision products	$14 billion
Home health care	$12 billion
Construction	$12 billion

Will anyone escape these costs? If possible, it is the 37 million Americans who have no health insurance. They most likely won't have to pay because they cannot afford the costs. Only those with assets of less than $1,000 will quality for federal Medicaid; the others are in trouble.

Health Insurers
Overhead Skyrocketing

In administering health insurance, for once the government is operating more efficiently than the private sector, and a study reported that the U.S. government and the Canadian health system spent far less than private companies. For every dollar paid in benefits, the private group spent 37.2 cents for administration, marketing, and overhead, while Medicare spent 2.1 cents per dollar and the Canadians, 0.9 cents.

In the last decade, administrative spending by private health insurance companies increased approximately 125% while benefits increased 80%, according to Citizen Action, the public interest group that ran the study. The biggest chunk of the costs went to salaries, sales commissions, employee benefits, and overhead for rent and advertising. These costs for the private group were even higher for individual health plans: 68.2 cents to deliver a dollar in benefits in 1990; in 1981, it was 30.7 cents.

According to the same study, American businesses and consumers would have saved about $120 billion from 1981 to 1990 if the private group had been as efficient as Medicare.

Highway Mileage

Each year Americans travel more than 1.4 trillion miles on the nation's major highways in about 190 million vehicles. Sometimes it seems as though everyone in the country is behind the wheel and that you are on the most crowded stretch of highway of all. That may be the case, at least if you are on the Beltway around Washington, D.C.; it's the nation's most crowded road.

Following are the states with the most-traveled roads, and the number of cars per thousand residents.

Washington, D.C.	n/a
New Jersey	731
California	737
Hawaii	696
Maryland	754
Connecticut	798
Massachusetts	619
Florida	714

The next list cites the number of various kind of vehicles on the nation's roads, as determined by the Department of Transportation.

Automobiles	142,500,000
Trucks	43,000,000
Motorcycles	4,200,000
Buses	600,000

Homeless People
More Trouble in Their Ranks

The Biggest Controversy: It's universally agreed that the plight of the homeless is a national disgrace, but there is almost no agreement as to how many people are homeless. The Department of Housing and Urban Development says there are 50,000. Homeless advocacy groups say 3 million. The Census Bureau has its own count.

March 20, 1990: The Census Bureau undertook a two-day count, visiting 11,000 shelters and 24,000 street sites. The census takers found far fewer homeless people to survey than others who have done head counts, such as those working with the homeless. The bureau's survey, however, is the best estimate we have of the nation's homeless population: 228,261 — 178,828 in emergency shelters and 49,793 at "preidentified street locations."

A 21-city survey by the U.S. Conference of Mayors found that 33% of the homeless who were surveyed were severely mentally ill; of that group, 37% were addicted to alcohol or illegal drugs. Among the cities, New York had the highest number of mentally ill, with 18,150; Louisville had the most drug users, 5,254.

This list cites the numbers of homeless people in major American cities,

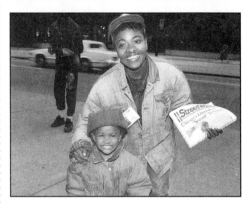

The newspaper <u>Streetwise</u> informs the public about homelessness as well as earns income for its homeless vendors. Photo, courtesy of Steve Nozicka.

according to the official count on March 20–21, 1990.

Alexandria, Va.	220
Boston	3,613
Charleston, S.C.	600
Chicago	6,764
Cleveland	10,000
Kansas City, Mo.	13,000
Los Angeles	31,000
Louisville	11,442
Nashville	942
New York City	55,000
Philadelphia	35,000
Phoenix	6,300
St. Paul	1,023
Salt Lake City	2,000

San Diego	7,000
San Francisco	3,000+
Santa Monica, Calif.	4,000
Seattle	1,350+
Trenton, N.J.	600
Washington, D.C.	7,500

Home Prices
The Bubble Bursts

At one time in America, to build a nest egg all you needed to do was buy a house, wait a few years for the 10%–15% real estate inflation to take effect, and count your money with a smile. Profits of $100,000 or more were realized by average homeowners between 1970 and 1980, when the real estate boom was at its peak. The boom is over now, and house prices more or less keep pace with inflation.

The median price for an existing single-family home in America was $104,200 in May 1993, according to the National Association of Realtors, which represents an increase in value of 5.1% from the first three months of 1992. Considering that inflation in the 1990s has been 3.9%, that isn't too bad for homeowners looking for a profit. In the decade thus far, however, prices are up only 3.5%; therefore they

are up only 0.4% over inflation. In the 1980s, home prices rose 4.8% and inflation averaged 5.1% — a *loss*, which seemed impossible at one time!

According to the NAR, the biggest increases and decreases in home prices in 1992 vs. 1993 were as follows:

Biggest Increases

Richland, Wash.	24.5%
Detroit	19.0%
Syracuse, N.Y.	11.2%
Spokane	10.9%
Charleston, W.Va.	10.2%
Fort Myers, Fla.	10.2%

Biggest Decreases

Toledo	−11.2%
Springfield, Mass.	−9.1%
Philadelphia	−9.0%
Los Angeles	−8.0%
Atlantic City	−7.8%

Median home prices vary enormously across the nation. This list shows the median prices in the 10 most and least expensive metropolitan areas during the first quarter of 1993, according to the NAR.

Most Expensive

| Honolulu | $347,000 |
| San Francisco | $249,300 |

Anaheim, Calif.	$222,200
Los Angeles	$199,700
Bergen-Passaic, N.J.	$182,800
New York	$168,000
Boston	$165,200
Middlesex County, N.J.	$158,400
Nassau–Suffolk County, N.Y.	$158,000
Washington, D.C.	$153,500

Least Expensive

Waterloo, Iowa	$44,300
Davenport, Iowa	$54,500
Peoria, Ill.	$57,500
Youngstown, Ohio	$58,600
Amarillo, Tex.	$59,700
Beaumont, Tex.	$60,300
Oklahoma City	$61,000
Topeka, Kans.	$62,900
South Bend, Ind.	$63,000
Omaha	$64,300

Homosexuals

Fewer Than Thought

Since the movement often called "coming out of the closet" has begun to emerge, many gays pegged the percentage of homosexuals in the U.S. at 10%. That estimate may be far off the mark.

Since the early 1980s, when the AIDS epidemic and the gay rights movement began to gain national momentum, many researchers have been more interested in getting a reliable count of the number of gay people in America. In 1950, the Alfred Kinsey team reported that 37% of males had had homosexual experiences and that 4% of Americans considered their primary sexual orientation to be homosexual. In 1988, the American Sociological Association reported that 3.7% of the nation was gay. Recently, several sophisticated surveys have come up with much smaller numbers.

The 1990 census counted 69,200 lesbian couples and 88,200 gay male couples —well below 1% of the nation. In 1993, one of the most respected behavioral research organizations, the Alan Guttmacher Institute, reported that 2% of the males have had homosexual experiences and 1% consider themselves primarily homosexual in their preferences.

Undoubtedly, gay activists are disappointed that, quantitatively, estimates are so low, but qualitatively, gay demographics are above average. For example, according to the census report released in 1993, 40% of the partners of homosexual couples have college degrees compared to 13% for heterosexual spouses.

The Homosexual Income Advantage: While married heterosexual couples have long been considered the highest income group in the nation, gay male couples have higher incomes than any other cohabiting group, according to the census report. One reason is that homosexual couples are more likely to have two working partners than are heterosexual ones, and gays are also more likely to live in big cities, where salaries are higher.

Further, male homosexual live-in partners, which represent 56% of homosexual couples, have the advantage of the income gender gap. According to the Bureau of Labor Statistics, women earn only 75% of what men do. When sexual orientation and living status are taken into account, the household incomes of male homosexual partners have the highest annual average earnings ($56,863); households of unmarried heterosexuals have the lowest ($37,602).

The list below represents a comparison of the average annual household incomes of heterosexuals and homosexuals, according to the 1993 census report.

Married heterosexuals	$47,012
Unmarried heterosexuals	$37,602
Male homosexuals	$56,863
Female homosexuals	$44,793

Gay Couples: Though the majority of Americans are opposed to gays serving in the military, they have a more liberal attitude toward whether homosexuals should be able to be legally married. According to a poll of 1,000 adults age 25 and over conducted by the Wirthin Group, 46% of singles and 30% of married couples say they should have that right.

Hospital Stays
Outpatient Services on the Rise

At one time, surgical patients were almost certain to stay in the hospital for at least one night. No longer, according to the American Hospital Association.

Its statistics indicate that there is almost an equal number of inpatient and outpatient operations: of 24 million annual operations, 11 million are performed on an outpatient basis, 11 million on an inpatient basis, and somewhat more than 2 million at locations removed from hospitals.

In 1980, only 16% of all hospital surgery was done on an outpatient basis. By 1985, with the increasing scrutiny of hospital costs by insurers and the Medicare program, that figure jumped to 36%. New England led the outpatient rate, with 42%; Illinois had the lowest rate, 27%.

Following are six surgical procedures that accounted for 2.4 million hospital days in 1990; all of them are rapidly becoming very short stay or outpatient procedures.

Gall bladder removal
Inguinal (above the testes) hernia repair
Hysterectomy
Prostatectomy
Appendectomy
Removal of part of the stomach

By the end of the century, 85% of all surgical procedures will be done on an outpatient basis, according to Jeff Goldsmith, the president of Health Futures, Inc.

Hotels for Nonsmokers
Clearing the Air

With only 26% of U.S. adults still smoking, hotels are catching up to the nonsmoking trend, reserving more nonsmoking rooms for the majority of their guests. It's smart business rather than a sudden concern for their guests' health.

Hotels cannot convert rooms to nonsmoking status fast enough to meet the demand, for considerable expense is involved. The hotels must shampoo carpets, dry-clean drapes and bedspreads, change pillows, and wash linens; some even throw out mattresses, bedspreads, and drapes and repaint the entire room. It is then sealed and air fresheners are brought in. All of this costs between $150 and $600 per room, according to hotel operators.

The percentages of nonsmoking rooms in major hotel chains are:

Marriott	60%
Hilton	50%
Ritz-Carlton	50%
Sheraton	40%
Hampton Inns	40%
Holiday Inn	30%
Radisson	25%

Choice	15%
Hyatt	10%
Stouffer	10%

Nonsmoking Contracts: Some hotels require guests to sign contracts, promising not to smoke in nonsmoking rooms. If guests do smoke (and get caught), the hotel has the right to charge them for cleaning the room again. Making the agreement formal poses a potential problem: When the smoking rooms are full, what happens when smokers must take a nonsmoking room? In the face of a legal contract, will they cheat or simply go to another hotel? The problem is likely to be greater for international travelers, a higher percentage of whom smoke. They account for 10% of U.S. hotel visitors.

Hotel Telephone Surcharges

Bane to Travelers,
Boon to Management

Many travelers are visibly shaken when they see that their hotel bill reflects surcharges on it for each phone call they made (sometimes even those that didn't go through). It is not uncommon for such surcharges to total as much as $50 for a two- or three-day stay by a business person who is on the phone constantly. It's the cost of doing business, hotel management says; phone systems are expensive to install and maintain.

But many guests consider the surcharges unprincipled gouging, and in response to their growing clamor, some hotels are looking for solutions that will not increase room rates. Stouffer has dropped its surcharges on credit card and collect calls as well as those to 800 numbers. Four Seasons, on the other hand, charges almost a dollar to call a *toll-free* number. Some budget hotels now offer unlimited free local calls.

The following list indicates how much different hotel chains charge for local calls and the surcharge for calling-card calls, as compiled by *USA Today*.

	Local	Calling Card
Courtyard by Marriott	$.50	$.00
Four Seasons	$.95	$.95
Hampton Inns	$.00	$.00
Hilton (company-owned)	$1.00	$.00
Hyatt	$.75	$.75

Marriott	$.75	$.75
Red Roof	$.00	$.00
Sheraton (USA, Canada)	$.75	$1.00
Stouffer	$.75	$.00

Household Injuries

Product-related Mishaps

Each year manufactured goods send almost 5 million Americans to the hospital. Some 15,000 of these injuries result from ill-advised uses of baby strollers, according to the Consumer Product Safety Commission. But babies are not the most at risk. Stairs and steps, used by normal adults, account for a million hospitalizations annually. Bikes and bike accessories are the second leading cause of product injuries, with 600,000, followed by knives (500,000), tables (350,000), and chairs (300,000).

Oddball Injuries: Many common objects, which are not generally regarded as dangerous, inflict serious injuries. Perhaps the greatest danger is not realizing that certain things can be hazardous. Wheelchairs, for example, annually cause 50,000 injuries requir-

ing hospitalization, and bunk beds injure 40,000. Even the most innocuous things at home can be dangerous. Burns from hot water cause 40,000 trips to the hospital. Televisions injure 30,000; telephones, 16,000; and jewelry, 40,000.

The following products frequently cause about the annual number of injuries listed beside them, according to data adapted from the CPSC.

Nails, screws, tacks	250,000
Bathtubs, showers	140,000
Drinking glasses	130,000
Ladders	130,000
Fences, fence posts	120,000
Drugs, medications	110,000
Bottles, jars	110,000
Metal containers	100,000

Other goods causing 50,000 or more injuries annually include carpets and rugs, footwear, lawn mowers, skateboards, sinks, toilets, and hammers.

Hurricanes

Though the effectiveness of speedy warning systems has doubled and redoubled in recent decades, hurricanes still are engines of tragedy

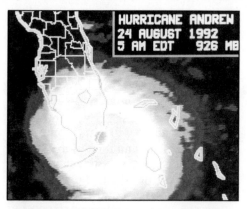

HURRICANE ANDREW
24 AUGUST 1992
5 AM EDT   926 MB

Like a bull's-eye, Miami was almost in the eye of Hurricane Andrew, America's worst national disaster.

with but a single benefit: they are a major source of rain for those continental corners they unpredictably strike. The costliest natural disaster ever to strike the U.S. was Hurricane Andrew, which hit South Florida and Louisiana in August 1992, killing 30 persons in Florida and 4 in Louisiana and causing an estimated $20 billion in property damage.

The number of deaths caused by hurricane-related injuries has greatly diminished in modern times. Earlier in this century, thousands could die in the storms. The highest death toll in U.S. history was recorded in Galveston, Tex., in 1900 when 6,000 died.

Once radio and television transmissions became common and warnings could be broadcast, however, the number of deaths dropped, and most of the worst storms registered fewer than 100 deaths. In 1969 Hurricane Camille, one of the strongest ever recorded, caused 256 deaths.

Here are the costliest hurricanes and the damage inflicted, according to the U.S. Weather Service.

- Andrew (Fla., S.C.; 1992) — $20 billion
- Hugo (S.C.; 1989) — $7 billion
- Frederick (Ala., Miss.; 1979) — $2.3 billion
- Agnes (northeast U.S.; 1972) — $2.1 billion
- Alicia (Tex.; 1983) — $2 billion
- Juan (La.; 1985) — $1.5 billion
- Camille (Miss., Ala.; 1969) — $1.42 billion
- Betsy (Fla., La.; 1965) — $1.42 billion
- Elena (Miss., Ala., Fla.; 1985) — $1.25 billion
- Gloria (eastern U.S.; 1985) —$900 million

Incomes

Personal Compensation

Other than their deepest personal feelings, the thing Americans lie about the most is their income. According to the book *The Day America Told the Truth*, 43% of Americans have lied about it. Those who know statistics and want to have flexibility when stating their income can have a field day with the issue of compensation because income can be expressed in many ways. A few of them include household income, average worker compensation, and per capita income.

To show how figures can be deceiving yet absolutely correct, consider the following facts about annual incomes in the U.S. from various sources. (The figures have been adjusted to reflect 1993 dollars at the beginning of the year.)

- The average pay of the most common jobs in America is $44,014. — *The Jobs Rated Almanac*
- The median family income in the U.S. is $36,731. — U.S. Census Bureau
- The per capita income in metropolitan areas in America is $20,117. — Bureau of Economic Analysis
- The per capita income in America is $19,841. — U.S. Department of Commerce

Perhaps the most meaningful measurement is per capita income, because it takes into account individuals who don't work, most of whom rely on the family breadwinner. Hence it represents how much money average Americans have to represent themselves in the marketplace.

Below are the states with highest and lowest per capita incomes in the U.S. at the beginning of 1993, according to the Department of Commerce.

Highest Incomes

Connecticut	$26,979
New Jersey	$26,457
District of Columbia	$26,360
Massachusetts	$24,059
New York	$23,534

Lowest Incomes

West Virginia	$15,065
Utah	$15,325
New Mexico	$15,353
Arkansas	$15,439
Louisiana	$15,712

Another significant measure of income is how well it keeps pace with inflation. In 1991, for example, per capita income rose 2.4%, but the inflation rate was 3.1%. Hence individuals with average per capita incomes had less to show for it when their bills were paid. In 1992, income increases surpassed the inflation rate — up 3.9% in the face of 2.9% inflation — the first year in the last three in which a real gain was made. In the 1980s, however, American incomes fared well in relation to inflation: per capita incomes rose 7.0% in the face of 5.1% inflation.

Perhaps the worst aspect of income statistics is the disparity in incomes among various minorities in America. Also, despite a growing trend of women succeeding in the work force, they earn about three quarters of what men do.

Below are the family incomes of the three principal racial groups in the U.S., according to the Census Bureau. (The figures have been adjusted to reflect 1993 dollars at the beginning of the year.)

Whites	$38,355
Hispanics	$24,345
Blacks	$22,258

Incomes — Cities vs. Suburbs

Question: The riots in Los Angeles appear to be revealing once again that the needs of some urban citizens are not being met. What's the most pressing need for the cities? *Answer:* Jobs and skills. — Richard Nathan, political scientist, in interview with *USA Today*

Those living in the inner city in America are earning from one third to one half of the salary earned by those in the nearby suburbs. Under the Reagan and Bush administrations, federal aid to cities declined more than 50%, from $50 billion to $21.7 billion, forcing them to raise taxes by 72% and cut services by 42%. Adding even further damage where there was high unemployment, the cities cut back their work forces by 32% over the same period. The result has been growing poverty and bitterness in areas with high percentages of jobless people.

The suburban areas of major U.S. cities fared better, mainly because their median incomes are larger, more than 50% higher around San Francisco, Newark, El Paso, and Boston. This table shows how some major cities stand in per capita income compared to their suburbs, as compiled by the League of Cities and the U.S. Conference of Mayors.

	City	Suburbs
Atlanta	$11,689	$17,892
Boston	$12,984	$30,158
Charlotte	$13,970	$15,519
Dallas	$13,489	$20,415
El Paso	$8,027	$19,049
Miami	$9,830	$16,689
Newark	$7,622	$23,747
San Antonio	$12,592	$12,893
San Fran-cisco	$15,137	$32,315

Income Taxes

During the average workday (9 a.m. to 5 p.m.), it will take Americans almost 3 hours to pay their taxes —1 hour and 46 minutes to pay federal taxes and another 59 minutes for all other taxes.

Tax Facts: Death and you-know-what are inevitable, but a few other things happen with regularity. The following events took place in 1992 and can be expected to continue similarly in the years to come.

- Returns filed —115 million
- Late filings —30 million taxpayers waited until the final week to file their returns.
- Returns audited —990,000
- Criminal charges filed —3,477
- Persons sent to prison —1,814

Did You Read His Lips . . . or His Mind? Withholding taxes can be a tricky business. The trick is to make citizens "feel" that the rates have gone down when in fact they have not. Here's how the Bush administration did it. In 1992, the average single taxpayer gained an extra $172.50 each paycheck. Married couples filing jointly picked up $342. What's the catch? The tax liability was generally the same, but the withholding was lowered. At tax time, everyone paid at the same rate as they did the year before. Only those who increased their withholding by filing a new W-4 form came out even. Those who relied on previous withholding rates either owed taxes or received a smaller refund.

So how much do we pay Uncle Sam? On average, workers paid about $4,000 in 1991, which was slightly less than they paid in 1990 because the recession and its effects on production brought down individual earnings. Nonetheless, personal taxes paid since 1985 were up 27%. This table represents personal income tax (in billions) paid by American workers in recent years.

1985	$336
1986	$350
1987	$393
1988	$401
1989	$452
1990	$470
1991	$461

The Installment Plan: Uncle Sam knows that if you make it hard enough on those who cannot pay their taxes, many will simply avoid filing or put it off as long as possible. For those who owe but can't pay, a deal is available by filing IRS form 9465 (an installment request), which should be attached to the 1040 form with a check for as much as you can afford. The IRS will contact you within 30 days and tell you how much to pay. It's not a free ride, however; there's a 6% penalty plus 7% interest to pay as well.

Income Tax Refunds
Withholding Cut Backfires

In a quaint turn of economic events, the cut in tax withholding that President Bush ordered in 1992 to inject some life into the economy via consumer spending actually hindered economic recovery in 1993, according to David Levy, the vice chairman of Jerome Levy Economics. He estimated that consumers' spendable income after the tax cut was decreased 2% a year by the president's action.

In 1992, an average 1991 income tax refund check of $1,000 went out to 86 million Americans. But after the tax cut, according to the American Payroll Association, 80% of all workers took Bush's bait and spent the amount saved thanks to the lower withholding rate — an average of $345 per married couple filing jointly and $172.50 for single taxpayers. Inevitably, those free spenders had to account for that money on their income tax reports at the end of the year, thus reducing the refund they received in 1993. Levy estimated the total amount at up to $20 billion taken out of the already sluggish economy. Rosalind Wells of the NPD Group added that Christmas spending in 1992 left many consumers overextended, starting the New Year riding on their charge cards.

Indian Youths

"This is the most devastated group of adolescents in the United States." — *Michael Resnick, researcher at the University of Minnesota*

Alarming problems have been found in a study of Native American youths. Broken homes, suicides, premature deaths, sexual abuse, and other ills plague these young people far more than they do other youths. So concluded a study conducted on nearly 14,000 rural teens from 50 tribes in 15 states who answered a questionnaire that was circulated by the American Medical Association. The study was confined to those living on reservations.

Native American teens are twice as likely to die during their youth as other teens, and 1 in 6 have attempted suicide between grades 7 and 12, four times the rate of other teens, according to a 1992 report in the *Journal of the American Medical Association*. And 1 in 5 of the teens say they are in poor health, although they don't experience more health problems than other young people until they reach the ninth grade, when their lack of role models begins to show. As many as 18% say they have been victims of sexual abuse.

Presently, there are only 17 mental health workers for the nation's 400,000 Native American youth, and Senator Daniel Inouye (D-Hawaii) said 200 are needed. Congressman George Miller (D-California), the chair of the House Interior Committee, said the AMA study "strips the charade away" that Native Americans are doing all right.

And the answer? According to the researchers who conducted the study, it may be found in improved health services, better education, stronger cultural ties, and the creation of mentorship programs to provide the role models that many Native American children need.

Individual Retirement Accounts

The popularity wanes but the pie is huge, even after the government changed the deductibility status. Nonetheless, the number of dollars currently invested in IRAs is still large enough to influence the stock market.

Money magazine estimates that $39 billion in fresh dollars was contributed to IRAs in 1992, down from $72 billion in 1991. Even so, the total IRA investment in 1993 was $725 billion, up from $199 billion in 1985, according to the Investment Company Institute.

Mutual Funds Soaking Up Dollars: From 1990 through 1992, stocks rallied briskly in May when IRA holders began switching their savings into mutual funds; many more Americans went down to the wire with their tax returns, including those holding IRAs, who simply delayed decisions on their accounts. The giant Fidelity Investment group of mutual funds reported opening 60% more IRA accounts since January 1993. Vanguard Group said IRA accounts were up 35% over the levels of the year before.

The mutual fund industry claims to have 29.1% of those assets, double its share in 1985. According to Kathryn Hopkins, an executive vice president at Fidelity, 80% of the IRA money at Fidelity is targeted for stock funds. The most popular IRA choices, she says, are conservative stocks and Fidelity's Asset Manager funds, which emphasize stocks but include bonds and cash investments as well.

Industries
A Little Service?

Service industries today dwarf those involved in the manufacture of goods (durable and nondurable). This list cites the 10 largest industries in the U.S. today and the number of workers they employ, according to the Department of Labor.

Health services	8.1 million
Eating and drinking places	6.5 million
Business services	5.9 million
Durable goods	3.8 million
Transportation	3.8 million
Food stores	3.8 million
Finance	3.4 million
Nondurable goods	2.6 million
General merchandise stores	2.4 million
Insurance	2.2 million

At one time or another, agriculture, manufacturing (durable and nondurable goods), and railroads were the largest U.S. industries. Now, a whole new class of smaller industries is emerging. The next list shows the annual rate of increase of the fastest-growing subindustries in the U.S.

Electromedical equipment	9.0%
Surgical and medical	8.2%
Medicinals and botanicals	8.0%
Semiconductors and related devices	7.8%
X-ray apparatus and tubes	7.8%
Motorcycles, bicycles, and parts	7.7%
Farm machinery and equipment	7.7%
Oil and gas field machinery	7.7%
Household audio and video equipment	6.8%
Poultry slaughtering and processing	6.6%

Inflation

"Gold will be over $2,000 an ounce . . . interest rates will exceed 40% . . . Social Security pension benefits will exceed $100,000 a year . . . inflation will cause a constitutional crisis by 1987." — *Howard Ruff, predictions from his 1981 book,* Survive and Win in the Inflationary Eighties

Those who bet on inflation in the eighties made a giant miscalculation. Millions of "savvy" investors, including the inflation-hedge guru Howard Ruff, did just that. In the late 1970s and early 1980s, inflation in the U.S. was at its worst in modern history, averaging about 10% annually. When it reached its peak of 13.5% in 1980, economists and financial writers warned about the "inflationary eighties"; in retrospect, however, the 1980s was a period of disinflation.

So far in the 1990s, annual inflation rates have averaged 3.9%. This list shows inflation in the 1990s, as computed by the Bureau of Labor Statistics.

1990	5.4%
1991	4.2%
1992	3.0%
1993	3.5%–4.5%*

*estimated range

Even inflation that stays in the 4%–5% range increases costs dramatically over time. During the 1980s, inflation averaged 5.1%. In that same period, however, wages and salaries more or less kept pace with inflation. Barring interruptions in their employment status, the average consumer did not feel a pinch. The result is that by the early 1990s, wages and prices had increased about an average of 60%; hence few felt inflation's grip unless they suffered from a period of unemployment.

Why is it, then, that prices seem to being going up? One reason is that the Consumer Price Index, on which the federal government bases its annual inflation figures, assumes that a consumer is buying a mixed basket of goods and services. Few consumers, however, buy the same basket that government economists put into their equation. In the real world, each consumer has different priorities for spending. Those who spend their money, for example, on a house, college tuition, and other items that have increased beyond the inflation rate will come up short. Food is the only item that has historically kept pace with inflation since World War II.

This list shows the cost increases in different categories since 1980, according to the BLS.

Clothing	41%
New cars	48%
Food	61%
Housing	91%
Medical care	164%

Price Multiples, 1950–1991: Those who have heard their grandmother remi-nisce about when eggs were 10 cents a dozen during the Great Depression can play a similar game with the table below. The numbers in the right-hand column represent the multiple by which prices increased from different years compared to the prices in 1991. For example, something that sold for $1 in 1950 cost $5.66 in 1991.

1950	5.66
1960	4.60
1970	3.51
1980	1.65
1990	1.04

Intercourse

Some 150 million Americans (88% of adults) engage in sexual intercourse at least once each year. The average frequency is 57 times annually. Women have intercourse an average of 51 times annually, men, 66 times.

Some 85% have participated in oral sex; 24% have participated in interracial sex, and 31% have had intercourse in public places. The following list represents various situations involving sexual intercourse among American men and women. (The figures do not total 100% because of the variance in groups surveyed and multiple answers.)

Adult Preferences

With spouse	80%
With lights off	62%
Missionary position	61%
Woman on top	26%

For Females

Have any orgasm	92%
Premarital	72%
Before age 20	67%
Regular orgasms	60%
Orgasms while penetrated	37%
Never done it	32%
Anal penetration	32%

For Males

Premarital	81%
Done before age 20	78%
Performed cunnilingus	76%
Done with prostitute	34%
Never done it	29%

Sources: National Center for Health Statistics; Alfred Kinsey Report; Singles, the New Americans, by Jacqueline Simenauer and David Carroll

Interracial Marriage

Before the passage of the 1965 Civil Rights Act, many interracial couples lived in fear of being discovered by an intolerant public, and only some 1 in 200 marriages were between couples of different races. By 1970, 1 in 145 marriages were interracial, by 1980, 1 in 75; and by 1990, 1 in 53. Today, slightly more than 20% of interracial marriages are between blacks and whites; the others involve other races as well.

This list shows various interracial marriage combinations, according to the Census Bureau, and the approximate proportions of them among interracial couples ("other" refers to Asians, Native Americans, and mixed races).

White man and woman (other)	50%
White woman and man (other)	25%
Black man and white woman	16%
White man and black woman	6%
Black man and woman (other)	3%
Black woman and man (other)	1%

Jails

More Room to Grow

In addition to more than 800,000 men and women who are serving out their sentences in prison, a large contingent of the nation's incarcerated population is in city and county jails.

A total of 426,479 men and women were in jails in 1991. Some 51% were awaiting trial, a 5.2% increase from 1990. Life inside is not just a matter of waiting to go home or to prison, however. Some never get out at all. In 1991, 546 inmates died in jail: 54% from natural causes, 15% from AIDS, 24% by suicide, and 3% from homicide by their peers.

A Day in Jail: Unlike state and federal prisons — which, at least in theory, aim to rehabilitate criminals — city and county jails are primarily detention centers for those serving light sentences or awaiting trial for more serious crimes. The chief activity of most inmates is waiting.

This table shows the daily average population of jails and a breakdown of their inmates, according to Bureau of Justice statistics.

	1990	1991
Men	365,821	384,628
Women	37,198	39,501
Juveniles	2,301	2,350
Total	405,320	426,479

Though more people are in jail every year, a boom in jail construction has reduced the problem of overcrowding from 104% of capacity to 101%.

Job Growth

Postwar Boom Runs Out of Steam

Slow job growth now, slow job growth later, is the gloomy forecast of the president of a leading consulting firm, David Birch, of Cognetics, Inc.

Against the prevailing optimistic view of most economic analysts — slow growth in the early nineties but fast growth later — Birch predicts that the rate of job growth in the U.S. will be 1% for the next ten years, not the 7% that followed the recession of 1983–84. He maintains that the U.S. will never again reach that 7% figure because of a steady decline in the birth rate in the 20th century (interrupted by the postwar baby boom, which increased the population's growth rate from less than 1% a year to 2%).

The trend toward job growth is spent, Birch says, and the work force now is growing by only 1.2% a year. The National Federation of Independent Businesses confirms this

Dangerous? The Chicago Police Department's lakefront bike patrol is not quite as perilous as other beats.

view. Its 1992 survey showed that only 17% of small firms planned to expand hiring, and they were the firms behind the 1970s and '80s job growth, selling appliances, such as air conditioners and microwave ovens, to the boomers, who now have all they need and are busy paying off their credit card bills.

Of the 20 business categories that had large declines, the largest was suffered by appliance dealers. Birch's parting comment: "It's not so bad. Everybody's waiting for the big surge [after the 1990s recession], and it's not happening. When people accept that it's going to be a slow recovery, they'll settle into an economy that will be healthy, but just slower."

Job Hazards
Some Literally Work to Death

Some people leave home for work and don't return, for death and injury on the job are more commonplace than we think. Though a policeman's job is often considered the quintessential dangerous occupation, it is not the only one.

Here is a list of the jobs at which the most deaths occur and the approximate odds that a worker will be killed at them, according to figures from the National Institute for Occupational Health and Safety.

Police	1 in 2,500
Taxi driver	1 in 30,000
Convenience store clerk	1 in 45,000
Trucker	1 in 60,000
Gas station attendant	1 in 75,000
Retail store clerk	1 in 110,000
Restaurant/ bar worker	1 in 140,000

Ordinary cops have the most dangerous occupation of all: each year almost 400,000 are assaulted. In the city, the odds of their being killed is about the same as those of a soldier in battle. Law enforcement officers working for the federal government have the lowest incidence of being assaulted.

The next list represents the number of assaults on federal officers reported by the FBI in 1990, the latest available statistics.

Fewest Assaults

IRS agent	3
Bureau of Indian Affairs agent	5
Postal inspector	6

Most Assaults

Immigration & Naturalization Service agent	409
U.S. attorney	269
Bureau of Prisons officer	185

Judgeships
Help Wanted

It is hard to imagine a plum job with a near-six-figure salary, excellent perks and prestige, and *a 14% vacancy rate*, but the federal court system, with 846 judgeships, has 117 vacancies at this writing.

Though there are 66 nominations pending for these jobs, the U.S. court system is hanging the Vacancy sign out for federal district court judgeships in most of the country. Surprisingly, the states with the most vacancies are those that traditionally attract voluntary transferees: Florida, California, and New York. Only 16 states have

The U.S. Supreme Court building is home base for the federal district court, with more than 100 judges. Photo, courtesy Washington, D.C., Convention and Visitors Association.

their full quota of judges; the rest have anywhere from 1 to more than 4 posts to fill at $96,000 annually. Some states are especially hard pressed because they have a small judicial system and need between 1 and 3 judges. Among them are Delaware, with only 3 district courts; Idaho, with 2; South Dakota, with 3; and Wyoming, with 2.

The courts are often criticized for not having enough minorities on the bench. Presently, 21.4% judges are from minority groups, including women. According to the Administra-tive Office of U.S. Courts, Alliance for Justice, the number of minority judges is as follows:

Women	76
Blacks	44
Hispanics	30
Asians	4
Disabled	2

Junk Mail
Deluge Piles Up in Landfills

One person's junk may be another's treasure, but the proliferation of advertising mail ultimately results in 156 million tons of direct mail, cat-alogues, and newspaper inserts clog-ging the nation's landfills annually, says John Ruston, an economic analyst at the Environmental Defense Fund.

Catalogue mailings, for example, in-creased from about 12 billion in 1986 to 14 billion today, and this represents only one quarter of all the advertising mail. Brochures top the outpouring, with 55%; 5% are coupons, 7%, charity, and 7%, "other."

Surveys taken by the Direct Marketing Association, Simmons Market Research Bureau, Marketing Logistics, Inc., and the Postal Service show other trends in advertiser mail:

- The amount of junk mail depends on the recipient's income. Persons earning less than $15,000 a year receive approximately 12 pieces a week; those earning $65,000 and more, 35 or more.
- Total U.S. mail order sales are approximately $200 billion.
- About 100 million American adults shop by mail, an increase of almost 75% in ten years.

Language Studies
Americans Too Smug About English

Let *them* learn to speak English — that is the attitude of most Americans toward learning a foreign language. Unfortunately, there is evidence that this sentiment is hurting Americans abroad.

In Japan, France, Germany, Italy, and the Scandinavian countries, many people know English well enough to get along, placing them some steps ahead of Americans in their ability to participate fully in today's global economy.

The Japanese have a strong advantage in dealing with the U.S. because of their widespread knowledge of English. Slowly, Americans are discovering that doing business in more than one language makes sense. However, the idea has not yet caught on among students who will soon be entering the business world.

According to the Modern Language Association, scarcely more than a million university students in the country are enrolled in the six principal language courses available. Below is a breakdown of the languages and the number of students studying them.

Language	Students
Spanish	533,607
French	272,555
German	133,380
Italian	49,726
Japanese	45,717
Russian	44,384

Languages Spoken at Home
Foreign Languages Near Record High

Not since World War II have so many Americans spoken a foreign language at home. Today, 1 in 7 U.S. residents speaks a language other than English. Spanish is the leading tongue, spoken by 17 million Americans — 54% of those who do not use English at home. All told, 31.8 million American residents speak 329 foreign languages in their households. This represents an increase of 34% in foreign language usage since 1980.

Asian languages account for 14% of foreign language speakers, reflecting the new wave of immigration. European languages have declined the most, as the descendants of the old immigrants abandon such languages as German, Yiddish, Polish, and Italian.

This list represents the 20 most common foreign languages in use in the home and the states with the highest percentage of speakers, according to the U.S. Census Bureau.

Spanish	7,339,172	N. Mexico
French	1,702,176	Maine
German	1,547,099	N. Dakota
Italian	1,308,648	New York
Chinese	1,249,213	Hawaii
Tagalog	843,251	Hawaii
Polish	723,483	Illinois
Korean	626,478	Hawaii
Vietnamese	507,069	California
Portuguese	429,860	Rhode Is.
Japanese	427,657	Hawaii
Greek	388,260	Mass.
Arabic	355,150	Michigan
Hindi	331,484	New Jersey
Russian	241,798	New York
Yiddish	213,064	New York
Thai/Lao	206,266	California
Persian	201,865	California
Creole	187,658	Florida
Armenian	149,694	California

Other languages spoken by more than 100,000 American residents and the states in which they are chiefly used are: Navajo (New Mexico), Hungarian (New Jersey), Hebrew (New York), Dutch (Utah), Mon-Khmer (Rhode Island), and Gujarathi (New Jersey).

Below are the 5 states that have the most and the fewest foreign language speakers in the home, according to the U.S. Census.

Most Foreign Speakers

New Mexico	35.5%
California	31.5%
Texas	25.4%
Hawaii	24.8%
New York	23.3%

Fewest Foreign Speakers

Kentucky	2.5%
West Virginia	2.6%
Arkansas	2.8%
Alabama	2.9%
Tennessee	2.9%

Most of those who speak foreign languages at home, 94.2%, speak some English. More than half of foreign language users, 56.1%, speak English "very well," 23% speak it "well," and 15.2% speak it "not very well." Only 5.8% speak no English at all.

Layoffs

"Stormy Mondays"

It turns out that there is yet another reason to hate Mondays. No longer are they just "blue," some of them are the darkest shade of gray.

Employers announce more layoffs on Mondays than on any other day in the week, according to Challenger, Gray & Christman, a job replacement consulting firm. Its report on the first three months of 1993 indicates that of 170,615 layoffs announced by 150 companies, 67,487, or 40%, were announced on a Monday, launching the now widely used label for the day:

"Stormy Mondays." Tuesday came in second, with 55,168 layoffs (32%), Thursday third, with 18,514 (11%), and Friday fourth, with 16,935 (10%).

"Announcing layoffs on Monday makes more of a 'clean break' and gives the employee an opportunity to get an early start on planning his or her search for a new job," said James E. Challenger, the president of the consulting firm. The cleanest break of all came one Monday in Illinois, which suffered 56,789 layoffs in the first quarter of 1993; 50,000 of them were at one company, Sears, Roebuck.

Lefties

Study Finds "Risk Factors"

The Aristera Organization of Westport, Conn., has found that both the mentally retarded and the academically superior include more left-handers than the general population. But left-handedness brings its share of problems. A disproportionate share of lefties winds up in hospital emergency rooms. Why? Door injuries, one of the most common, affect left-handed people more because most doors open from the right.

Some 1 in 10 people are naturally left-handed. Among children, 1 in 7 are; however, many are pressured to change and therefore go through a "clumsy" period while in transition.

When Dr. Charles Graham of the University of Little Rock studied 761 children treated at emergency rooms, he concluded that being a lefty carries a decided "risk factor." He found that accident patients were 1.7 times more likely to be lefties, and male lefties (who outnumber females 2 to 1) were twice as likely to have accidents as females. Previous studies have found that lefties die younger, presumably from accidental deaths.

Once grown up, however, left-handers have a great advantage: they are less in danger of strokes incapacitating them because, unlike right-handers, they have speech control on both sides of the brain, so damage to one side can be offset.

Lies, Lies, Lies

"Just about everyone lies — 91% of us lie regularly."(Trust me on this)

So say the authors of *The Day America Told the Truth*, a book reveal-ing some of America's darkest secrets. When we don't lie, the researchers tell us, 45% of the time it is because we feel that lying is wrong; only 17% of the time do we refrain from lying for fear of being caught.

The Truly Serious Liar: The above study defines serious lies as those that "hurt people, violate a trust, have legal consequences, or are totally self-serving." Who would do such a thing? According to the findings, the most serious liars are :

- Men (40%) vs. women (31%)
- Homosexuals/bisexuals (52%) vs. heterosexuals (33%)
- Blacks (51%) vs. whites (33%)
- Catholics (36%) vs. Protestants (34%) vs. Jews (25%)
- Unemployed (42%) vs. employed (34%)
- Liberals (37%) vs. conservatives (29%)
- Ages 18–24 (50%)
- Ages 25–44 (34%)
- Ages 45–64 (29%)
- Ages 65 and older (19%)
- People earning less than $10,000 annually (49%) vs. those making $45,000 or more (31%)

. . . and about what

True feelings	81%
Income	43%
Accomplishments	42%
Sex life	40%
Age	31%
Education	23%
Family background	22%
Marital status	16%
Race	14%

Lightning Strikes

Lightning only strikes once, but after that, who or what is on the hot side of the bolt from the heavens? The reality is that on an average day, lightning strikes one unlucky person in America. Surprisingly, about 2 in 3 people who get zapped live to tell about it, although most have no recollection of the actual impact because the usual dose of about 3,000 million kilowatts causes an instant blackout.

With about three bolts per second striking American soil, the odds of someone's getting hit by one of them on any given day is a comfortable 250 million to 1. This is little comfort, however, for the 376 men who have been killed by lightning since 1985, according to the National Weather Service. In the same period, 63 women met the same fate. The discrepancy, says the service, is caused by the jobs and recreational activities of men, who expose themselves to lightning more often than women do.

The Big Hit: The average bolt of lightning has a life of between 1/30 and 1/10 of a second. The reasons we don't miss seeing something that brief are its magnificent luminosity and sheer length, between 1,000 feet and almost 2 miles. The point of impact is almost always open water or vegetation. The most common land strike is a tree. What do you think is one of the most common impact sites of all man-made objects? (Hint: It is in New York City, King Kong climbed all over it, and it gets hit an average of 20 times each year). The Empire State Building.

Love for Sale
Going Rate: $50 –$1,000

Each year about 100,000 individuals are arrested for prostitution or

Even a bride has her price, according to Betsy Nolan (played by Sarah Jessica Parker) in Castle Rock Entertainment's production of Honeymoon in Vegas.

Robert Redford, eat your heart out! Taking a lead from the film *Indecent Proposal*, in which Redford offered a man $1 million to make love to his wife, *Men's Health* magazine conducted a survey of 3,000 men and women which showed that nearly 3 out of 4 male respondents said they would offer their services for only $100. Women asked a higher price for their favors: 82% wanted $1,000; 9%, $500; 9%, $100; and 1%, $50. Among the men, 3% would sell themselves for $50, 71% for $100, 1% for $500, and 26% for $1,000.

Despite the obvious dangers, 1 in 3 men admits to having had sex with a prostitute. Meeting men in bars is the most common way female prostitutes obtain clients. Another frequent practice for some is to use classified ads. According to the noted sex researchers Masters and Johnson, women who run ads for sexual solicitation (for either fun or money) receive an average of 49 calls per ad. Men who advertise average 15 calls.

"commercial vice," according to the FBI *Uniform Crime Reports*. Among those arrested, men numbered 1 in 3. Only 1 in 51 men was under the age of 18. Among women, who account for 2 in 3 prostitution-related arrests, 1 in 82 was under 18.

Magazine Circulation

Time, Life, People, Fortune —judging by the choice of names, there is no doubt that Time-Life's founder, Henry Luce, and his successors knew that magazines that address the pulse of American life would be the best-selling ones.

After World War II, however, all that changed. Television *was* the pulse of America and, subsequently, the circulation of magazines fell, and some of the largest — *Look, Saturday Evening Post,* and *Collier's* — folded.

Big-circulation magazines are back today, but in a different way. The biggest ones address specific needs of readers rather than focusing on the news of the day.

The largest, *Modern Maturity,* is an organ of the largest association in the country, the American Association of Retired Persons. Armed with this mouthpiece, AARP has in recent years become a strong political lobbying force for the rights of the elderly. Running the home is a focus of millions of readers, and "the shelter books" (trade jargon for today's women's service magazines) are also among the largest.

This table shows the 10 largest magazines and their paid circulation, according to *Advertising Age.*

Modern Maturity	22,879,886
Reader's Digest	16,258,476
TV Guide	14,498,341
National Geographic	9,708,254
Better Homes and Gardens	8,002,585
Cable Guide	5,889,947
Family Circle	5,283,660
Good Housekeeping	5,139,355
Ladies' Home Journal	5,041,143
Woman's Day	4,810,445

Magazines for Every Taste
New Magazine Boom

The magazine industry seems to be on the rebound, according to Samir Husni, a journalism professor at the University of Mississippi and the nation's premier magazine tracker: he publishes *Guide to New Consumer Magazines.* He reports that with the increasing specialization in our society comes a slew of relevant magazines. Where once sports, music, and computers were considered specialties, now there are magazines for just about every subspecialty: mountain biking, rap music, electronic bulletin boards, and thousands more. Husni believes this trend has peaked; hardly any subject, no matter how arcane, does not have a periodical devoted to it.

He notes that 1992 was a record year for the launching of new magazines; a total of 679 new titles hit the stands after two somewhat depressed years, with 557 entries in 1990 and 553 in 1991. The market has been growing steadily since 1985, the year Husni began his tracking, when there were only 231 new magazines.

The average cover price for a 1992 startup was $3.89, and the subscription price was $19.78 a year. Almost all of the major categories tracked in Husni's annual, which lists 66,000 assorted periodicals and 3,600 consumer publications, registered growth except the following: military (after a leap in 1991 due to the Persian Gulf War), lesbianism, women's fashion, and beauty.

Not surprisingly, magazine startups devoted to sex — with such titillating names as *Leggy*, *Family Heat*, and *Future Sex* — led the pack with 97, followed by lifestyle and service magazines (60), sports publications (40), magazines devoted to crafts, games, and hobbies (35), and celebrity magazines (33). Husni believes that baby boomers looking for advice on parenthood are chiefly behind the strength of 1992's lifestyle and service category, which included two magazines devoted to outlet shopping.

But do they make any money? Half a given year's magazine launchings fail before the end of the year, and only 3 out of 10 are still around after four years.

Male Impotence

*"You should, if you want it, have a satisfactory sexual relationship into your 90s."
—Dr. James Barada, urologist, Albany, N.Y., at the national meeting of the American Urological Association*

More than a million American males are currently being treated for sexual impotence, many of them relatively young. In addition to those who have been diagnosed as impotent, an estimated 30 million men have problems getting or maintaining an erection.

The most common treatment for impotence is self-injection with an erection-producing drug, which is used by about a million sufferers. Another 30,000 use a vacuum device to achieve an erection, while 20,000 choose penile implants. According to Dr. Barada, the number of men seeking some form of treatment has increased fivefold in the last few years.

Twenty years ago, doctors thought impotence was caused by psychological problems in 95% of cases. Sleep research that monitors the penis has proved otherwise. Erections during sleep are natural in men. The average male's penis, even for many who claim to be impotent, is erect during periods of dreaming for about three hours each night, as the penis is filled with oxygen-rich blood. Only a small number of men cannot achieve an erection during sleep, usually the result of a vascular problem. Half the males who have undergone coronary bypass surgery are impotent.

According to Dr. Erwin Goldstein, a urologist at the Boston University School of Medicine and the author of *The Potent Male*, other reasons for impotence include the following:

- Many drugs used to treat heart disease interfere with blood flow, prohibiting erections.
- Smoking, lack of exercise, sleep deprivation, sexual abstinence, diabetes, and injuries keep oxygen from the penis.

- Diabetes or prostate surgery may cause nerve damage.
- Hormone imbalances and steroid overdoses can cause impotence.

Male Sexuality
Zeroing in on the Male Libido

One of the most comprehensive surveys yet of male sexual behavior has found that the typical male under 40 years of age has had a total of 7 sex partners and has both received and performed oral sex, though not nearly as often as he has had intercourse. Anal sex proved to be less common: 20% have tried it, most of them with a woman.

This $1.8 million study, funded by the federal government and conducted by the Battelle Human Affairs Research Center in Seattle in 1991, interviewed 3,321 men nationally aged 20–39. It also found that:

- Only 12% are virgins.
- 23% of bachelors have had more than 20 partners in their lives.
- The typical married man has sex five times a month and does not cheat on his wife, although he has had 4 other partners in his life.

- 75% of white males both perform and receive oral sex; only 43% of black men perform it, while 66% receive it.
- Anal sex has been practiced by 20%, but fewer practice it regularly.
- Anal sex is a mainly heterosexual activity; 90% did it the first time with a woman; 50% have done it with just one person, and 20% with more than four.
- Condoms are used by 50% of gay men.
- 75% agree that using condoms "shows you are a caring person"; the same number agree that condoms reduce sensation, while 27% admit they are embarrassed to buy them.

Marches in the Capital

G ot a gripe? Something troubling you? Take your troubles to Washington, D.C., and show the nation how many share your concern. Millions of Americans have gone to stand up and be counted, but the count may be way off. An examination of crowd estimates of marches in Washington

The National Mall, with the Capitol and Lincoln Memorial at either end, has plenty of room for political rallies. Photo, courtesy of Washington, D.C., Convention and Visitors Association.

reveals that who is doing the counting may influence the official report.

Who's Doing the Counting: The Gay Rights March of April 25, 1993, may have been one of the largest marches on Washington — or one of the smallest. The National Park Service estimated that 300,000 people attended; however, the local government in Washington estimated it at 1 million, leaving 700,000 people possibly swinging in the wind around the Washington Monument. In April 1992, Park Service and D.C. police initially estimated a National Organization for Women abortion-rights crowd at

500,000. The Park police later lowered its estimate to 250,000, then returned to its original figure. In May 1992, local police estimated that a protest demanding more federal aid to cities drew 150,000 demonstrators; the Park police estimate was 600,000. And so it goes.

This is a list of the largest marches or rallies in Washington and the number of attendees, according to the National Park Service police.

- Vietnam War Moratorium Rally (11/15/69) — 600,000
- Abortion Rights March (4/5/92) — 500,000
- Vietnam War "Out Now" rally (4/24/71) — 500,000
- 20th Anniversary of Martin Luther King Jr.'s Rights March (8/20/83) — 300,000
- Abortion Rights March (4/9/89) — 300,000
- Gay Rights March (4/25/93) — 300,000
- Solidarity Day Labor March (9/19/91) — 260,000
- Civil Rights March (8/28/63) — 250,000
- Solidarity Day Labor March (8/31/91) — 250,000

- Anti-abortion March (4/28/90) — 200,000
- Abortion Rights March (11/12/89) — 200,000
- Gay Rights March (10/14/87) — 200,000
- King Holiday March (1/15/81) — 200,000

Marriage
Fewer Take the Plunge

Nearly a quarter of all adults, 22.6%, have never been married, according to the Census Bureau, and the odds an individual will marry in the near future is dropping. The number of Americans over age 18 who have never taken a stroll down the aisle is 41 million, almost double the number in 1970, 21 million.

Some 72% of the adult population was married in 1970 but only 61% in 1991, according to the Census Bureau. It said that the median age for marrying is also rising. Today it is 24, up from 21 in 1970. For men, the median age is 26 years, up from 23 in 1970. For women, the median age is 24, up from 21 in 1970. Today's median age at marriage for all adults is about the

Marriage may be on the decline, but not in Las Vegas, which has countless chapels where no appointment is necessary. Photo, courtesy Las Vegas News Bureau.

same as it was at the turn of the century, hence the trend toward getting married earlier in life has reversed itself.

Other significant changes in marriage trends, according to the Census Bureau, are as follows.

Marital Status	1970	1991
Married	71.7%	61.4%

	1970	1991
Never Married	16.2%	22.6%
Divorced	3.2%	8.6%
Widowed	8.9%	7.4%

Never Married

Race	1970	1980	1991
White	15.6%	18.9%	20.5%
Black	20.6%	30.5%	37.1%
Hispanic	18.6%	24.1%	27.3%

Alternatives: One reason marriages are on the decline is the increasing incidence — and acceptability — of couples cohabiting. Twenty years ago, about 10% of adults lived with an unmarried mate before their first marriage. Today almost half do, 9 in 20. The younger a woman is, the more likely she is to live with her male lover. Among unmarried women born in the 1940s, 3% have lived with an unmarried male. Among women born in the 1960s, approximately one third will live with a male before marriage.

Math Skills
School Failures Add Up

We may be an ingenious nation in many ways, but we need our calculators by our side. Math has never been emphasized in our schools, as it has been in Europe and Asia, and this lack is showing up on U.S. report cards.

According to the National Assessment of Educational Progress, a testing program for public school students, a dismal 25% of American children are proficient at their grade level in mathematical skills.

In 1992, the NAEP tested 250,000 fourth-, eighth-, and twelfth-graders from 10,000 schools in 44 states. The results of the exams showed that:

- 82% of fourth-graders do not have a sufficient grasp of fractions and decimals.
- 80% of eighth-graders and 50% of twelfth-graders cannot solve problems involving fractions, decimals, and percentages.
- 30%–40% of Asian American students are proficient in math.
- 20%–30% of white students are proficient.
- 10% of Native American, black, and Hispanic students are proficient.

The scores in different parts of the country varied enormously. Those in the Midwest were the highest; the lowest were in the South. This list represents the rank of eighth-graders in the 44 states. Because of ties, the lowest rank was 41.

Best States

Iowa	1
Minnesota	1
North Dakota	3
Nebraska	4
Wisconsin	4

Worst States

Mississippi	41
Louisiana	40
Alabama	39
Arkansas	38
West Virginia	38

Medicare and Medicaid

Eligible Seniors Miss Out on Full Benefits

Today's low-income seniors are the most secure group in America when it comes to receiving medical treatment for life-threatening illnesses. The combination of state and federal Medicaid programs and the national Medicare program have virtually guaranteed that medical attention is available. Millions of seniors, however, are not taking advantage of the government programs that cover small items.

Nearly half of low-income seniors do not apply for out-of-pocket medical expenses, according to Families USA, a national health care advocacy group. These include such items as medicine and treatment for minor illnesses. For major medical expenses, most doctors and hospitals help seniors to get aid, but for lesser procedures, most of them must put in their own claims to be covered by Medicare and Medicaid.

Some 4.25 million people are eligible; however, about 42% of them — 1.8 million seniors — fail to do the necessary paperwork. Administrators blame the problem on not enough public awareness of the specific programs. Seniors see it differently, however: the paperwork is so exhaustive that many of them simply find it more than they can handle. So far, the only answer has been local social service agencies, who help seniors wade through the paper jungle.

Medical Malpractice

"In my specialty, general surgery, doctors have seen premiums rise from $9,900 in 1982 to $22,500 in 1991. Yet a recent Harvard study shows that the vast majority of claims bear no evidence of bad medical care. In fact, 60% to 75% of claims are resolved in favor of the physician." — *Dr. D. Smoak, Jr., Orangeburg, S.C.*

Some say malpractice suits against the nation's physicians have gotten out of hand. Roughly speaking, the current rates paid by surgeons add $100 to the cost of every operation. Though the cost of liability insurance adds significantly to health care costs, according to *USA Today*, if we stopped every single negligence lawsuit, only about 1% of America's health care costs would be saved.

In fact, the real cost to patients is the preponderance of "defensive treatments" — that is, extra (and possibly unnecessary) tests performed by doctors. According to the American Medical Association, the cost of tests the doctors order primarily to protect themselves from possible court cases has escalated from $4.8 million in 1982 to $15.5 million in 1990.

But doctors have good cause to be careful. Today's average award for patients who win malpractice suits is $1.17 million. According to the AMA, the most frequent malpractice allegations and the number of suits filed in 1990 were:

Surgery/postoperative complications	922
Failure to diagnose cancer	498
Improper treatment/ birth-related	416
Surgery/inadvertent act	283
Improper treatment/ infection	232
Improper treatment during examination	202
Improper treatment/drug side effects	195
Failure to diagnose circu- latory problems/thrombosis	181
Failure to diagnose fracture or dislocation	179

The New York Hospital Study: New Yorkers generally believe that they have the best health care facilities in the nation. That may be true of the *facilities*, but the quality of hospital care has been called into question by researchers from Harvard University. In 1990, a team studying cases at New York state hospitals from the year 1984 found an incredible 27,000 injuries and 7,000 deaths attributed to negligence. Surprisingly, only 1 in 8 victims of the purported negligence actually filed suit. The researchers concluded, "We do not now have a problem of too many claims; if anything, there are too few."

Are many doctors not operating up to snuff? One study in Florida indicated that a very small number of doctors is responsible: only 3% of all doctors accounted for 85% of all the awards to plaintiffs in malpractice suits.

Military Induction Standards
Road out of Poverty Closing

In America's shrinking military, recruiters are taking a tougher stand against high school dropouts, men and women with police records, and those who can't pass a mandatory test for drug use. These criteria bar a passage out of poverty for many young Americans, especially blacks.

Some of the most hardened inner-city youth have long seen the military as one of the last open doors out of the violence and blight of their surroundings, and the army is one of the few institutions in which whites are routinely supervised by blacks. A quarter of the army's first sergeants are black, and in the Marines, 20% are black. In the other branches of the military, blacks are far less prevalent in supervisory capacities.

Sergeant First Class Charles Davis, 38, one of thousands of blacks who joined the army in the early 1970s and who now is a recruiter in Hollywood, said, "In [white] Santa Monica, the kids weren't as willing to join the army, but they could easily pass the qualification tests. In the South L.A. area, we may have had 150 who wanted to join, but only 2 could pass the test."

Throughout the inner cities of the U.S., few youths score in the upper half, said Charles Moskos, a leading military sociologist. The average score on the test for all males 18 to 23 years old is 51. The average for whites is 56; for blacks, 24.

Minority Explosion
Forecast for the Year 2050

Not too long ago, some demographers at the University of Chicago predicted that Chicago would be a dominantly black-Hispanic Catholic city by the year 2025. The Census Bureau, forecasting what the American population will be like 25 years later, in 2050, confirms the projection of a dramatic rise in the Hispanic population, attributed in part to an influx of nearly 900,000 Hispanic immigrants a year (both legal and illegal).

The U.S. population is expected to grow by a staggering 50% — from 255 million to 383 million — by 2050, and with that increase will come a change in the complexion of the populace, literally. The Hispanic population is expected to grow more than threefold, from its current 24 million to 81 million, eventually accounting for more than 1 in 5 Americans. The black population will nearly double, from its current 32 million to 62 million; however, its proportion of the overall population will rise only modestly, from 12% to 16%. Non-Hispanic whites will increase just a fraction, from 192 million to 208 million. This means that whites in the U.S. will drop from 75% of the population to 53%, a bare majority. In 1940, whites accounted for 90% of the population.

The tide of immigration from Asia and the Pacific islands will also swell. Asian Americans currently make up 3% of the nation's population, with 8 million people; by 2050 this group will grow to 41 million — 13%. And although the Native American population will remain at about 1% of the populace, the number of Native Americans will more than double by 2050, from 2 million to 5 million.

Mobile Homes

"Dens of disease, bribery, corruption, crookedness, rape, white slavery, thievery, and murder." — *J. Edgar Hoover*

Are you old enough to remember when mobile homes were eyesores on the landscape? If so, take another look, for times have changed.

Today they have "ambiance," and they have become not only affordable (average price, $27,800) but livable and, in fact, comfortable. According to the Census Bureau, they are the fastest-growing type of housing nationwide, increasing 59% in ten years compared to 13% for all other types of homes.

Almost 1 in 5 homes built in the 1980s were mobile homes —now often called "manufactured housing" by those in the industry. Nearly half of the 195,000 sold in 1990 were double-wides, averaging 1,440 square feet in area. Additions like porches are common; air conditioning is standard.

Two thirds of all mobile homes have three or more bedrooms, and nearly all are made in the U.S.

Mobile homes are primarily a post–World War II phenomenon. Starting in the 1950s, they gradually increased twenty-five times in number. This table shows the growth in mobile homes between 1950 and 1990.

1950	315,218
1960	766,565
1970	2,073,994
1980	4,663,457
1990	7,399,855

Tornado Catchers? There is a simple way to save your community from the ravages of killer twisters, according to weather watchers. They like to tell the story of a mayor in a town plagued by tornado damage. To protect his community from further disaster, he used the city treasury to invest in a mobile home park and placed the trailers just outside the town to act as "tornado catchers." No one knows if the ruse worked, but we do know that between 1985 and 1991, 341 Americans were killed by tornadoes and 35% of them were in mobile homes, according to the National Weather Service. Though a mobile home is no more likely to be struck by a twister than any other, it is less likely to be able to withstand the impact.

Moon Rocks
Collecting Earth Dust

Twelve Apollo astronauts walked, drove, and played golf on the moon during the glory years of the U.S. space program, between 1969 and 1972. In all, 842 pounds of moon rock and dust were collected in the six moon landings and brought back to Earth. But what happened to that lunar lode?

Today, only 2% of the treasure — less than 15 pounds — is available for scientific study; 3%, about 24 pounds, is on loan to educators and museums; and 2%, about 16 pounds, has been destroyed in the process of scientific analysis. Meanwhile, 673 pounds of moon rock — 80% of the total on Earth — rests in airtight vaults at NASA's Johnson Space Center in Houston, and another 114 pounds, 13%, is in a special vault at Brooks Air Force Base. (The Apollo crews were not allowed to keep samples.)

The biggest rock haul came on the last lunar Apollo flight, Apollo 17, launched from Florida on December 7, 1972, and manned by Eugene Cernan, Harrison Schmitt, and Ronald Evans. Cernan and Schmitt gathered a record 244 pounds of lunar relics on December 11. The "Genesis Rock" is the most famous of all the moon samples, since it was given a name. A half-pound piece of soda-lime feldspar found by Apollo 15's James Irwin, it has been estimated by geologists to be 4.4 billion years old, as old as the solar system itself.

Now NASA ponders a return to the moon in preparation for the Mars sweep it hopes to make by 2019, but the outlook for such a project is grim. Many point to a lack of "spiritual desire" among Americans for costly space probes in the face of social and economic problems at home. Cernan is more pragmatic. He blames NASA for not having enough vision to present a good case to Congress and the people for making the trip to the moon and Mars, which could easily cost $500 billion.

This table summarizes the manned moon flights and the number of hours each crew spent on the surface of the moon.

Apollo 11 (July 1969)	22
Apollo 12 (November 1969)	32
Apollo 13 (April 1970)	aborted
Apollo 14 (January-February 1971)	34
Apollo 15 (July-August 1971)	67
Apollo 16 (April 1972)	71
Apollo 17 (December 1972)	75

Morality

Cheap Wanton Sex Plus . . .

Sexual indiscretions lead the list of what shames Americans the most, even though more people admit to sins such as lying and stealing. The biggest change has been not just what we do but what we find acceptable, even when they may be things we clearly recognize as unsavory.

This list presents what Americans are most ashamed of (by percentage), according to Patterson and Kim's findings as reported in *The Day America Told the Truth.*

Adultery/affairs	18%
Fornication/premarital sex	14%
Lying	11%

Stealing	10%
Cheating/taking advantage of others	6%
Drunkenness	5%
Abortion	3%
Shoplifting	3%
Wicked thoughts	3%
Verbal cruelty	2%
Masturbation	2%
Stealing from work	2%
Kinky sex	2%
Pornography	2%

Motherhood

American Women Have Fewer Children

Women in the U.S. have far fewer children than those in other countries. The average American woman will have 1.9 children versus 3.3, the world average. The highest fertility rates are in Africa, where women have an average of 5.1 children; the lowest, in Western Europe, where they have 1.6. Throughout the world, 80% of women bear children. In America, however, only 60% do, which represents a decline. In 1976, 65% of American women had children. By 1988, only 62% were mothers.

This list, compiled by the National Center for Health Statistics, represents the proportions of American women in different categories who will have a child in a year.

Blacks	94 in 1,000
Hispanics	87 in 1,000
Whites	66 in 1,000

The next list represents the odds that a first birth will take place during various age periods in a woman's life.

Under 20	1 in 4
20–24	1 in 3
25–29	1 in 4
30–34	1 in 8
35+	1 in 25

Mother's Day

Hello, Mother

On Mother's Day, 1993, AT&T reported a record number of phone calls, 110.5 million, up 8.5% from the previous year. Sprint reported that calls were up 45% over normal, and although MCI did not report a tally, it said an average call lasted longer than an hour.

Some companies will do anything to promote their sales. MCI used the foremost American institution, motherhood, as a draw by polling its callers to publicize its long-distance service just before Mother's Day, 1993. According to the poll, the following women are America's favorite mothers. Also shown is the percentage of respondents who indicated that they would like to call that mother, along with their own, on Mother's Day.

Favorite Mothers

Barbara Bush	29%
Hillary Rodham Clinton	12%
Princess Diana	7%

According to the same poll:

Most Admired Mom in History

Virgin Mary	14%
Mother Teresa	10%
Eleanor Roosevelt	5%

TV Moms

Kathie Lee Gifford	16%
Cindy Walsch	14%
Murphy Brown	14%
Roseanne	7%

| Marge Simpson | 5% |
| June Cleaver | 3% |

Most in Need of a Mother's Advice

Madonna	31%
Saddam Hussein	20%
Mike Tyson	16%
Howard Stern	6%
Joey Buttafuoco	5%
Woody Allen	4%

And How Much Is She Worth? If how much Americans spend on their mothers is any indication, Mom's a mighty fat cat. Below is the tally of money spent on Mother's Day, according to the Mother's Day Council, Ayer Public Relations.

Candy	$329 million
Cards	$225 million
Phone calls	$76 million
Flowers	$61 million

Motorcycles

A motorcycle is more than transportation. It is a way of life for more than 4 million Americans who like the wind in their face and the feel of the open road at their feet.

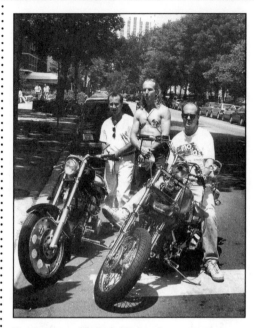

Don't mess with their Harleys!

Industry sources often ballyhoo the "new popularity" of biking. Most would interpret it as a dynamic growth in ownership, but the only thing new about motorcycling is the marked affluence of many riders. A growing white-collar crowd takes to the road on weekends; a declining base of blue-collar riders, affected by the recession, can no longer afford to buy bikes. So, due primarily to poor economic times, motorcycle registrations have dropped drastically — 25% since 1980. The number of registrations compiled by the Department of Transportation is:

1980	5,694,000
1985	5,444,000
1989	4,434,000
1990	4,259,000

Fatal motorcycle accidents have also declined sharply: 45% between 1985 and 1991. Many people attribute this to the new state laws that mandate the use of helmets. (The only states that do not require a helmet are Illinois, Iowa, and Colorado.) Most of these laws went into effect in the 1970s, when motorcycle sales were booming and too many drivers and state legislators had witnessed ghastly accidents.

This table represents the number of fatalities caused by motorcycle accidents, according to the National Highway Traffic Safety Administration.

1976	3,189
1980	5,144
1992	2,325

This dramatic drop in deaths is also due to the following:

- More riders are taking courses in motorcycle safety, possibly due to an increased percentage of more educated riders than in the past. In 1992 alone, 105,000 cyclists attended courses given by the Motorcycle Safety Foundation.
- In the last fifteen years, the average age of cyclists has increased and they are more experienced.
- The recession of the early 1990s has caused a decline in ridership.

Mount McKinley

"If a climber dies, you feel sad, but you hope he made it to the summit first."
—*Thomas Villars, veteran climber*

It is regarded by many as one of the nation's most beautiful natural paradises —and the deadliest. Famous as the highest point in North America, it is also infamous among experienced mountain climbers: an incredible 61% who attempt to scale McKinley fail, and a significant number of them die in the process.

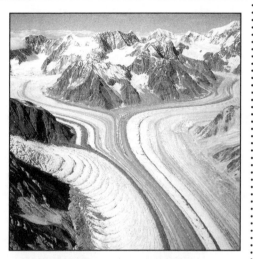

A thousand climbers a year try to scale America's highest summit, Mount McKinley.

The beckoning 20,320-foot (2,032-story) mountain lies near the rustic bush town of Talkeeta, Alaska, populated by 500 residents and 1,000 transient climbers each year. On Main Street sits the Fairview Inn, with a mural of the mountain behind the bar, handmade flags marking successful climbs, and a bulletin board message center. One wall at the inn is studded with photographs of 48 dead climbers. The year 1992 saw 11 of those photographs added to the wall, a record number, as a record 1,024 climb-

ers tried to scale the coldest mountain in North America. "This year has been brutal," said the ranger Scott Gill, but he gave no reason why so many people died.

This table cites the number of attempts made on McKinley and the death toll since 1980, compiled by the National Park Service.

Year	Climbers	Successes	Deaths
1980	659	283	8
1981	612	310	6
1982	696	310	0
1983	709	474	2
1984	695	324	2
1985	645	321	2
1986	755	406	4
1987	817	251	2
1988	916	551	2
1989	1,009	517	6
1990	998	573	3
1991	935	553	0
1992	1,024	398	11

Movie Production
A White Male World

Among minorities working in films in the last ten years, women and blacks did not fare well in the production end of the business. Women directors account for 8% and minority directors for about 5% of all films, in spite of a flurry of movies made by black directors in the last few years. "If these figures were translated to represent a five-day work week," said Glenn J. Gumpel, head of the Directors Guild of America, "women directors would control the set for no more than a few hours after lunch on Friday."

The Good Ol' Boys of New York: The producer Warren Hudlin, who collaborated with his director brother, Reginald, on *House Party* and its sequel, got an unpleasant surprise during the filming of *Boomerang* in New York. As president of the Black Filmmakers Foundation, he was in a position to do something for blacks in the industry, so he tried to find a black production trainee, with no success. "I thought it was astounding that there was nobody black in the training program in *New York*," he said.

Looking ahead, minorities "still face an uphill battle in competing for jobs," according to Warren Adler, executive secretary of the DGA. Women directors accounted for 8% of all hours worked by union directors in 1990, up from 3% in 1983.

In the category of unit production manager, minorities working in the field maintained a 3% share of total employment, with women increasing their share from 5% to 15%.

Movies
Most Expensive Ever Made

No one knows better than Hollywood's moguls that money doesn't always buy success. After spending more than $40 million on a half-dozen or more movies that flopped like pancakes, the once sure-thing megabudget film is looked on with a jaundiced eye by financiers.

The Michael Cimino Story: It was a classic case of the overbudget movie — Michael Cimino's *Heaven's Gate*. After Cimino won critical acclaim, including the Best Picture and Best Director Oscars for *The Deer Hunter*, his studio, United Artists, gave him free rein to achieve his artistic vision. The resulting $40 million megaflop led to the dissolution of the long-established UA studios, which had been founded by Charlie Chaplin and Mary Pickford in the days of the silent movies.

A mere ten years later, Cimino's $40 million seems like a bargain when such flops as *Days of Thunder, Tango and Cash, Ishtar,* and *Santa Claus,* which previously would have broken most studios, simply get passed over in silence.

This table lists the movies with budgets of $50 million or more, according to the *New York Times.*

Terminator II	$100 million
Die Hard	$70 million
Who Framed Roger Rabbit?	$70 million
Total Recall	$65 million
The Godfather, Part III	$65 million
Rambo III	$58 million
Days of Thunder	$55 million
Tango and Cash	$55 million
Ishtar	$55 million
Superman	$55 million
Superman II	$54 million
The Adventures of Baron Munchausen	$52 million
Annie	$51 million
The Cotton Club	$51 million
Hudson Hawk	$51 million
Another 48 Hours	$50 million
Batman	$50 million
Coming to America	$50 million
Santa Claus	$50 million

Movie Stars
Quick-Draw Artists

Today's movies are judged as much by their first-week ticket sales as by their critical acclaim (or lack thereof). Getting a big initial draw is often the launching pad to success in filmland, so the studios like to go with the stars who pack 'em in the first week.

Eddie Murphy is tops at packing theaters the first week his movies hit the street. Photo, courtesy Terri Williams Agency.

Those who can do it earn big bucks. Two quick-draw artists, Arnold Schwarzenegger and Eddie Murphy, command $15 million and $9 million respectively per film. Sigourney Weaver, another proven attraction, nearly ties with big Arnold and consistently disproves the theory that women can't outdraw men.

This list, compiled by *Variety*, represents the top 10 quick-draw artists and the average box office take for their pictures during the first weekend.

Eddie Murphy	$16.9 million
Arnold Schwarzenegger	$15.4 million
Sigourney Weaver	$15.2 million
Michael Keaton	$14.2 million
Bill Murray	$12.5 million
Mel Gibson	$14.2 million
Harrison Ford	$12.0 million
Tom Cruise	$11.4 million
Julia Roberts	$11.2 million
Michael J. Fox	$10.8 million

Multiple Births

U.S. Leads in Twins and Trips

Worldwide, about 1 in 100 pregnancies involves either the splitting of an egg or two or more eggs being fertilized. About 1 in 90 births results in twins and 1 in 9,000, triplets. In America, however, the rate of multiple births is just about double the world average.

The reason is that in America, women are having children much later in life than women elsewhere, and as a woman ages, multiple births are more likely due to the decreased regularity of menstruation; often two or even three eggs are passed instead of one. Add to this the fact that many older women cannot conceive without fertility drugs, which also increase the frequency of multiple births.

These figures, compiled by the American College of Obstetricians and Gynecologists, represents the proportions of various multiple births in 1990, the year for which the latest data are available. The numbers in parentheses represent the proportions in 1973.

Twins — 1 in 43 (1 in 50)
Triplets — 1 in 1,341 (1 in 3,500)

Quadruplets and quintuplets are quite rare. In 1989, 229 quads and 40 quints were born in the U.S.; in 1990, there were fewer —185 quads and 13 quints.

Musical Instruments

Since 1980, not too many instrumentalists have made the popular music charts. Many who grew up during the sixties and seventies, however, cut their musical teeth on the music of greats as disparate as Al Hirt, Chet Atkins, and Liberace. Music lessons were a regular after-school activity for almost a quarter of American kids.

More than 57 million adults play at least one instrument; half of them play two or more. Three quarters do it regularly. This list shows the different instruments Americans play and the numbers involved.

Piano	21 million
Guitar	19 million
Organ	6 million
Flute	4 million
Clarinet	4 million
Drums	3 million
Trumpet	3 million
Violin	2 million
Harmonica	1.7 million

Saxophone	1 million
Electronic keyboard	600,000

Mutual Funds

In 1955, 82% of the outstanding shares on the New York Stock Exchange were owned by private citizens, most of whom were relatively unschooled in financial management. At the same time, institutional buyers held a meager 18%. In three tumultuous decades, those percentages have reversed, and as the 1990s dawned, institutionally managed stock funds proliferated.

In 1993, U.S. mutual funds manage more than $700 billion in negotiable securities. Before the debacle of Black October 1987, more than 844 Americans had invested in funds offering shares in lucrative portfolios of stocks and bonds; the demand was so great that new funds were appearing at the rate of one each day.

As we approach the mid-nineties, that trend has returned. There are now 4,006 mutual funds, which translates to there being more funds than individual stocks on both the New York Stock Exchange (2,726 stocks) and the

American Stock Exchange (972 stocks) combined.

This table shows some of the largest mutual funds now trading, according to the upcoming book *Who Really Owns America.*

	Assets (in billions)	Share-holders
Fidelity Magellan	$12.0	1,000,000
Windsor Fund	$6.0	250,000
Fidelity Puritan Fund	$5.0	500,000
Investment Company of America	$5.0	250,000
Templeton World Fund	$4.5	350,000
Fidelity Equity Income	$4.5	250,000
Pioneer II	$4.0	650,000
Affiliated Fund	$4.0	200,000
Merrill Lynch	$3.0	350,000
American Capital Fund Pace	$3.0	450,000

Here is a spectrum of the market choices that mutuals invest in and their average annual profits from 1926 to 1992, as compiled by Ibbotson Associates, in Chicago.

Small company stocks	17.6%
Common stocks	12.4%
Long-term corporate bonds	5.8%
Intermediate term government bonds	5.3%
U.S. Treasury bills	3.8%
Inflation	3.2%

National Parks
3% of U.S. Land Area is Reserved

Alaska has 550,000 residents and 20 million annual visitors to its national parks. This largest state also has more state parks and recreation areas than any other. But for all its acres devoted to scenic beauty, the National Park Service in Alaska brings in annual revenues of only $1.5 million, less than 20% of the state's operating budget, set by the service. In contrast, tiny Rhode Island brings in more money — $2 million, 25% of its budget — from 7 million visitors, according to the National Association of State Park Directors.

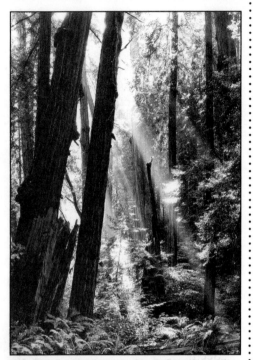

Muir Woods, with its towering redwoods north of San Francisco, is one of the National Park Service's most popular attractions.

The national park system comprises 354 areas covering about 76 million acres, 3% of the total U.S. land area, across the 50 states, the District of Columbia, Guam, Puerto Rico, Saipan, and the U.S. Virgin Islands. The state leader by far in drawing visitors is California, with beautiful weather and 1.3 million acres of parks. Each year, some 80 million people pay more than $45 million, more than 25% of the state's National Park Service budget. Though the service is known principally for its scenic parks, more than half of its total area is given over to the preservation and commemoration of important historical events.

These tables list the five states with the most and the least park acreage, the number of visitors they attract, and the estimated annual income from them, adapted from National Park Service data.

Most Acreage

	Acreage (1,000s)	Visitors (millions)	income (millions)
Alaska	3,169	20	$1.5
California	1,300	80	$45.0
New York	259	60	$30.0
Washington	236	40	$7.0
Oregon	88	40	$9.0

Least Acreage

Rhode Island	9	0.8	$2.0
North Dakota	17	1.0	$0.8
Mississippi	23	4.0	$5.0
Hawaii	25	20.0	$1.5
N. Hampshire	31	33.3	$0.8

Net Worth
Rich Getting Richer
Poor Getting Poorer

According to the Department of Labor, the net worth of the average American at mid-1993 is $38,469, only a modest improvement since 1986. When inflation is factored into the equation, the average American made virtually no gain; 80% have actually suffered losses in their net worth.

For the first time since World War II, the poor are getting poorer and so are middle- and upper-middle-income Americans. Among the poorest, net worths have dropped more than 15%; among the upper middle class, more than 7%.

Those with the highest incomes are, indeed, getting richer, much richer. Not just the millionaires, but those who earn more than $45,000 a year. Their net worths are up significantly, when everyone else's is down.

As we move through the nineties, the five-year table clearly indicates that many upper-middle-income families are slipping into the middle class at an alarming rate. Many in the highest-income classes, on the other hand, are moving into the ranks of the truly wealthy.

Today, 2.8% of American families have net worths of more than $500,000. The median value of their assets is about $900,000. Approximately half of this elite group, 3.5 million people, are "millionaires," that is, members of families with $1 million or more in net assets.

The Department of Commerce subdivides the net worth of Americans into equal-quantity quintiles, as shown below, with the numbers and percentages of American households.

Median Net Worth

Quintile*	Net Worth	Distribution
Lowest	$4,324	7.0%
Second	$19,694	12.3%
Third	$28,040	15.7%
Fourth	$46,253	20.6%
Highest	$111,770	44.4%

*Quintiles: 1990 quintile upper limits for monthly income were: lowest quintile, $939; second quintile, $1,699; third quintile, $2,568; fourth quintile, $3,883; highest quintile, $3,884 or more.

Distribution: The percentage of the combined net worth of American households.

In its 1990 report, the Department of Commerce noted that the net worth of the average American dropped 3.4% over the last reported five-year period. Not only have net worths dropped — and during an essentially inflationary period — but four of the five quintiles have dropped, and only the wealthiest quintile has increased. This table below represents the change over the five-year period:

Median Net Worth

Quintile	1990	1986	Change
Overall U.S.	$35,752	$37,012	–3.4%
Lowest	4,324	5,103	–15.7%
Second	19,694	21,248	–7.3%
Third	28,044	29,459	–4.8%
Fourth	46,253	49,253	–7.4%
Highest	111,770	98,411	+13.6%

Newspapers

At the close of World War II, there were more than 3,000 daily newspapers in America. Today, about half survive and a few new ones have appeared, most notably *USA Today*; it has the highest circulation of all with its weekend edition, which comes out on Fridays.

In general, the circulations of individual newspapers have risen in the past few decades. Industry analysts say the chief reason is the folding of rival papers. Most recently, Americans have been engrossed by news events, particularly the colorful political campaigns, high-profile scandals of every sort, and America's military exploits, all of which have translated to increased newspaper sales.

Following are the 20 largest newspapers in the U.S. and their daily and Sunday circulations, according to the March 31, 1993, reports of the Audit Bureau of Circulations.

	Daily	Sunday
Wall Street Journal	1,852,967	none
USA Today	1,632,345	2,003,620*
New York Times	1,230,461	1,812,458
Los Angeles Times	1,38,353	1,812,458
Washington Post	855,171	1,170,150

*USA Today *has a weekend rather than a Sunday edition.*

	Daily	Sunday
New York		
Daily News	769,801	977,599
Newsday	762,043	851,685
Chicago		
Tribune	691,941	1,117,816
Detroit Free		
Press	574,817	none
San Francisco		
Chronicle	564,374	715,299
Chicago		
Sun-Times	553,355	549,038
Dallas Morning		
News	527,816	834,035
Boston Globe	504,869	811,409
Philadelphia		
Inquirer	502,740	965,350
Newark		
Star-Ledger	483,012	728,579
New York Post	427,319	none
Houston		
Chronicle	423,256	608,429
Miami Herald	414,216	542,450
Minneapolis–		
St. Paul Star		
Tribune	413,603	695,710
Cleveland		
Plain Dealer	408,829	548,789

Not-for-profit Execs

One fourth of America's 117 top not-for-profit organizations richly reward their top executives, paying them an amount equal to or more than the salary of the president of the not-for-profit U.S. ($200,000 annually).

The issue of beefy salaries for cash-cow charities and public service organizations became common knowledge when William Aramony resigned as the president of United Way amid controversy over his $463,000 annual salary, generous benefits, and extravagant travels. Soon after, a survey conducted by the Chronicle of Philanthropy found that Harold Williams, president of the J. Paul Getty Trust, profited the most with his unusual dollar-added salary figure of $509,001. It was also learned that the Ford Foundation's president, Franklin A. Thomas, was second, at $422,426, and the Rockefeller Foundation's chief, Peter C. Goldmark, Jr., was third, raking in $346,500.

James N. Wood of the Art Institute of Chicago was paid $236,642. Institute officials disputed that, although it was reported that they admitted he does make more than $200,000. Salaries of an even $200,000 were paid to Elizabeth Dole, the head of the American Red Cross, and Faye Wattleton of Planned Parenthood. In all, 33 of the organizations surveyed paid their leaders $200,000 or more. The lowest-paid executive surveyed was the Reverend Val Peter, executive director of Father Flanagan's Boys' Town in Nebraska, who received $20,000.

Nudity

The Bare Facts Uncovered

The naked truth is that many Americans take off their clothes for reasons other than bathing and sex. The largest percentage of naked Americans are sleeping men — 53% of American males sleep nude versus 27% of women, according to *Do You Do It with the Lights On!* by Mel Poretz and Barry Sinrod. Overall, they say, 40% of the nation is naked while asleep.

Other times, though not too frequently, a large contingent is naked to have some fun: 55% have done strip teases for their mates, most of whom (65%) are women, according to the researchers. More than one third of couples have taken videos or snapshots of their mate while naked — 39% of the men and 34% of the women, and the pictures are not necessarily kept private. Some 21% of the men and 28% of the women have shown the tapes and pictures to others.

The next most popular activity in the buff is swimming. About 1 in 10 Americans report having gone skinny-dipping. There are 200 nude beaches in the U.S., most of them (50) in California. The least popular activity in which clothes are optional is nudism, engaged in by 17,500 Americans who belong to the Naturist Society, which keeps tabs on American's bare facts, from swimming to sunbathing.

Following are the five best and worst body parts of Americans, as rated by the individuals and reported in Poretz and Sinrod's book.

The Best Body Parts

Men	Women
Buttocks	Breasts
Legs	Face
Face	Legs
Arms	Buttocks
Head	Eyes

The Worst Body Parts

Men	Women
Stomach	Stomach
Feet	Buttocks

Chest   Hips
Knees   Legs
Legs   Thighs

Office Building Pollution
Indoor Air Quality on the Carpet

"There's something going on in modern, air-conditioned buildings that's making people more sick than they were in old-fashioned buildings." — *Stephen Hokanson, president of the Building Owners and Managers Association International.*

Analyses by Healthy Buildings International and Boelter Associates of 813 buildings with indoor air quality problems found that one third had significant amounts of allergy-causing fungi. They also found that 75.6% of the buildings have operating faults and/or poor maintenance, the chief cause of the pollution. The second biggest cause is inefficient filtration of the air supply. Other causes and the percentage of buildings affected by them include:

Poor ventilation due to energy conservation 54.1%
Poor air distribution 20.9%
Design errors 16.5%

Combination office/residential buildings, such as the John Hancock Center in Chicago, would be doubly dangerous if their closed environments were contaminated.

Contaminated ductwork 12.2 %

They're Everywhere: The sources of the pollution present a real problem: it would be impossible to dispense with almost any of them and still run an efficient, comfortable office. They are:

Contaminated water
Fabrics
Particleboard
Fireproofing
Plaster
Furnishings
Cleaning products
Engine exhaust (from
    underground garages)
Copy machines
Laser printers

This table lists the major pollutants and the percentages of buildings that have them, according to the study. (The numbers total more than 100% because multiple pollutants are present in many locations.)

Allergic fungi	33.4%
Dust	26.6%
Low humidity	18.5%
Bacteria	10.2%
Formaldehyde	8.5%
Fiberglass	6.6%
Vehicle exhaust	5.6%
Volatile organic compounds	4.1%
Tobacco smoke	2.8%

Organ Donors
The Wait Can Be Killing

L'Tany Davis wants a more fulfilling life, free of needles and tubes. She is physically tired from the twice-a-week dialysis that is keeping her alive until a kidney transplant is possible. But there is little hope because of another problem — she is black.

Most organ donors are white, and the issue of compatibility requires that the donor be the same race as the recipient, thus stacking the odds against nonwhites getting needed organs.

According to the United Network for Organ Sharing, blacks gave only 9.2% of all kidneys donated in the nation in 1992. Of the 19,851 individuals of all races on waiting lists, 31.8% are black. However, whites donated 82.8% of the available kidneys, even though 47% of those needing them are nonwhite. Hispanic donors accounted for 9.6%, with 6.1% seeking a kidney, and Asians gave 0.9%, with 4.8% needing them.

The federal government spends about $35,000 a year keeping each needy person on dialysis. For each kidney recipient, the cost is about $5,000 for drugs the first year and often much less after that, according to Dr. Raymond Pollak, chief of the transplant division at the University of Illinois Hospital. Despite gains made through educational programs designed to increase the number of black donors, the problem grows worse because the number of blacks needing kidneys continues to rise.

Peanuts

Anything but a Shell Game

Use any laundry soap lately? You're probably using peanuts. Any baby massage cream? You're probably using peanuts. How about cloth dyes, diesel fuel, insecticides, dandruff treatments, instant coffee, silicone in some breast implants? In a large number of instances, these products contain peanuts, one of the most versatile crops grown in the world and the ninth most valuable cash crop in the U.S.: in 1991 it represented a farm value of $4.9 billion.

Not Just Peanuts in Dixie: Five states — Georgia, Alabama, Florida, Texas, and Oklahoma — have a corner on the

Peanuts in Plains, Ga. Photo, courtesy of Georgia Bureau of Industry and Trade.

global peanut market. The famed agronomist George Washington Carter (1864–1943) established peanuts, along with soybeans and sweet potatoes, as the money crops when boll weevils and depleted soil threatened the South's cotton plantings in the late 1800s. His experiments and those of later scientists have found hundreds of uses for the peanut. Carver said, "I doubt if there is any other foodstuff that can be so universally eaten, in some form, by every individual." He wasn't just whistling "Dixie." He found 300 uses for them, including two of today's favorite treats, peanut ice cream and peanut butter cookies. He also found many uses for peanut oil and even the hulls, which are used in making charcoal and fertilizers.

Today, 4.9 billion pounds are grown in the U.S. annually, up from 2.9 billion in 1970, and nearly half of them in Jimmy Carter's Georgia, according to the Department of Agriculture. It reports that farmers are paid about 28 cents a pound for peanuts, a price that has remained fairly steady since 1984. Some 40 million Americans enjoy peanut butter in some form daily (about half of each year's crop ends up in the spread), and more than 85% of American homes stock it, according to the 1992 *Old Farmer's Almanac*. How many peanuts in each box of Cracker Jack? Nine nuts per ounce of Jack.

Pension Funds

The assets of all U.S. pension funds have increased fourfold in the last decade to total a staggering $2 trillion. To put it in perspective, the gross national product is approximately $5.4 trillion. More than a third of the $2 trillion is invested by independent money management firms.

This table shows the largest corporate pension funds and the approximate value of the securities (in billions) between 1990 and 1993, according to the upcoming book *Who Really Owns America*.

General Motors	$35–$40
AT&T	$33–$40
General Electric	$28–$30
Ford Motor Co.	$18–$20
IBM	$18–$20

In addition, there are many pension funds — private, state, and federal — that number in the tens of thousands.

The portfolio manager of the California Public Employees Retirement System, for example, is responsible for $43 billion — just slightly less than the deposits of Manufacturers Hanover Trust, the fourth largest bank in the nation. And there are 49 other states with pension funds, some with several separate funds. AT&T's chief pension manager must oversee $35 billion — $3 billion more than the company's gross annual revenue.

Pizza
Acres of Slices

Among the young and the hungry, it's more American than anything.

Not the world's biggest, but no small fry either—Pizza Hut's "Big Foot" measures 12" x 24".

Some 85% of all telephone orders for food to go are for pizza. Among kids aged 3 to 11, pizza tops their list of favorite foods, according to a Gallup poll, which indicated that 82% prefer pizza. According to *USA Today*, pizza is a $17.7 billion industry. The world of pizza even has its own publication, *Pizza Today*, which reports the following important pizza facts:

- Lorenzo Amato cooked the world's largest pizza on October 11, 1989 — it covered more than 5,000 square feet.
- Americans eat 90 acres of pizza every day.
- The average American eats 7.5 pizzas a year.

- Nearly 96% of all Americans eat pizza about 30 times a year.

Who Makes All the Dough? Almost gone from the urban landscape is the family-run pizza parlor. Today, almost half of all pizza is served by the three giants, who control the following shares of the market, according to Technomic:

	1991	1992
Pizza Hut	24.1%	24.3%
Domino's	14.1%	13.0%
Little Caesar's	9.8%	11.2%

Pizza Trends of the Nineties: Anchovies are definitely out. Thin crust is still in but losing ground to thick crust and pan pizza. Below are the favorites according to the pizza bible, *Pizza Today*.

Type of Crust

Thin	48%
Thick	46%
No preference	6%

Favorite Toppings (in order)
Pepperoni
Mushrooms
Extra cheese

Sausage
Green pepper
Onion

What's the newest trend in pizza? It's a new gimmick brought to you by Pizza Hut in an effort to step on Little Caesar's, king of the cheap pizza. The Hut has unleashed Big Foot, a 21-slice, 2-by-1-foot pie priced at $9 to $11, depending on location.

Police Brutality

Slugfests with the Cops

A government study undertaken after the Rodney King beating in Los Angeles in 1991 shows that the New Orleans police averaged 35 brutality cases a year, the most in the nation. The Los Angeles Police Department averaged 14 complaints a year, to place eleventh in the country, whereas the Los Angeles County Sheriff's Office came in second, with 34 complaints a year.

These rankings were compiled by the Justice Department from a review of 15,000 complaints of misconduct in 4,400 of the nation's 16,000 police departments received between 1984 and 1990, including those from jails and prisons. The Jefferson Parish, La., Sheriff's Office ranked third, with 23 complaints a year, followed by the San Antonio police, who averaged 21. Congressman John Conyers (D-Michigan) called the report disappointing because it did not include a breakdown on what percentages of the victims were black.

Justice Department rankings on police brutality in cities between October 1984 and September 1990 are shown below, along with the number of complaints reported annually.

New Orleans	35
Los Angeles County	34
Jefferson Parish, La.	23
San Antonio	21
El Paso	18
Houston	18
Chicago	17
St. Louis	15
San Diego	15
New York	14
Los Angeles	14
Puerto Rico	14

Popcorn
10 Billion Quarts

Five thousand years ago, long before the first real American dream was even envisioned, the Native Americans knew and perfected the second real American dream — a delicious, filling, low-fat, salt-free, high-fiber munchable. By the mid-1950s, when both dreams had been realized by millions, 2 out of 3 Americans watching television munched on home-popped popcorn as often as four nights a week.

Today, Americans are the largest per capita consumers of popcorn in the world, eating more than 10 billion quarts annually and generating more than $1 billion in sales.

The Duds Are the Real Problem: How can you tell a real popcorn aficionado? It's the person howling about the "duds," the charred, unpopped kernels usually found at the bottom of the bucket. One of the unfortunate facts of popcorn history is that until modern times, not all corn was poppable; it must have at least 14% water content so that it can expand into puffs.

The answer has been a new, dudless corn, often marketed as "gourmet" popcorn, prepared by the discriminating few. This hybrid has a swelling ratio of 40 times its kernel size compared to ordinary popcorn's average 35–38 times.

About 70% of all popcorn is consumed in the home and 30% in theaters, at carnivals, amusement parks, and stadiums. One quarter of all popcorn sales in the U.S., $250 million worth, take place in movie theaters, with an 86% profit margin for the theater owner. He pays 5 cents for the popcorn, 2 cents for the "butter" (almost always a cheap imitation). How much would real butter cost? Three more cents . . . but that would cut into the profit.

Population Shifts
"Rust Belt" Cities Decline

The population of the U.S. grew from 226,545,805 in 1980 to 248,709,873 in 1990. The 1993 population estimate is 255 million. The West had the largest population growth (22.3%) and the Midwest the least (1.4%). The Northeast grew by 3.4%, the South by 13.4%.

Some 3 of the 8 American cities with more than 1 million people have suffered substantial losses in population since 1980. At the same time, 33% of the cities of 250,000–500,000 population increased in size, while cities of 500,000 — 1 million or more remained stable.

Former large manufacturing cities, such as St. Louis and Pittsburgh, are now shrinking in the direction of midsize cities. The bigger, million-plus cities — Philadelphia, Chicago, and Detroit — were down substantially. Dallas joined the million-plus club in 1990, growing from 904,087 persons in 1980 to 1,006,877 in 1990, a 9.7% increase. New York gained 250,925 persons in the 1980s and remained by far the biggest city in the nation, with 7.3 million people. Its population gain in the 1980s still left it 572,999 people short of its all-time population high of 7.9 million, achieved in 1960.

The number of midsize cities — those with populations between 250,000 and 500,000 — increased from 30 to 40. Among the states, California continued its record growth, with 12% of all Americans now living there. It grew by 6.1 million people in the 1980s, a 26% growth, which is unique in U.S. history.

These tables list those cities with the biggest shifts in population, according to the 1990 census.

Biggest Losers

City	1990	1980	Change
Gary, Ind.	116,646	151,968	−23%
Newark	275,221	329,248	−16.4%
Detroit	1,027,974	1,203,369	−14.6%
Pittsburgh	369,879	423,960	−12.8%
St. Louis	396,685	452,804	−12.4%
Cleveland	505,616	573,822	−11.9%
Flint, Mich.	140,761	159,611	−11.8%
New Orleans	496,938	557,927	−10.9%
Warren, Mi.	144,864	161,134	−10.1%
Chattanooga, Tenn.	152,466	169,514	−10.1%

Biggest Gainers

City	1990	1980	Change
Morena Valley, Calif.	118,779	28,309	319.6%
Mesa, Ariz.	288,091	152,404	89.0%
Rancho Cucamonga, Calif.	101,409	55,250	83.5%
Plano, Tex.	128,713	72,331	77.9%
Irvine, Calif.	110,330	62,134	77.6%
Escondido, Calif.	108,635	64,355	68.8%
Oceanside, Calif.	128,398	76,698	67.4%
Santa Clarita, Calif.	110,642	66,730	65.8%
Bakersfield, Calif.	174,820	105,611	65.5%

Postal Service

"Neither snow, nor rain, nor heat, nor gloom of night stays these couriers from the swift completion of their appointed rounds."

If you think lost letters, misdirected mail, and long lines at the post office window are the rule rather than the exception, 30% of Americans interviewed in a Roper poll agree with you. The Postal Service, however, claims punctual delivery rates of 95% for local mail and 90% for cross-country mail.

The Case of Pearl's Postcard: It was the first full day of spring, March 22, 1911. Pearl Wild of Cannonsburg, Mich., was thinking of her sister Estella, who lived a buggy ride or two away in Grand Rapids. Estella liked to prepare food for her family, which is probably why Pearl obtained a very special postcard for her sibling to ask her a favor. That day, Pearl mailed her sister the dainty card embossed with apple blossoms with a simple request: would she make some butter. No one knows if Estella ever delivered any spread to Pearl. By 1993, when the card was delivered, Estella had been dead for fifteen years (even though she lived to age 93). Her grandson Gordon, who lives across the street, received the card in his mailbox — technically misdelivered, but with good intentions. As for Pearl, nothing more was reported about her except her husband's occupation: he was a postal worker.

The Postal Service employs 800,000 people and moves more than 160 billion pieces of mail annually — 661 envelopes and boxes per capita — which accounts for 40% of all the world's mail. The mail is moved at a consumer cost lower than that in any other industrial nation. But that can change any time the 5-member Postal Rate Commission and the 11-member Board of Governors deem it necessary.

Between 1979 and 1988, the post office had five years of profits and five years of losses. In 1989, it earned $61 million, but it lost $874 million in 1990 and *$1.47 billion* in 1991. Losses for 1992 are still being counted by the auditors at this writing.

This list shows the average annual number of pieces of various classifications of mail, according to Postal Service data.

First class	90 billion
Third class	60 billion

Second class	10 billion
Fourth class	700 million
Priority mail	500 million
Express mail	50 million
Mailgram	10 million

In addition, the Postal Service moves 800 million pieces of international mail, 600 million pieces of its own correspondence ("U.S. Postal Service" mail), and 35 million pieces that are free for the blind. In 1992 the service printed some 50 billion stamps — more than 600,000 miles worth — enough to circle the earth 25 times.

Poverty

Highest Since 1960s

About 36 million Americans are trapped in poverty, an increase of 2 million since the beginning of the decade, which is more than at any time since 1964, when President Lyndon Johnson declared a war on poverty.

About 15% of Americans are officially classified as "poor," which the Census Bureau defined in 1991 as those in a family of four with an annual income of less than $13,924, or $6,932 for a single person. In 1989, 12.7% of the population was classified as poor. It was also reported that the purchasing power of American households is shrinking by more than $1,000 per year as the 1990s progress.

In 1992, the Census Bureau issued a special report on poverty comparing 1991 to 1990. Some of its findings are:

- The number of poor families increased to 7.7 million, up from 7.1 million.
- The poverty rate for whites rose to 11.3% from 10.7%; for blacks it rose to 32.7% from 31.9%; for Hispanics, 28.7% from 28.1%; and for Asian Americans, 13.8% from 12.2%.
- 40% of the poor were children; 11% elderly.
- 29% of the poor lacked medical insurance.

Poverty Among the Elderly

The General Accounting Office estimates that 5.7 million elderly Americans are poor or close to it.

Across all racial and ethnic groups, people over 75 years of age are more likely to be poor or near poor than any other age group. Elderly women are nearly twice as likely to be poor than elderly men, and elderly minorities are 75% more likely to be poor than elderly nonminorities. The plight of the aged poor can hardly be more poignantly presented than it was by one Maryland woman, Rose Taylor.

The Case of Ms. Taylor: According to official government policy, Ms. Taylor is worth more dead than alive. She has lived in her home for forty-seven years but cannot afford running water and indoor plumbing. The county offered to pay $3,000 for those fundamental needs but demanded that she give her home to the county when she died. She consented. Her only other asset is a small insurance policy, which she has paid in full to make sure that her funeral expenses are covered. With only $442 a month in Social Security income, she is unlikely to be able to save for it.

Her local Social Security office calls her frequently, checking to see if she has cashed in her insurance — money everyone would agree she could use. She dare not do it, however; if she does, she will lose her eligibility for her medical card, which she needs to pay for her medications. Even if she is foolish enough to do so, the amount she would receive from the insurance company would be deducted from her Social Security income, hence she would have no gain whatsoever. The only way she can get the money is by dying.

In response to her plight, Congressman Edward Roybal (D-California), the chairman of the Select Committee on Aging, said, "I'm convinced that a false impression is developing in this country that most elderly persons are well off, and that those few who are not are being adequately provided for through an extensive network of federal programs. In fact, this is not the case."

Pregnant Women Abused

Abuse against pregnant women is on the rise. A study involving nearly 700 women, published in the *Journal of the American Medical Association,* found that 17% of them — 1 in 6 — suffered physical or sexual abuse before coming to term; previous estimates have ranged from 3% to 8%.

Judith McFarland, a doctor of public health at Texas Women's University in Houston and the senior author of the report, called the results "just the tip of the iceberg." Multiple cases of abuse were common, the report said. More than 60% of the victims were beaten at least twice during their pregnancies and more than 33% four or more times. About 75% of the batterers were husbands, ex-husbands, or boyfriends, the remainder relatives or neighbors.

White women tended to be attacked more frequently and more severely than Hispanic or black women. Hispanic women were beaten more frequently but less severely than blacks, but only 7% of the black women were married, compared to 62% of the Hispanics and 40% of the whites.

Premature Babies

Ten years ago, a premature birth was the most frightening event that could befall parents. With recent technological developments, however, many babies born as early as 28 weeks after conception are surviving and growing into healthy toddlers. Even some born only 24 weeks after conception are being saved.

According to the National Center for Health Statistics, 10% of all babies born are "preemies" — hospital jargon for an infant born before the full 37-week gestation period. In 1990, some 430,000 babies were preemies.

Most neonatal intensive care units are not just using more sophisticated techniques and equipment, they are now using parents as a medical tool. According to Dr. Heidelise Als of Harvard Medical School, a leading researcher in premature births, the involvement of parents in hospital care is the major factor in the increased success with preemies. Als found that babies who were given routine incubator care by their mothers and fathers spent about half as much time on respirators as those who were cared for solely by the hospital staff. They were able to begin bottle or breast feeding earlier and had a lower incidence of brain hemorrhaging and lung disorders, the most common ailments among newborns.

Kangaroo Care: One of the most innovative developments in saving the lives of newborns has been "kangaroo care." The mother takes the child from the incubator at frequent intervals and nestles the baby against her body and breasts. Developed in

Bogotá, Colombia, the process has been shown to increase the development of premature babies while decreasing complications. The method has proven so effective that its use is growing in the U.S.; sometimes an infant is even taken off a respirator for a short period to be cuddled by the mother.

Presidential Life Expectancy
A Killing Job

Few would doubt that the president of the United States has one of the most stressful jobs possible, and now comes statistical evidence that the position is, in fact, hazardous to his health — not to mention the possibility of his being assassinated. Of the 42 presidents thus far, 3 have been fatally shot — 7% of those who held the office. By contrast .04% of policemen are killed in the line of duty, which means that the president's risk of being killed is 175 times greater than that of a law enforcement officer.

In a 1992 article in *Science*, Professor Robert Gilbert of Boston's Northeastern University calls the longevity of U.S. presidents "lackluster" and argues that "an alarming number of U.S. presidents have died prematurely and suffered from debilitating problems in office." That hasn't always been so. The first 10 presidents, from George Washington through John Tyler, enjoyed above-average life spans of 77.9 years; the average, according to an account of Gilbert's findings in the *Chicago Tribune*, was 74.2 years for an educated white man.

The next 10 chief executives who were not assassinated — from James Polk through Grover Cleveland — lived the shortest lives, dying at an average age of 66.3, considerably below the average. The situation improved slightly in the next century, but the presidency still was debilitating. From Benjamin Harrison through Lyndon Johnson (of those who were not assassinated), presidents lived 4.6 years shorter than their life expectancy, succumbing at an average age of 71. Cardiovascular disease was blamed for the deaths of 7 of the presidents who died prematurely during this century, including Teddy Roosevelt, Franklin Roosevelt, Woodrow Wilson, Warren Harding, Calvin Coolidge, and Lyndon Johnson.

To offset the health problems inherent in the world's most important job, Gilbert advises that a mental health unit be established in the White House to monitor and curb the stress levels of both the president and vice president.

Presidential Pardons
Pardon Me?

The president of the United States has almost unlimited power to pardon those convicted or accused of a crime and to shorten prison sentences, so bypassing the Justice Department's screening process and years of delay. Compared to his predecessors, President Bush certainly did not abuse the privilege, giving few breaks to defendants who appealed to him during his term. Of 969 requests for mercy, he approved only 38 pardons and 1 commutation, according to the Justice Department — by far the lowest record in modern history.

In the midst of a reelection campaign and not wanting to look soft on crime or be accused of cronyism, Bush granted no pardons during his last year

Franklin D. Roosevelt, the most forgiving man to occupy the White House, pardoned about 300 offenders each year. Photo, courtesy VOA.

and a half in office — until he lost the election. Then he issued pardons for many of those involved in the Iran-contra scandal, including Caspar Weinberger, the former secretary of defense.

Bush was in an especially forgiving mood on three days in the course of his term: 10 persons were pardoned on

August 14, 1989; 17 on March 5, 1991; and 12 on July 5, 1991.

In November 1992, hundreds of requests were still pending. The most famous one was that of Patty Hearst, the notorious heiress who turned bank robber after being kidnapped by the Symbionese Liberation Army, a terrorist group. Hearst received a twenty-five-year prison sentence in 1976, of which she served three years. President Carter commuted her sentence but would not pardon her.

Well-known individuals who did get presidential pardons include Armand Hammer (by Bush), Jimmy Hoffa (by Nixon), Yankee owner George Steinbrenner (by Reagan), President Nixon (by Ford), and Tokyo Rose (also by Ford).

This table cites the pardons and commutations granted by modern presidents, according to the Justice Department.

	Total	Annual Average
Franklin Roosevelt	3,687	307
Harry Truman	2,044	264
Dwight Eisenhower	1,157	145
John Kennedy	575	203
Lyndon Johnson	1,187	230
Richard Nixon	926	161
Gerald Ford	409	182
Jimmy Carter	566	141
Ronald Reagan	406	51
George Bush	39	10

Prison Inmates
More Drug Offenders, Fewer Serious Criminals

America imprisons more of its citizens than any other country in the world. According to statistics from the Justice Department, 1 of every 200 Americans has been incarcerated at least once. Among young black males, an incredible 1 in 7 has been in jail.

Today's prison population is over 800,000, up more than 150% from that of ten years ago. The rate per 100,000 population is now 310, up from 139 in 1980.

Most of the increases are due to drug-related rather than serious crimes (murder, manslaughter, sexual assault, assault, and burglary). In 1980, more than 60% of the prison population was convicted of serious crimes; today, it is 40%. The space once occupied by serious offenders is now being used to house criminals convicted of drug crimes, who account for about 30% of inmates, up from 10% in 1980.

Those convicted of serious drug offenses are guaranteed to serve time. The percentage of drug offenders imprisoned is now close to 90%, up from 77% in 1986. In 1980, 1 in 13 new inmates was convicted of a drug offense. Today, one third of all new inmates are drug offenders.

Offenders who break federal laws and go to prison stay there longer than those in state prisons. Those who receive federal sentences serve about 85% of their time, whereas those in state prisons serve about half. Approximately three quarters of the convicted criminals covered by the Sentencing Reform Act of 1985 are sent to prison compared with 52% in 1986, the last year before the law took effect.

Federal prisoners released now have served an average of 19 months, 29% longer than the average term served by prisoners released in 1986. The act eliminated early release on parole and gave judges guidelines for adding prison time in proportion to the seriousness of the crime and the defendant's record.

Professor's Salaries
Pay Raises at Record Low

Although there's a broad range of salary scales at the nation's colleges and universities, one thing is consistent: few professors received significant raises to begin the 1993 academic year. The average increase was 3.5%, the smallest in twenty years.

Raises were smaller at state universities (2.9%) than at private schools (4.7%) — the biggest difference in a decade, according to a report from the American Association of University Professors. It said the average faculty salary in 1991–92 was $45,360, with schools that grant doctorates paying an average of $51,080, baccalaureate schools paying $37,260, and two-year colleges paying $37,760. Harvard pays $91,000 annually to full professors. The lowest-paying schools offer full professors about $40,000.

The ProfScam Theory: Charles Sykes, who pummeled higher education in his 1988 book *ProfScam*, charges that faculty salaries have been rising while teaching loads have been declining. Not so, says James Appleberry, of the

American Association of State Universities, who claims workloads have increased. Sykes maintains that it is the tenured professors who have the plum jobs: "It's a little hard to feel sorry for the tenured faculty members who may teach one or two classes a week."

This list of faculty salaries in 1992 was compiled by the American Association of University Professors.

Public Institutions

	Men	Women
Professor	$62,580	$56,340
Associate Professor	$45,720	$43,070
Instructor	$27,910	$25,810

Private Institutions

	Men	Women
Professor	$77,750	$69,250
Associate	$52,740	$48,680
Instructor	$34,200	$32,190

Property Seizures

Crimes That Pay

The war on drugs has many profiteers. Changes in criminal law during the 1980s have created a new and important source of revenue for law enforcement agencies, and they are making the most of it. The inventory of seized property held by the Justice Department reached a record $2 billion in 1992, up from $33 million in 1979, according to a U.S. Marshals Service study. It also noted that billions more in confiscated property had already been sold by the department. Seizures by state and local agencies may be even higher, but no figures are available.

The law that allows for confiscations was enacted by the first Congress in 1789, but it was never widely used until federal and state governments stepped up their crackdowns on drugs and money-laundering violations. More than 100 laws authorizing such seizures were enacted in the 1980s, and it quickly became clear that not just drug pushers and users would see their lives impounded. Illegal immigrants and their smugglers, white-collar criminals, owners of adult bookstore owners, and racketeers have also lost homes, cars, and other valuable property under the new laws, often without the formality of a court conviction.

The Case of Lyle Austin: Compared to other places, South Dakota didn't have much of a drug problem . . . until Lyle

Austin was charged with possession of cocaine. Austin was not alleged to have very much, and he didn't contest the charge. One count of possession is often passed over in most U.S. courts, so Austin thought it was in everybody's interest for him simply to plead guilty. But when he did, the roof caved in over him.

Federal agents seized his business, a body shop worth $40,000. With no business, Austin could have stayed at home all day, but he had another problem — they seized his home, too. With no business and no home, he got mad. "Cruel and unusual punishment," he cried. Too bad, the authorities said, maintaining that payment to a sovereign for some offenses is within the law. But the issue of "how much is enough" got the attention of the Supreme Court, which said Austin might have a point. The case was sent back to the lower courts, where it is yet unresolved, but they are expected to rule that the case of Lyle Austin went too far, indeed.

In addition to the law enforcement agencies, which simply keep and assign confiscated goods, other beneficiaries of the new laws have included schools, libraries, and many discount shoppers, who bought the more than 17,000 cars seized from the smugglers of illegal aliens in 1992 alone. The most common confiscated properties sold at federal auctions are vehicles, jewelry, financial instruments, currency, and real estate.

Property Theft
A Most Personal Offense

Next to a bodily attack, the most emotionally traumatic crime against Americans may be the theft of personal possessions. Almost 13 million individuals have been victims, according to the FBI. Arrests for such crimes total almost 1.5 million persons a year, including more than half a million juveniles and more than 100,000 women.

The total loss of property in America due to theft is more than $16 billion annually, about half of which comes from automobile heists, the most expensive property crime. Thankfully, almost two thirds of stolen autos are recovered. Next on the list is jewels, the most difficult goods for police to recover. Following is a breakdown of the approximate value of stolen goods and the percentage recovered, adapted from FBI statistics.

Motor vehicles	$8.5 billion	65%
Jewelry and precious metals	$1.4 billion	4%
Televisions, stereos, etc.	$1.2 billion	5%
Currency, notes, etc.	$1.0 billion	6%
Clothing and furs	$390 million	13%
Office equipment	$320 million	7%
Household goods	$280 million	7%
Firearms	$130 million	10%
Consumable goods	$110 million	12%
Livestock	$20 million	17%
Miscellaneous	$2.9 billion	10%

Of the total $16.25 billion, 38%, or about $6 billion, is recovered.

Prostate Cancer
Tests Failing to Halt Climb

The American Cancer Society predicts that 34,000 men will die of prostate cancer this year. With the death rate from this disease rising from 19,095 in 1980 to 24,175 for white men in 1988, and from 3,670 to 4,581 among blacks, doctors at the Centers for Disease Control fear that newer and more expensive tests are not doing the job.

Ron Aubert, an epidemiologist at the center, said, "We're not at the point where organizations feel comfortable making recommendations that people get these early screenings. There is clearly something going on. It's becoming a public health problem." Two decades ago, prostate cancer was seen mostly in older men, with an average age of 73 at the time of diagnosis. Now it is widespread in men in their early fifties and even some men in their middle thirties.

The cause of prostatic cancer is unknown, but according to the Columbia College of Physicians and Surgeons' *Complete Home Medical Guide*, predisposing factors include heredity and perhaps viral, sexual, and dietary factors. A high-fat diet seems to increase the risk.

Race Relations
U.S. In a Worried Mood

The overwhelming mood of Americans responding to a *New York Times* survey of 1,253 adults is "Wake up to the problems of minorities." To the question, "How good are race relations today?" 71% of whites and 75% of the blacks responded, "Generally bad."

Perhaps the rioting in Los Angeles in 1992 caused by the acquittal of the police in the beating of Rodney G. King, a black, was a warning to the nation to improve its conduct of race relationships; 71% of the whites and 75% of the blacks called it "a warning," and only 21% of the whites and 19% of the blacks called it "an isolated incident."

Continuing the grim mood, 53% of the whites and 55% of the blacks said that there will always be prejudice and discrimination in America, and more than half of both whites and blacks believed there would still be race riots in American cities twenty-five years from now. A lack of jobs was blamed as the root of the trouble, most respondents agreed. When asked what steps to take to improve the situation, the respondents listed jobs and training at the top, followed by better police training, more blacks in government, stronger civil rights laws, black and Hispanic ownership of local businesses, and, last, more police.

Racial Geography
Blacks In South, Asians In West

Though the racial climate has changed since World War II, America's major racial groups have remained relatively static in their geographic preferences. Even the migration of many black families to the North has not changed the fact that most blacks still live in the South. Likewise, Hispanics have remained mainly in the South and West.

Asian Americans represent a different and changing geographic pattern. Before the turn of the century, they came to the U.S. through western entry points, and, like most immigrants, they settled and remain relatively close to those ports. Now Asians, unlike other groups, represent a new wave of immigration and are settling virtually all over the nation.

They are coming to the U.S. primarily from the Philippines, Korea, Vietnam, India, and China.

This table shows the percentage of the major racial groups living in various parts of the nation, according to the Census Bureau.

	West	South	Midwest	N'east
Black	9.4%	52.8%	19.1%	18.7%
Asian	55.6%	15.4%	10.6%	18.4%
Hispanic	45.9%	30.8%	7.8%	15.5%
White	18.7%	32.6%	27.2%	21.5%

Radon Gas

In Homes, Now Schools, Too

In late 1988, radon became a household word. That year the Environmental Protection Agency released a study showing that at least 8 million homes in the country could contain excessive levels of the odorless, colorless, cancer-causing gas, which leaks into dwellings from the underlying soil.

In a 1993 survey of 1,000 schools, the EPA found that 20% contained potentially dangerous levels of radon. It estimated from the study that 11 million students nationwide in 70,000 classrooms are exposed to radon, and that some classrooms have gas levels almost fifteen times above federal limits. Problem areas in schools often varied greatly from room to room, depending on ventilation and other factors, but were always found on the first floor.

Studies show that radon causes about 14,000 of the nation's cancer deaths a year — about 2.6% of the 520,000 in 1992. The EPA survey was taken under a mandate of the 100th Congress, which created a national radon program following the EPA's 1988 study.

Railroad Fatalities

Many a nervous traveler opts for the train, thinking it is the safest way to travel. Statistics support this belief. The odds of being killed on a train ride are an incredible 1 in 9 million. You are more likely to win the state lottery, get struck by lightning, or be the parent of quintuplets.

Why, then, do we occasionally read accounts of a massive number of deaths in a train accident? Perhaps it is because a fatal train wreck is almost always a front-page story. The media are more prone to cover rare occurrences, especially when many lose their lives. This list cites the major train accidents since 1960, as compiled by the Associated Press.

- 45 killed, Chicago, Oct. 30, 1972
- 19 killed, Steelton, Pa., July 28, 1962
- 16 killed, Chevy Chase, Md., Jan. 4, 1987
- 14 killed, Bakersfield, Calif., Mar. 14, 1960
- 13 killed, Everett, Mass., Dec. 28, 1966
- 11 killed, Chicago (elevated), Feb. 4, 1977
- 11 killed, Salem, Ill., June 10, 1971
- 8 killed, Camden, S.C., July 31, 1991
- 5 killed, New York City (subway), Aug. 28, 1991
- 5 killed, Williston, Vt., July 7, 1984

Rain or Shine

Soggy Vacation Tales

The U.S. has a range of climates from tropical to arid. Some of its top vacation spots are at both ends of the spectrum, from rainy Miami and New Orleans to the desert-like reaches of Phoenix and Reno. Here is a list of the wettest and driest places in America and their annual rainfall in inches, according to the *Statistical Abstract of the United States.*

The Rainiest

Mobile, Ala.	64.64
New Orleans	59.74
Miami	57.75
San Juan, P.R.	53.99
Juneau	53.15
Jackson, Miss.	52.82
Jacksonville, Fla.	52.76
Memphis	51.57
Little Rock	49.20
Columbia, S.C.	49.12

The Driest

Phoenix	7.11
Reno	7.49
El Paso	7.82
Albuquerque	8.12
San Diego	9.32
Boise	11.71
Cheyenne	13.31
Great Falls, Mont.	15.24
Salt Lake City	15.31
Bismarck, N.Dak.	15.36

Rapes

84% Not Reported

A government-funded study done in 1990 was finally released in 1993 by the National Victim Center and the Crime Victims Research and Treatment Center of the Medical University of South Carolina, after interviews with 4,000 women across the country. (One can only imagine how many bureaucratic agencies it had to go through before it was cleared for publication.) It revealed that 683,000 U.S. women were raped in 1990 and that 12.1 million adult women had been raped at least once in their lives. About 62% of the victims said they were attacked when they were minors, with about 29% of that group saying they were 10 or younger at the time.

The list below represents the relationships of the victims and the offenders by percentage of cases, according to the center.

Neighbors/friends	29%
Strangers	22%
Relatives (other than immediate family)	16%
Fathers or stepfathers	11%
Boyfriends or ex-boyfriends	11%
Husbands or ex-husbands	9%
Refused to answer or were unsure	3%

Other findings were as follows:

- Of 12.1 million women raped, 6.8 million were raped once and 4.7 million more than once; 600,000 were unsure of the number of times.
- Only 16% reported the crime to police; 69% feared being blamed for somehow causing the rape.
- About 66% said they would have reported the crime if there were a law prohibiting the media from disclosing their identity.

Rape Penalties Are Tougher on Robbers Than Rapists: For six months a Senate Judiciary Committee compiled federal and state records on rapes and their aftermath. The panel also interviewed workers in rape crisis centers in 12 states. Experts on sexual assault and family violence appeared before the committee as well. Their conclusion: judges, prosecutors, and police throw up roadblocks to accusers and show too much leniency to those convicted.

Persons standing trial for murder or robbery are much more likely to be convicted than those accused of rape: accused murderers face a conviction rate of 69%, robbers, 61%, and rapists, 46%. Of those ultimately convicted of rape, 25% are released on probation and *never serve prison time.* Only 2% of rape victims will ever see their attackers imprisoned.

Rape in the Military
Navy Is Hardest Hit

With men and women in the U.S. military now doing some of the same jobs and living in closer quarters than ever before, more women are reporting assaults or are showing a heightened sensitivity about date rape.

On navy ships and bases around the world, despite cuts in the number of sailors, rape is on the rise, whereas in the army and air force it has decreased. Documents obtained under the Freedom of Information Act and published by the *Orange County Register* in California show that rapes nearly tripled in the last five years, and most rapists and victims were navy personnel. This compares to a 10% increase in the general population, up from 90,000 in 1987 to more than 100,000 now, according to the Justice Department.

Among other findings in the navy:

- 495 cases of reported rapes are "closed" due to charges being unsubstantiated or found false.
- 46 alleged rapes took place in 1987, 134 in 1990, and 130 in 1991.
- 299 cases were "unresolved" after five years because no witnesses were found or there was no evidence.

Recycling
At Last, "Politically Correct"

Twenty-five years ago the U.S. adopted recycling on a large scale, and today the practice has become "politically correct" and even fashionable. With the average American producing 3.5 pounds of garbage daily, landfills are bulging to capacity. According to the Environmental Protection Agency, there were 20,000 landfills in the U.S. in 1978. By 1988, all but 7,000 were full. In 1993, 16 states have fewer than five years of capacity left. America is responding by recycling everything from soda bottles to newsprint.

Corporations, like individuals, are getting on the bandwagon. In 1988, several manufacturers of plastic foam containers formed the National Polystyrene Recycling Corporation, aiming to increase the amount of recycled plastic foam waste 25% by 1995. In 1989, Procter & Gamble started marketing Spic and Span in recycled plastic bottles. In 1990, McDonald's stopped using polystyrene containers, and Pepsi-Cola and Coca-Cola began using 25% recycled plastic for their bottles.

Dents in the National Garbage Can: Below are some of the most significant effects that the emphasis on recycling has had in America, according to Debi Kimball in *Recycling in America*.

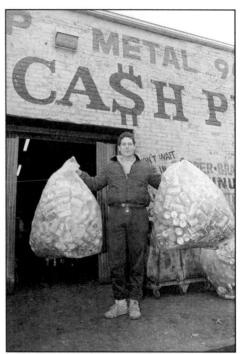

Keith Bell, who heads Recycling Programs, Inc., proudly displays the aluminum cans his crews collected. Photo © Robert C. V. Lieberman.

- Recycling one aluminum can saves the energy equivalent of a TV set running for three hours. In 1989, Americans recycled 49.5 billion aluminum beverage cans, bringing aluminum's recycling rate to 60.8%.
- In 1989, steel "tin" cans were being recycled at a rate of 21.6% nationwide; each minute of every

day, more than 9,000 steel cans are recycled.

- Every glass bottle recycled saves enough energy to light a 100-watt bulb for four hours; Americans recycle approximately 13 million glass bottles and jars every day.
- Americans throw away 2.5 million plastic bottles every hour of the day; of the 14.4 million tons of all types of plastics generated in 1988, only .2 million tons, 1.1%, were recycled.
- Americans use more than 75 million tons of paper and paperboard every year; about 20 million tons is recycled, a process that reduces air pollution by 74% and water pollution by 35%.
- About 9 million old cars were recycled in 1988, while 3 million were abandoned. This has led to the present situation, in which more than 50% of all steel manufactured in the U.S. is made from recycled material, thus reducing air pollution from steel mills by 86% and using 40% less water.

Religion
God's American Guises

God takes many forms and speaks many languages in the contemporary U.S. Each Sunday (or Saturday), 147.5 million Americans — 61% of the population — commune with some form of deity. There are hundreds of religious denominations that fall under the umbrella of 21 major subgroups of Judaism, Christianity, and Islam. The three major religions of the nation share many traits, including an adherence to the laws of the Old Testament and a belief in the holy status of the ancient city of Jerusalem.

There are 141 million Christians, 95.8% of the religious affiliated; 6 million are Jewish, and 300,000 are estimated to be Muslims, though no reliable statistics exist for the latter. The Roman Catholic church is the largest single denomination in the country, with 57 million followers, 39% of all the religiously affiliated; they represent 23% of the total population. Baptists are the largest Protestant group, with 28.4 million adherents, 19.3% of the nation's worshipers. Methodists are the next largest, with 13.2 million members, 9% of the religious, followed by 8.4 million Lutherans, who represent 5.7% of the churchgoers.

This table shows where most religiously affiliated Christians and Jews live, according to the Glenmary Research Center and *American Jewish Yearbook* respectively.

Top 10 Christian States

	% Christian	Number
Utah	75%	1,097,000
Rhode Island	75%	710,000
North Dakota	73.8%	482,000
South Dakota	66.9%	462,000
Minnesota	64.9%	2,644,000
Wisconsin	64.4%	3,029,000
Massachusetts	64.0%	3,669,000
Nebraska	63.1%	990,000
Iowa	60.8%	1,890,000
Connecticut	60.8%	1,890,000

Top 10 Jewish States

New York	1,844,000
California	909,000
Florida	585,000
New Jersey	411,000
Pennsylvania	346,000
Massachusetts	276,000
Illinois	258,000
Maryland	210,000
Ohio	131,000
Texas	107,000

Reproductive Health Among Minorities

A survey, sponsored by the Consortium Media Center and the National Council of Negro Women for the Women of Color Reproductive Poll, questioned 1,157 black, Asian, Hispanic, and Native American women age 18 and older in 1992.

Some 59% of the women did not practice birth control; 32% of the 302 black women questioned said they could not afford contraceptive devices, were afraid of them, or didn't like them. Some 22% of the Native American women reported having been sterilized compared to 6% of all the respondents. This compares to 25% of all American women who have been sterilized, a finding by the Guttmacher Institute.

The survey also reported that:

- More than 66% of black respondents said they had a gynecologist; 36% of the Native American women had one.
- 90% of black women had had Pap smears to screen for cervical cancer; 71% of Asian females had had one.

- 52% of black women had undergone mammograms to test for breast cancer; 40% of Asians and 32% of the Indians had undergone one.

Restaurant Chains
Family Favorites

No fair peeking in the kitchen to see if the floors and walls are scrubbed, the cookware shiny, the produce rinsed, and the dishes clean. We're talking here about the menus offered, the service provided, the atmosphere, and the cost for a family who wants to eat out without going to some elegant, pricey palace. We're talking about good ol' American chains.

Consumer Reports surveyed about 98,000 readers to rate 38 casual dining spots based on a 100-point scale (none scored higher than 75 or lower than 54). The top three in each category and their scores were as follows:

Family Restaurants
Cracker Barrel	75
Bob Evans	69
Po-Folks	65

Steak/Buffet Houses
Mr. Steak	64
Ryan's	64
Golden Corral	63

Casual Dinner Houses
Stuart Anderson's	71
Olive Garden	70
Steak and Ale	69

Retailing
The City vs. the Suburbs

There was a time in America, before World War II, when the suburbs were mainly bedroom communities. Most suburbanites worked and shopped in the city, for there was little commerce beyond the city limits.

In the 1950s that changed. Chain stores, discount outlets, and branches of the city's department stores began to sprout in affluent suburbs. This trend became so intense that by the 1980s, many city dwellers were forced to do much of their shopping in the suburbs. Now, in the 1990s, another change is taking place: the cities are appealing to the nation's big retailers to open stores within the city limits.

And they are doing it in record numbers.

New York's deputy mayor for finance and economic development, Barry F. Sullivan, expressed the phenomenon best, saying, "My belief is

Urban shopping malls, such as Las Vegas's Forum, offer unusual embellishments to attract suburban shoppers. Photo, courtesy Las Vegas News Bureau.

that we are watching the gradual reentry into the city of the business that went to the suburbs in the post–World War II market. That market is

relatively saturated. Now they're looking for ways to begin to come back."

Today, in major metropolitan areas, almost half of all retail transactions (48%) are in the suburbs, with the remainder in the cities.

This table, compiled by the City Planning Department of the Census Bureau, represents the amounts in the suburbs and the cities per $1,000 of personal spending in major metropolitan areas.

	Suburbs	City
Boston	$448	$468
Chicago	$432	$365
Dallas	$404	$574
Detroit	$459	$348
Houston	$285	$643
Los Angeles	$412	$382
New York	$395	$298
San Francisco	$366	$422

Richest of Them All
How Do They Do It?

The 3-Step Process: "1. Go to work early. 2. Stay late. 3. Find oil." — *John D. Rockefeller*

Below are the people on *Forbes* magazine's 1992 list of the richest

Americans and the area in which their fortune was acquired.

Bill Gates (computer software)	$6.3 billion
John Kluge (media)	$5.5 billion
Walton family (retailing)	$5.1 billion*
Warren Buffet (investing)	$4.4 billion
Samuel and Donald Newhouse (publishing)	$3.5 billion

Five members of the family occupy spots 3–7 of Forbes's 10 richest, the result of inheriting Sam Walton's fortune (estimated at more than $15 billion), which the patriarch earned by founding and building the Walmart chain.

Bill Gates, 36 years old, is the youngest ever to reach the top of the list. His considerable assets grew $1.5 billion over the previous year, the result of making money from each computer that uses MS-DOS, the most widely used operating system in personal computers (often called "IBM compatibles"). John Kluge, the owner of Metro Media, owns many radio and television stations and cellular phone interests as well as the Harlem Globetrotters and the Ice Capades.

The Biggest Losers: While some fortunes grow, others decline. John Kluge fell from the first spot when his assets dropped a hefty $400 million, due to the slump in broadcast revenues and competition with cable TV. Ross Perot

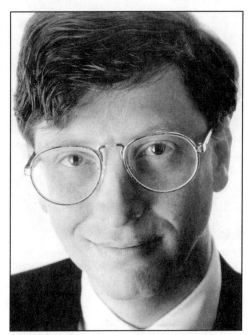

Bill Gates made $1.5 billion last year, seven times more than Ross Perot.

was once the sixth richest American but is now in nineteenth place. The good news for him is that last year his wealth grew from $2.2 billion to $2.4 billion. The junk bond king Michael Milken earned 30 cents an hour during his 22 months in prison. His cut in pay along with a $1.1 billion fine for securities violations reduced his nest egg to a relatively modest $700 million.

Overall, the fortunes of *Forbes*'s richest 400 Americans grew at an annual rate of 4.3%, about 50% greater than the incomes of average Americans, which grew at a rate of 2.9%. Those on the elite list experienced an average increase of $31 million last year for a net gain of $300 billion.

The Steel Phantom at Kennywood Park, near Pittsburgh, has the longest drop of all roller coasters (22 stories) and reaches a speed of 80 mph, making it the world's fastest.

Roller Coasters

Back in Style

People have been coasting on man-made devices ever since 102 B.C., when the Teutons slid down the Alps on their shields on their way to attack Rome. It took the French, however, to put "coasters" on wheels 1,900 years later, when they built the first made-for-fun wooden tracks in a Paris public garden. The idea was brought over to America in 1870, when an abandoned mine train in Pennsylvania was used to carry passengers down a slight mountain grade. The idea so delighted the passengers that inventors began building "scenic railways" — a moniker the Patent Office still uses rather than the more common "roller coaster" — to thrill and delight riders.

According to Todd H. Throgmorton's book *Roller Coasters*, in the "golden age" of coasters, the 1920s, the U.S. boasted about 1,500 of the twisting, turning, dropping, climbing fun machines. Their popularity declined during the Depression and World War II, but today a second golden age for coasters is upon us, a revival that began in the 1950s with the opening of Disneyland.

There are 376 coasters in the U.S. today, 108 of which have been built since 1970. Speeds have increased to 80 miles an hour, heights to 22 stories, first drops to 61 degrees, and G-forces to as high as 6.5 (astronauts can withstand G-forces of 11 before they black out). The longest ride in the nation is 4 minutes, 4 seconds, on the Beast in King Island, Ohio. The shortest ride Throgmorton records is 36 seconds on the Tidal Wave at Paramount's Great America in Santa Clara, Calif., but riders get their money's worth: they hurtle from 0 to 55 mph in 4.2 seconds. Of the total coasters, excluding traveling kid-park coasters, California leads the nation with 44. Pennsylvania is second, with 38, followed by Ohio (34), Texas (26), and North Carolina (20). Only 15 of the 50 states have no roller coasters at all!

Other roller coaster facts, from *Roller Coaster*:

- The fastest: the Steel Phantom, West Mifflin, Pa. —80 mph
- The longest drop: the Steel Phantom —22 stories
- The roughest ride: the Riverside Cyclone, Agawam, Mass. — first drop from 0 to 60 mph in 3 seconds
- The smoothest ride: the Yankee Cannonball, Salem, N.H. — 2,000 feet long, 35 mph, 2-minute ride
- The oldest: the Leap-the-Dips, Altoona, Pa. — 1902
- The newest: the Rattler, San Antonio, Tex. — 1992; Vortex, Charlotte, N.C. — 1992; the Ninja, Atlanta, Ga. — 1992; the Ripsaw, Bloomington, Minn., 1992; Batman, the Ride, Gurnee, Ill. — 1992
- The most terrifying: the Twister, Denver—twisting ride that includes a 65-mph plunge into a tunnel along a high-banked curve
- The most bizarre: the Dragon Coaster, Rye, N.Y. — a 2-minute ride through the mouth of a dragon

SAT Scores
First Rise Since 1985

I s it an upward trend or a temporary aberration? Scholastic Aptitude Test scores, which may help predict a student's academic performance in college, rose in 1992 for the first time in seven years.

Nationally, averages for the verbal portion rose to 423, 1 point above the previous year's record low. Since 1969, verbal scores had dropped 40 points, according to the College Board. In math, the average was 476, 2 points above the previous year's score and 10 points above 1981's record low. The last year that both verbal and math scores rose was 1985, when the verbal score went up from 426 to 431 and the math score, from 471 to 475.

The president of the College Board, Donald M. Stewart, put it in perspective, saying, "One or two points may not seem like much, but each point is meaningful on a test taken by more than a million students who represent roughly two thirds of all entering college freshmen."

The board's report included the following highlights:

- Minority students accounted for 29% of those tested, which is double the 15% of 1975, the year the board began officially recognizing differences in the scores of various ethnic groups.

- Since 1976, the mean scores of blacks have risen 20 points on the verbal portion and 31 on the math portion. The mean scores of whites fell 9 points on the verbal and 2 on the math.

- Mexican Americans' scores fell 5 points in the verbal portion and 2 points in math. The averages for Native Americans rose 5 points and 2 points, respectively.

- For students from private schools, average scores were 469 for the verbal portion and 526 for math. The students at church-affiliated schools scored 439 and 474 respectively and public school students, 420 and 475 respectively.

- Foreign students tested very high in math, 533, or 57 points above the U.S. average. In the verbal section, they averaged only 389.

Stewart also noted that SAT scores in large cities and rural areas were sharply below those in suburbs, mid-size cities, and small cities and towns.

Schools at Home

"I'm sort of like a butcher who doesn't eat red meat." —*Clarence Williams, an administrator at Antioch (Ill.) High School, whose four children have never entered a classroom*

America's schools are in crisis, fiscally and academically, and to make matters worse, there is a discipline problem at inner-city schools. Administrators have few realistic solutions for the short term, but some families do: keep the kids at home!

The parents of more than 300,000 school-age children in the U.S. are teaching their youngsters at home, according to a 1992 study by the Department of Education. Though fewer than 1% of children are following this course, there were only 15,000 such children in 1982, hence a 20-fold increase has occurred in a decade.

Advocates of home teaching believe their students are learning more than they would in school, and a report by the National Home Education Research Institute concurs. Its sampling of 2,163 families showed students who attend school at home, on average, score at or above the 80th percentile on standard achievement tests. And more colleges are accepting students schooled at home, depending on no more than "an interview, a portfolio, and what you've done with your life,"

said Pat Farenga, the publisher of *Growing Without Schools.*

Science Studies
Young Einstein Was No Wizard, Either

Only 51% of America's eighth-graders know that the sun rises in the east and sets in the west; 34% know that running water causes erosion; and 35% of fourth-graders know that a microscope is not used for air temperature, wind speed, or distant stars.

A national report on science achievement shows disappointingly low results on how well U.S. students understand even basic science, and the blame is put on schools and the way teachers present their information, using dry lectures rather than hands-on experiments.

The 1990 report "The Science Report Card," issued by the National Assessment of Education Progress, is based on a survey of 20,000 students in grades 4, 8, and 12. It reported that about 66% of the eighth-graders and about 33% of the fourth-graders understood basic science and had a primary ability to interpret the results of experiments. Fewer than 33% of twelfth-graders attended high schools that gave science the same priority as math and reading. While 80% of the fourth-graders said they liked science, interest dwindled to 68% for the eighth-graders and 65% for the twelfth-graders. For their part, 39% of the eighth-grade science teachers said their lab spaces were inadequate.

Secretaries
Take a Letter, Miss Jones

That's the way it used to be. Today *Ms.* Jones might not even be a woman, and it's not likely that he or she will be taking a letter. Today's 4 million secretaries have a different job and, in fact, are even being called administrative assistants.

There was a time when the boss's secretary just answered phones and typed all day on a manual typewriter. Now, thanks to computers, voice mail, tough economic times, and staff reductions, secretaries are freed from such menial tasks. Instead they can train workers, organize events, make travel arrangements, and perform administrative duties.

This list describes the varied tasks of the modern secretary, according to a poll taken by Gannett News Service.

- 16% handle financial software.
- 18.9% use desktop publishing software.
- 33% supervise others.
- 46.2% run database software.
- 48.5% train workers.
- 64.2% make travel arrangements.
- 72.9% use spreadsheet software.
- 80.8% buy office supplies.
- 93% use personal computers.
- 95.4% buy office furniture.
- 95.4% use word processing software.

Who Has the Sleaziest Boss: The heat against bosses has risen so high that 9 to 5 is planning a National Boss Contest to showcase the best and sleaziest bosses. The latter is not likely to be regarded as a great honor by the company of the winner.

Senior Drivers
When Do You Cut Them Off?

Authorities throughout the nation are at a loss about how to deal with a mushrooming road safety problem: identifying older drivers who might pose a hazard while not discriminating against those who do not.

Of the 167 million licensed drivers in the U.S., somewhat more than 22 million are over the age of 65, twice the number that existed twenty years ago.

In a retirement haven like Florida, for example, accidents in which older drivers lose control of their vehicles are so common that they are referred to as SEA — sudden elder acceleration. Fatalities per million drivers in the 70-plus age group numbered about 150 in 1990, placing seniors fourth among twelve age groups; the top group was the drivers from 16 to 19, who caused 350 fatalities, according to the National Highway Traffic Safety Administration. Only 16 states have laws monitoring their older driving population.

Those who believe in screening elderly drivers argue that after age 75, drivers are twice as likely to have accidents as those in other age groups, and their reflexes and cognitive skills are not easily corrected or have faded permanently. Most difficult for elderly drivers is the complex maneuver of left turns, which requires several judgments at once. Many elderly drivers, in fact, circle a block in order to avoid making left turns, realizing their limits.

Sexual Harassment
Students Report Hostile Hallways

Official Definition: "[Behavior or remarks] in the workplace which interfere with work performance or create an intimidating, hostile or offensive working environment." —*Section VII of the 1964 Civil Rights Act*

Once thought to be a problem faced primarily by women at work, sexual harassment is now known to be suffered by men and schoolchildren as well. Some 8 in 10 students in the eighth through eleventh grades report being victims. Almost as many boys as girls (76% and 85%, respectively) say they have been harassed, according to a 1993 report, *Hostile Hallways*, put out by Louis Harris and Associates for the American Association of University Women.

The most prevalent forms of sexual harassment are offensive sexual remarks rather than unwanted touching or other physical contact. The Women Employed, a national advocacy group, estimates that 45% of the women at work have been victims of sexual harassment. The American Women's Association of Female Doctors and Medical Students estimates the harassment of women to be 27%.

The *Women's Action Coalition Stats*, a fact book about women, reports that at least half of all women will be sexually harassed in their lifetime. It also reports that women are 9 times more prone to leave a job than men when they are victims and are 3 times more likely to lose their job. Though reports of men being victims are much rarer, court cases are beginning to emerge. In one such case, a Florida man won $1 million in damages from his employer.

Though about 1 in 3 women actually reports experiencing some sort of sexual harassment, it is believed this is the tip of the iceberg. Some believe that many women will not formalize their complaints because of fear of repercussions, and statistics confirm this. Incredibly, the odds that a man will be reported in any way for sexual harassment are 1 in 10. The incidence of an alleged offender being officially reported under the Civil Rights Act is dismal — only 1 in about 11,000 are reported.

Children are much more likely to be vocal about being harassed. The Harris/AAUW study reported the following about harassment of teens:

- 56% of girls and 76% of boys say they are the object of sexual comments, jokes, or looks.
- 65% of girls and 42% of boys are touched, grabbed, or pinched.
- 57% of girls and 36% of boys are intentionally touched casually in a sexual way.
- 49% of girls and 41% of boys are mooned or flashed.

Single-parent Families
Threefold Increase

"It is unlikely that we will return to the days when households with three or more persons are the rule, rather than the exception." — *Steve Rawlings, author of a census report on families*

Most Americans over 50 years old fondly remember the three-generation family: kids, parents, and grandparents, all under one roof. Things are vastly different today.

The increase in one-parent families, most headed by women, has nearly tripled since 1970, according to a census report based on 57,400 American families. This is one of the most profound changes in family composition that has occurred in American history.

In 1970, there were 3.8 million single-parent families, and in 1980, 6.9 million; today there are slightly more than 10 million, and the figure is increasing rapidly. Of today's single-parent families, 8.7 million are maintained by the mother, 1.4 million by the father.

Of the nation's 5.2 million black families, about 63% are maintained by one parent; of the 28.4 million white families, 23%. Among Hispanic families, 1 in 3 are headed by a single parent.

Women bear a staggering 86% of the burden, as they have since 1970, when 90% headed one-parent families. The bureau noted that about 1 in 6 white fathers raise children by themselves, while about 1 in 14 black fathers do.

Skyscrapers

Although New York is the undisputed skyscraper capital of the world, the tallest building of all is now in Chicago, where the nation's first skyscraper was built in 1883. The

The Sears Tower in Chicago (center) is the world's tallest building.

Big Apple, however, is the home of 5 of the 10 tallest buildings in America.

The nation's tallest, in order, are:

Sears Tower (Chicago)	1,454 feet
World Trade Center (NYC)	1,377 feet
Empire State Building (NYC)	1,250 feet
Standard Oil Building (Chicago)	1,136 feet
John Hancock Center (Chicago)	1,127 feet
Chrysler Building (NYC)	1,046 feet

Texas Building (Houston)	1,002 feet
Allied Bank Building (Houston)	985 feet
American International (NYC)	952 feet
Citicorp Center (NYC)	915 feet

Great Falls, Mont.	58.3
Salt Lake City	58.2

Source: U.S. National Oceanic and Atmospheric Administration

Social Security

On August 14, 1935, President Franklin D. Roosevelt signed Social Security into law. Under its provisions, workers pay the government a tax on their earnings that they may redeem in retirement. At the beginning, it was anticipated that, with every worker contributing, there would be a surplus, even when those in retirement took their pensions. It worked exactly as planned, which was not very difficult since there were more than 50 workers to each retiree. By 1945, there were 46 workers to each retiree; still, a surplus was growing each year. By 1950, there were only 16 workers to every retiree, and by 1992, only 3.

Today, there is still a "surplus." What this means is that Uncle Sam is collecting a bit more than is being disbursed, chiefly because mandatory payments have risen from an average of about $20 annually to almost $2,000 annually, a 100-fold increase.

Snowiest Places

Question: What happens when the ski slopes in the Rockies are bare and clouds roll in over the mountains?
Answer: It snows in Buffalo.

Do you abhor salt on your boots, skiing to work, shoveling your driveway? If so, the following places, shown with their annual snowfall (in inches), should be avoided between October and April.

Sault Ste. Marie, Mich.	114.9
Juneau	99.9
Buffalo	92.3
Burlington, Vt.	77.9
Portland, Me.	71.5
Albany, N.Y.	65.5
Concord, N.H.	64.3
Denver	60.3

Workers who earn more than $57,600 annually pay more than $4,406 (7.65%). Those who are self-employed must pay "the employer's share," too (an amount matching the *employee's* share), hence self-employed persons pay double. The self-employed who earn more than $57,700, then, must pay $8,812. Add to this the new and complicated Medicare deduction (1.45% — for *both* employer and employee), and a self-employed person earning $135,000 will pay an additional $2,244, for a total Social Security tax of $11,056 annually. All Social Security taxes are over and above normal income taxes, which range from 15% to 31%, depending on an individual's income bracket (the national average is 28%).

Due to these massive contributions, a surplus is collected, but it is not stashed away for retirement; rather, it is used for the general operation of the government. To masquerade the snatch, it is "invested" in special-issue U.S. Treasury bonds, which are nothing more than government IOUs — part of the national debt.

The Case of Ida Mae Fuller: This lovely senior citizen from Ludlow, Vt., was the nation's first claimant of Social Security. Fuller had the good fortune to live to age 99. She also was lucky enough to have her Social Security account "earn" almost one thousand times what she contributed. Having paid a grand total of $22, Fuller, collected more than $20,000 by the time she died.

Today, the average man will live to 71.5, the average woman to 78.7. In other words, it's not such a bad deal for seniors, but for those working, it's a travesty. Their money is simply transferred to the elderly, many of whom do not need it, though a substantial number could not live without it.

The average Social Security recipient collects $8,648. Those who have contributed the most during their working life get more. And most collect it whether they need it or not. The wealthiest third of recipients collect more than $100 billion annually. A 70-year-old millionaire, for example, can collect $1,120 monthly and his spouse, $560. Unfair? Perhaps. Average retirees who begin collecting at age 65 will get back every cent they put in — plus interest — by age 71.

Currently, 41 million Americans receive monthly checks totaling 20% of the entire federal budget. Each decade these benefits will double. By this decade's end, $500 billion will be spent, $1 trillion by 2010, and an incredible $20 trillion will be necessary when today's schoolchildren retire, starting in 2050.

Space Missions
U.S. Enthusiasm Waning

Public support for a planned space station and missions to the moon and Mars is declining, according to a poll commissioned by Rockwell International Corp., builders of the space shuttle fleet. Support is currently registered by 65% of Americans, down from 70% two years ago and 78% in 1988. The support for a Mars mission has slipped to 49%, from 64% in 1990 and 66% in 1988. The space shuttle program still rates high, with a 92% backing.

As a whole, much of the nation would like to see NASA's spending cut: 42% favor a cut, compared to 40% in 1990, 44% in 1989, and 36% in 1988. What do Americans favor? Satellites to monitor the earth's environment received 77% support. According to a survey of 1,006 voters conducted for Rockwell International Corp. by the Yankelovich Clancy Shulman market research firm, NASA ranks 7 on a scale of 10 in importance compared to other federal programs, which were led by education. Only defense, welfare, and farm subsidies ranked lower than the space program.

Sports Attendance

"If the people don't want to come out to the ball game, how ya gonna stop 'em?" — *Yogi Berra*

What's the most popular spectator sport in America? Contrary to the adage that baseball is "America's pastime," the ponies outdraw the boys of summer by a large margin, and Monday night football draws a far larger TV audience than almost any baseball game.

When it comes to actually being there, the list of America's favorite sporting events may be surprising. This table shows the 10 most popular spectator sports and their annual attendance, according to the *Statistical Abstract of the United States*.

Horse racing	69,946,000
Major league baseball	53,800,000
College football	35,581,000
Men's college basketball	32,504,000
Greyhound racing	26,477,000
National Football League	17,024,000
Professional basketball	14,051,000
National Hockey League	13,741,000
Jai alai	6,414,000
Women's college basketball	3,301,000

Another Surprising Sports Stat: In our exercise-conscious culture, noncompetitive pastimes like swimming, exercise walking, and bicycling garner far more participants than classic team activities like baseball, basketball, and football, perhaps because they can be done alone. The next table lists the most popular sports Americans like to play and the percentages that participate in them regularly, according to the National Sporting Goods Association.

Swimming	32.8%
Exercise walking	28.7%
Bicycling	24.8%
Camping	19.5%
Fishing (freshwater)	18.3%
Bowling	17.5%
Exercising with equipment	13.3%
Aerobic exercising	11.2%
Basketball	10.7%
Running/jogging	10.6%

Sports Franchises
Owners Get More Appreciation Than Players

Owning a team is a plum. Many successful business people regard this special investment as their most prestigious asset. It virtually guarantees them celebrity status, though some celebs don't always come out well in the papers; the baseball owners Marge Shatz and George Steinbrenner, to name two, have been as controversial as the worst-behaved ballplayers.

Nonetheless, owners get their own brand of appreciation. In addition to frequently earning millions of dollars in annual profits, the appreciation on their investment in a major sports franchise has grown enormously. In

1976, when free agency began in baseball, the average cost of a team was $10 million; it now averages $100 million, according to *Pay Dirt*. In this book, James Quirk and Rodney D. Fort report the following annual average increases in values as well as a comparison to a popular investment.

	Annual Appreciation
MLB (1901–90)	7.5%
NBA (1950–90)	16.5%
NFL (1920–90)	20.4%
Common stocks (1920–90)	10.3%

Owners face a new problem, which is likely to affect the value of their franchises: declining TV revenues. George Burman, a former National Football League player who is dean of the School of Management at Syracuse University, says, "It seems to me that it's the owners who are going to be left holding the bag [if they can't raise prices]. . . . Up until now they've had the opportunity to be stupid, and it didn't really cost them. They won't have that opportunity anymore."

Sports Tickets

Myth: High ticket prices are a way to get the fans to absorb the increasing costs of running a team, including the players' astronomical salaries.
Reality: According to the sports economist Gerald Scully, "There is no relationship between the cost of tickets and owner's costs." Ticket prices are based on whatever the market will bear.

Supply and demand are the major factors of ticket costs — nothing else. Consider baseball. In 1976, the free agency rule caused prices to soar because the owners had to bid for players on an open market. Over the next fifteen years, average salaries rose more than 1,000%. Average ticket prices, however, remained relatively stable, rising from $3.45 to $7.95. Adjusting these figures for inflation, the cost of tickets actually dropped below 1950 levels.

This table represents the current average ticket prices charged by major league teams, according to *Team Marketing Report*.

Baseball (1993)	$9.57
Basketball (1992–93)	$25.16
Hockey (1992–93)	$25.96
Football (1992)	$27.19

The Barry Bonds Solution: Though some teams can fill the stadium at the highest prices, others must become better marketers to survive. In San Francisco, the Giants had the problem of coping with Barry Bonds's $4.4 million salary. Their solution was to *cut* the cost of 24,000 seats, the ones in the upper deck. On the other hand, they will increase the cost of the premium seats, which are bought primarily by corporations that will spare no expense to impress their clients . . . or themselves.

Stock Ownership
The Great Divides in the Pie

The total outstanding stock in 1965 was valued at $713 billion; today, the value approaches $5 trillion. The New York Stock Exchange profiles its typical individual stockholder as follows: a 45-year-old, college-educated professional or manager with an annual income of $50,000 and a portfolio of stock valued at about $15,000.

About half of all stocks outstanding are owned by private individuals; the proportion is down drastically from 84% in 1965. The other half is owned by a variety of institutions, the largest being private pension funds, which own about 16%.

This table shows the various parties who own stocks and their values in 1965 and 1993, adapted from figures supplied by the Securities Industry Association.

	1965 (billions)	1993 (billions)
Households	$600	$26,000
Private pensions	$40	$800
Mutual funds	$30	$450
Foreign	$14	$330
Life insurance cos.	$12	$140
Other insurance cos.	$9.1	$120
Banks, brokers, dealers	$3.5	$33
Public pensions	$2.5	$420

The Clout Club: Giant pension and mutual funds are now the biggest owners of stock on the Big Board. Collectively, they own more than $1 trillion worth of stock in the largest companies in America, fully half the stock outstanding from these companies, and they account for about 80% of the volume of stock traded on any given day. Many institutional investors, due to their overwhelming presence, are taking more active roles in the management of the businesses they invest in. Large funds have started demanding seats on the board and management changes, where formerly they simply dumped disappointing stock.

Sears, General Motors, American Express, Digital Equipment, and IBM all succumbed to such pressures from the large funds in the early '90s. At one Sears annual meeting, for example, 23% to 41% of the shareholders voted against management on a variety of proposals; these were staggering numbers to a management used to single-digit nay votes. Many overdiversified companies have already knuckled under to the funds' pressure, according to Jack Coffee, a Columbia University law professor, who cites the example of Gulf & Western at the beginning of the '80s. G&W was forced to focus its resources and eventually became Paramount Communications by the next decade.

What befalls small investors trying to make their way against the avalanche of institutional buy and sell orders, which can affect a stock's price? Wall Street experts believe that small investors can choose to tag along and so ride the waves and reap the benefits of a developing insurgency among the funds.

Stressed Out
Who, What, Why, and Where

"If you can't stand the heat, get out of the kitchen." — *Harry Truman*

A Job from Hell: Give-em-hell Harry knew a lot about stress. According to the latest edition of *The Jobs Rated Almanac*, the job of the president of the United States is the most stressful of all the 250 jobs studied. The editors identified 22 stress factors, assigning a numerical weight to each one. The "mega-factors," according to their assessment, are deadlines, competitiveness, environmental conditions, risk to life, and meeting the public.

Below are the most and least stressful jobs that the almanac ranked, listed in order.

The 10 Most Stressful Jobs
President of the U.S.
Firefighter
Race car driver
Astronaut
Surgeon
Football player

Police officer
Osteopath
Highway patrol officer
Air traffic controller

The 10 Least Stressful Jobs
Musical instrument repairer
Industrial machine repairer
Medical records technician
Pharmacist
Software engineer
Typist/word processor
Librarian
Janitor
Bookkeeper
Fork-lift operator

A job can be the most or least stressful factor in one's life; however, where an individual lives is yet another. A college town, for example, is far more tranquil than a bustling city. A study conducted by *Psychology Today* ranked the relative psychological well-being of 286 cities by looking at four indicators of psychological and social pathology: alcoholism, suicide, divorce, and crime.

Interestingly, all of the 10 most stressful cities are in the West and South — Florida, California, Nevada, Texas, and Arkansas; indeed, of the 25 most stressful towns, only one —

New York City, of course — is in the Northeast. The most relaxed towns include a number with large universities, which attract well-educated middle- and upper-class residents. Below are the study's rankings of the most and least stressful communities in the U.S.

The 10 Most Stressful Cities
Reno
Las Vegas
Miami
Lakeland/Winter Haven, Fla.
North Little Rock/Little Rock
Panama City, Fla.
Odessa, Tex.
Jacksonville, Fla.
San Francisco/Oakland
Los Angeles/Long Beach

The 10 Least Stressful Cities
State College, Pa.
Grand Forks, N. Dak.
St. Cloud, Minn.
Rochester, Minn.
McAllen/Pharr/Edinburg, Tex.
Altoona, Pa.
Bloomington, Pa.
Provo/Orem, Utah
Utica, N.Y.
Akron, Ohio

Student Health Problems
Crisis in Grade Schools

More students are showing up too sick or too disturbed to perform well in grade school, according to a survey of 500 teachers from kindergarten through the sixth grade.

Some 64% of the teachers surveyed for the national PTA and the American Academy of Pediatrics said they are seeing more students with health problems than in the past. Only 5% said they are seeing fewer. Overall health and fitness are essential to a student's work performance, according to 94% of the teachers; 6% said they were somewhat important.

The ability to concentrate was cited by 66% as the factor most affected by poor health. Some 92% of the teachers listed psychological and emotional difficulties as the most common health problems. The researchers said these issues resulted mostly from divorce, neglect, low self-esteem, and the separation of family members.

Dr. Daniel Shea, the president of the academy, said, "Poor health is leading to poor academic performance. And poor academic performance is leading to . . . school dropouts, unemployment, poverty, and crime." He pointed out that high school dropouts were twice as likely as high school graduates and five times more likely than college graduates to be unemployed.

Student Leaders
Opinions Polled

"I wish we didn't have to put so much importance on a school's name, because we can get the same quality of academics from another school, but the big name will help with the career." — *Tim Macauley, West Linn (Oreg.) High School*

Young Mr. Macauley is among the 7% of teens who will choose a college based on its name. Most teenagers, however, are concerned with the more mundane, such as how to keep their friends (and sometimes themselves) sober. Alcohol is the number one teen problem, and it is getting worse. Students who couldn't care less about learning, called "the apathetics," are the second most serious problem, far ahead of others such as drugs and racism.

An annual poll of student government leaders, conducted during a meeting of the National Association of Student Councils by *USA Today*, indicates that alcohol, marijuana, and cigarette addiction has increased since 1990. Estimates of their use by students were 64% for beer, up from 58% in 1989; 52% for liquor, up from 46% in 1989; 20% for marijuana, up from 18% in 1991 but down 25% from 1988; 41% for cigarettes, up from 32% in 1989, with only 4% of the student leaders themselves addicted.

Below are some significant findings and the percentages of student leaders who:

- support the following: legalized abortion (59%), gun control (76%), the death penalty (81%).
- think most unemployed people could find jobs if they tried (37%).
- think a successful marriage will be the most important part of their adulthood (40%); 24% call success most important, 20%, acquiring knowledge, and 10%, making money.
- think America needs nuclear weapons (37%), down from 57%.
- And how do the teenage leaders rate the performance of their schools and teachers? C+.

Summer Vacations

More than 9 of every 10 Americans take one. During the 1993 summer vacation season, the American Automobile Association estimates that 231 million people traveled 100 or more miles from home. At the season's launching point, Memorial Day, the AAA estimated that 28.1 million people traveled: 24.2 million by car and 3.9 million by air, train, or bus.

The family car is the overwhelming transportation of choice, accounting for 82% of vacation travel. In the summer of 1992, when air fares were dis-

Visitors to Dollywood take a spin on the antique Dentzel Carousel while its 1901 Gavioli organ recalls our musical past.

counted by 50%, 80% still opted to drive.

Where's everybody going? A AAA survey indicates that driving vacations to the Southwest account for 30% of all trips taken. The West accounts for 21%, the Midwest for 20%, the Northeast for 14%, and the Great Lakes region for 13%. The remaining 2% of vacationers travel to Canada and Mexico.

These five top travel destinations, listed alphabetically, have a number of special features, according to the AAA.

- Branson, Mo. — more than 30 theaters that specialize in foot-stompin' country music
- Los Angeles — Disneyland and Knott's Berry Farm
- Orlando — Universal Studios, Walt Disney World, and the surrounding areas of Florida
- Washington, D.C. — the White House, the Capitol, the Smithsonian, and surrounding areas of Maryland and Virginia
- Yellowstone National Park — Old Faithful, wildlife watching, and nature trails

The Emerging Hot Spots: According to the AAA, more and more tourists are going to Minnesota to visit the giant 80-acre Mall of America in Bloomington, which includes the Camp Snoopy amusement park and a walk-through aquarium. Also in Minnesota is the town of Morton, where players flock for jackpot bingo. Another popular spot for gambling is Ledyard, Conn., which has a full-blown casino on the Native American reservation. Dollywood is Dolly Parton's own amusement park with everything from down-home music, country cookin', and rides aplenty.

The average American family of four spends $215.60 per day on vacation for "the basics":

Lodging	$89.00
Meals	$99.00
Auto expenses	$27.60

The recession that opened the decade has made Americans more cautious about spending. According to American Express, the nation travels in greater numbers, but vacations are shorter than in previous years. The average length is 4.8 days.

Teen Courts

New Concept in Juvenile Justice

Some 40% of the nation's 2 million juveniles who are annually arrested receive little more than a police record and a slap on the wrist, so authorities are looking for ways to dampen the youthful criminal activity with something more than stern warnings and probation. Enter Teen Courts, a mushrooming concept in smaller communities.

The Case of Bryan Couch: In Odessa, Tex., teen prosecutor Laurel Linde, 17, made short work of Bryan Couch, 16, who had been charged for driving under the influence. "How many beers were you drinking?" Linde asked. Couch replied eight to nine. "Did you know the legal age?" Couch did. "Were you trying to impress your friends?" "I shouldn't have done it," Couch replied. The jury of two males and two females sentenced Couch to 20 hours of community service and three stints on a jury. "He should have got the max," Linde said, shaking her head.

Since 1983, Odessa has been a model for other cities trying out this concept.

The Odessa court has passed judgment on 6,600 youths, issuing sentences on misdemeanor cases involving drugs or alcohol, traffic violations, shoplifting, or simple assault. They only issue sentences of up to 30 hours of community work and serve as many as four times on a teen jury. At the completion of the sentence, charges are dismissed.

Is it working? "Kids are much tougher than any adult," said Natalie Rothstein, the program coordinator. "If the jury thinks the defendant is lying, they'll usually nail him to the wall."

This list shows the leading juvenile offenses and the number of youths under 18 who were arrested in 1992, as compiled by the Department of Justice.

Theft	466,000
Runaways	174,000
Liquor violations	158,000
Assault	151,000
Burglary	143,000

Court Results	
Sent to juvenile court	64%
Handled internally, released	28%
Sent to adult criminal court	0.5%

Sent to welfare or
other agency   0.3%

Teen Gun Deaths

If you don't like guns, stay out of the army — and the nation's schools — where you will find as many as 135,000, according to an estimate by *USA Today*. As many as 2 million teenagers carry guns, knives, clubs, or razors. According to the National Center for Health Statistics, 4,173 American teenagers were fatally shot in 1990, the year for which the latest statistics are available. Only automobile accidents kill more of our nation's youth.

Will guns replace the automobile as the nation's number one killer of our young? We're moving in that direction. The figure of 4,200 killed in 1990 was up by almost 600 (about 17%) over the previous year. In 1985, 2,498 were killed.

Racial Lines: The bullet knows no racial boundaries. Among black males 15 to 19 years old, fatal gunshot wounds have increased from 37 deaths per 100,000 in 1985 to 105 deaths per 100,000 in 1990. Among white males,

the figure has nearly doubled, from 5 deaths per 100,000 to almost 10.

Teen Prejudices and Views on Race Relations
Clinging to Stereotypes

While most people agree that we as a society should teach our young that there is little or no difference between the races, there is one difference that cannot be denied: the races view racial problems through different-colored glasses.

Who's Who Among American High School Students polled 2,000 high-achieving high school students and found that 85% of blacks believe minorities have fewer opportunities, whereas only 30% of whites believe it to be true. By and large, whites were less aware of prejudices, actual or perceived. In addition, whites proved to be unaware that some of their actions are perceived as prejudice by people of color with whom they interact.

For example, as many as 6 in 10 blacks claim to have been victims of racial prejudice. Among whites, only 1 in 10 admitted to ever having acted openly prejudicial toward another racial or ethnic group.

Other findings were:

- About special educational opportunities: 60% of blacks and 10% of whites say blacks should have them.
- About confidence in police: 50% of blacks and 20% of whites do not trust the police.
- About interracial dating: 90% of blacks and 60% of whites approved of dating someone of a different race.

Today's youngsters have no firsthand memory of Dr. Martin Luther King, Jr., and the 1960s civil rights history. As the inheritors of the changes brought on by that era, the teens of the 1990s interact with members of other races far more frequently and more readily than their parents. Yet 48% of today's teens describe U.S. race relations as "generally bad"; only 42% said they were good.

A detailed study by Peter Hart Research Associates for People for the American Way showed that blacks were more pessimistic about race relations than whites, with 57% calling them bad; 49% of the Hispanics said the same. Of the 1,170 young people polled, 71% had at least one "close personal friendship" with a member of another race.

Among whites, 51% oppose colleges giving "special consideration to minority" students, and 65% are against giving "special consideration to minority job applicants." Almost half of the white youths, 49%, believe it is whites who are discriminated against, whereas 68% of blacks and 52% of Hispanics think their respective racial group is discriminated against.

This table shows the percentages of those polled who answered various questions in the following manner. (The numbers do not total 100% because some of those polled indicated they were "unsure" of their opinion.)

Relations generally good or bad?

	Good	Bad
Whites	44%	48%
Blacks	35%	57%
Hispanics	82%	16%

Discrimination prevalent?

	Agree	Disagree
Whites	81%	18%
Blacks	82%	17%
Hispanics	82%	16%

Telephone Technology
Junk Messages

"If you want service, press 1 *now*. If you want to inquire about your bill, press 2 *now*. If you're sick of this rigamorole, hang up *now!*"

First there was the party line, then the private line, then answering machines and also "caller option," which enables callers to hear a laundry list of things they couldn't care less about. The newest and certainly most annoying telephone innovation is the computer caller — the one with the friendly message that interrupts an afternoon nap with the inspirational message "You have just won a free prize in our sweepstakes. Please stay on the line; our operators are standing by to assist you in claiming your free gift."

Last year, 118 million Americans received 3 billion phone calls from telemarketers with computer messages. Surprisingly, 39% of those called stay on the line, and 6% actually bite the hook and take a deal from a microchip.

Robert Bulmash's Little War: You can fight back and get rid of those pests if you join Private Citizens, Inc., founded by Robert Bulmash of Warrensville, Ill. Membership costs $20, and with it comes a service. Private Citizens sends the following letter to more than 1,000 telemarketers: "I am unwilling to allow your free use of my time and telephone for such calls. I will accept junk calls, placed by or on your behalf, for a $100 fee, due within 30 days of such use. Your junk call will constitute your agreement to the reasonableness of my fee."

Though members report that the number of their junk phone callers dropped by 75%, some called anyway. You can collect, according to a book by Jay Kaye, *Light Your House with Potatoes*. Private Citzens reports that some telemarketers have actually paid the $100 fee. According to members, they are Sears, Roebuck and Chem-Lawn. J. C. Penney is a deadbeat.

Television Habits
$1 Million to Chuck the Tube?

Somebody at *TV Guide* got a bizarre notion: How much money would it take to induce you to give up watching TV? Surprisingly, enough people among the 1,007 persons polled took the question seriously enough to make their views into statistics.

Some of the findings include that 23% would be willing to sell their viewing habits for $25,000; 46% demanded $1 million; and 25% were stalwart enough to refuse even a cool million. Other results:

- Male adults are twice as likely to control the remote box as women (41% to 19% respectively).
- Some 63% of adults often watch television while eating; three quarters of them are 18- to 24-year-olds.
- More viewers are offended by too much violence (37%) than too much sex (27%). Other points of dissatisfaction are lack of creativity (14%), too many reruns (11%), and too many commercials (7%).
- A higher proportion of younger (32%) than older viewers (22%) found explicit sex more objectionable than excessive violence.

Television Programs
All-Time Highest Rated

"Do you, Tiny Tim, take this woman, Miss Vickie, to be your lawfully wedded wife?"

The wedding of falsetto-voiced Tiny Tim was one of the most watched shows of all time when it was televised on *The Tonight Show*. Tiny Tim, Miss Vickie, and Johnny Carson tiptoed through the tulips set up onstage for the wedding as an astonished and nearly dazed audience looked on. Since then, other shows have eclipsed its ratings.

The 10 top shows of all time, according to A. C. Nielsen, the television rating bureau, are (in order):

M*A*S*H (final episode) — 2/28/83
Dallas ("Who Shot J.R.?") —
   11/21/80
Cheers (final episode) — 5/20/93
Roots (Episode 8) — 1/30/77
Super Bowl XVI —1982
Super Bowl XVII — 1983
Super Bowl XX — 1986
Gone With the Wind, Part I —
   11/7/76

Gone With the Wind, Part II —
11/8/76
Super Bowl XII — 1978

The "Last Call": The final episode of *Cheers* made history when the 98-minute "Last Call" achieved a 45.5 rating and a 64-share. Nielsen estimated the audience at 42.4 million households, or 64% of actual viewers. NBC said it was the highest-rated episodic telecast in its history, but it did not beat out CBS's *M*A*S*H* in 1983 or its *Dallas* finale, which revealed who blew a hole in J.R.'s despicable hide.

The Tonight Show hitched on to the "Cheers" finale with a show that evening from the bar in Boston that inspired the show. It, too, set a record, achieving its third highest rating. It did not beat the ratings of Tiny Tim's nuptials, nor did it surpass Johnny Carson's finale.

Television vs. Children's Health
Cholesterol Levels Linked to TV

It took nine years for researchers at the University of California at Irvine to conclude that poor diet and not enough exercise take their toll on young people, just as they do on adults.

Their study involved 1,081 children between the ages of 2 and 20, television watchers all, and each with no family history of early heart attacks or cholesterol problems. Observed while watching TV, the kids just sat there in front of the television set, munching on junk food.

The survey concludes that 8% of the children had a cholesterol level of 200 milligrams or higher, a level considered dangerous for adults. Of those, 53% said they watched two or more hours of TV every day. If they watched TV for two to four hours a day, they were twice as likely to have high cholesterol levels, four times as likely if they watched for more than four hours.

Television Violence
It's Murder!

The watchdogs at the National Coalition on Television Violence began in 1980, and in March 1993, they reported that the murder rate had risen

27% in a year. Television watchers will see, on average, one murder every 78 minutes. A year ago, a murder enthusiast had to wait as long as 107 minutes to see a victim die.

So what? It's only a story and a bunch of actors. Some, including Dr. Carole Lieberman, the chairman of the NCTV, say otherwise. Lieberman says, "These figures correlate with other studies to show that violence in the media continues to grow. And there is incontestable proof that when there is violence in the media, it has a cumulative effect in causing viewers to become aggressive and desensitized to violence."

The coalition identified Fox as having the most violent programs during prime time, with 11 acts of violence per hour. The major networks keep the peace, by and large, compared to cable outlets and Fox. Last year, ABC, NBC, and CBS kept the level of violence in their programs to 7.7 savage incidents per hour. The previous year, there were as many as 8.6 in the average hour.

Who's Really Stomping 'em? Why, it's that kiddie idol of movies and TV, Indiana Jones, but of course he's still young and reckless on ABC's *Young Indiana Jones Chronicles*. Naturally, he'll grow up and become more responsible, but we hope he won't be watching television.

Therapist-Client Sex
Abuse of Power Behind Closed Doors

It's been called "a growing crisis of ethical abuse" among doctors, lawyers, professors, and psychiatrists. Surveys rate sexual misconduct among professionals overall at between 7% and 12% of practitioners, and a 1992 survey of family doctors, internists, gynecologists, and surgeons found as many guilty parties among them — 9% — as have been found among therapists.

According to *Psychology Today*, 90% of the victims are psychologically damaged by such conduct, many severely. One survey found that 11% of victims had been hospitalized due to their abuse, and 1% committed suicide. Some therapists have been characterized as calculating, predatory professionals, who may tell confused patients that their fear of sexual advances constitutes "resistance" to therapeutic change. Some therapists may leave a trail of 20, 50, or more victims, according to Dr. Glen Gabbard, director of the Menninger Clinic in Topeka, Kans. In 14% to 25% of the cases reported, patients initiated sex, according to *Psychology Today*, but every professional psychotherapy organization in America agrees that sex with clients is unprofessional — and in many states illegal. Nine states, California, Colorado, Florida, Georgia, Iowa, Maine, Minnesota, North Da-3kota, and Wisconsin, now classify sex with clients as felonies, with penalties that can include long prison terms.

One survey found that 7.1% of male psychiatrists admitted sexual misconduct, as did 3.1% of female psychiatrists. Another found that 80% of the exploitation involved a male therapist and a female client, while 13% involved a female therapist and a female client. Therapists were female and clients male in 5% of the cases.

Ross Perot came in second, not third; that is, among third-party candidates. (Teddy Roosevelt, as an Independent, got a higher percentage of the electoral vote in 1912.)

Third-Party Presidential Candidates

America Is All Ears

For almost a century, the American body politic has lived by a defining dictum: united we stand (behind the two-party system), and divided (by a third) we fall. Since 1900, eighteen third-party presidential hopefuls have received more than 1% of the popular vote, but only four reached double-digit figures: Teddy Roosevelt in 1912 (27%), Robert La Follette in 1924 (16.5%), George Wallace in 1968 (13.5%), and Ross Perot in 1992 (19%). The rest were left to quietly pay off their debts and vanish from the stage. But Perot's success in the most recent presidential parade and the growing disenchantment of the people with the entrenched powers may shake things up in the next election.

Five-Party Battle? Three independent parties are forming to make it a five-party battle in 1996: the America party, growing out of Perot's United We Stand organization; the Independence party, organized by Connecticut's Governor Lowell Weicker and the former third-party contender John Anderson (he received 6.6% of the popular vote in 1980); and the New party, formed by the union activist Sandy Pope and a University of Wisconsin professor, Joel Rogers. However, the pollster Frank Luntz gives the new parties little chance of breaking up the two-party monopoly.

This table names the independent candidates since 1900 who received more than 1% of votes, their parties, and the percentage of votes they received, according to *USA Today*.

Year	Candidate/Party	
1900	John Wooley Prohibition	1.5%
1904	Eugene Debs/Socialist	3%
1908	Eugene Debs/Socialist	3%
1912	Theodore Roosevelt/ Bull Moose	27%
1912	Eugene Debs/Socialist	6%
1916	Allan L. Benson/Socialist	3%
1916	Frank Hanley/Prohibition	1.2%
1920	Eugene Debs/Socialist	3.4%
1924	Robert La Follette/ Progressive	16.4%
1932	Norman Thomas/Socialist	2.2%
1936	William Lemke/Union	2%
1948	Strom Thurmond/States Rights	2.4%
1948	Henry Wallace/Progressive	2.4%
1968	George Wallace/American Independent	13.5%
1972	John G. Schmitz/American	1.4%
1976	Eugene McCarthy/ Independent	1%
1980	John Anderson/ Independent	6.6%
1980	Ed Clark/Libertarian	1.1%
1992	Ross Perot/Independent	19.0%

Traffic Deaths
Roads More Traveled, Less Dangerous

In 1992, for the first time in thirty years, deaths on the nation's highways were fewer than 40,000, according to the National Highway Traffic Safety Administration. This comes at a time when almost 90% of U.S. households have at least one car, van, or light truck; about 2.5 trillion passenger miles were traveled at last count; and 143 million cars roam U.S. roads.

1972, a Year That Will Live in Infamy: Highway fatalities in 1992 were way down from the most tragic year on U.S. highways, 1972, when 54,589 persons lost their lives. This continued a steady decline that began in 1988. Part of the reason is that an estimated 62% of all automobile occupants now use seat belts, an increase of 11% in a decade driven by crackdowns on seat belt laws and by the automatic seat belts in most new cars. Also contributing to the increase in road safety are better highway engineering, stricter overall safety standards for vehicles, and the development of air-bags and antilock brakes.

Before 1920, most automobiles were open chariots until the danger became obvious and Henry Ford began to produce his safer Model T. The earlier Model A is shown here. Photo, courtesy Henry Ford Museum, Dearborn, Mich.

The intense campaign against drunk driving seems to be hitting home as well: alcohol-related deaths nationwide dropped from a record 57.3% of all automobile fatalities in 1982 to 45.8% in 1992, another reason why highways have become safer. Still, drunk driving caused 18,000 traffic deaths in 1992, so thousands obviously still need to get the message.

Transportation Accidents

In 1992, an obscure figure in one of Les Krantz's books made headlines. The wire story carried by the Associated Press read: "Bus, Safest Way to Go." In *What the Odds Are*, the risks of death faced by travelers are computed as follows:

In an automobile	1 in 4 million
On an airplane	1 in 4.6 million
On a train	1 in 9 million
On a bus	1 in 500 million

Though the probability of one's dying in an air crash may seem high, airplanes don't often crash. This list shows the number of travel accidents in 1990 (the latest figures available) according to the Department of Transportation.

Motor vehicles	11.5 million
Railroads	2,879
Airlines	26

When airplanes do crash, the death toll is disastrous. The next list shows the odds that at least one person will die if the vehicle in which he or she is traveling is involved in a serious accident.

On an airplane	2 in 3
On a train	1 in 5
In a motor vehicle	1 in 258

Americans accumulate most of their travel miles in automobiles. Hence, the odds an average American will die in a car accident are a sobering 1 in 125. But during those less frequent trips in which you leave the operation of the vehicle to a professional — pilot, bus driver, or engineer — you can relax. And don't be afraid to let the gentle motion lull you to sleep. You are pretty safe.

UFOS

"The believability of the claims is less important than what we [as a society] make of them." — *Allen Ross, codirector of* Ordinary Conversations About Extraordinary Matters

Countless credible witnesses have seen UFOs, including President Carter. Each year there are 10,000 reports of unidentified flying objects, 4,000 of them in the U.S.; Florida and New York State lead the list in sightings. About 25 million Americans say they have seen at least one UFO. At

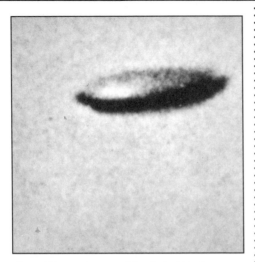

One of the many unexplained photos of objects over North America. Photo, Warren Smith; courtesy J. Allen Hynek Center for UFO Studies.

least one organization, the Center for UFO Studies in Chicago, investigates such reports with scientifically respected integrity. Most sightings, however, are not reported and most are not investigated at all.

April 8, 1992, Somewhere in Kansas: Charles Hodges was used to finding unusual things by the side of the road while working for the Kansas Department of Highways, but one day he made an unusual discovery: a piece of twisted, burned metal with a peculiar marking resembling a backward *R*. The ground around it was burnt and charred. Was it once and for all a piece of a UFO, the first ever found? In an effort to find out, the fragment was sent to the Kansas Cosmosphere and Space Center, which had been created as a tourist attraction but was increasing being taken seriously by UFO buffs. Disappointed believers soon got the "truth": it was a fragment of a Soviet rocket that had fallen from space. At least it was until a coworker of Hodges stepped forward. He had played a small prank that went too far. In fact, the "find" was a piece of a diesel tank. The misdiagnosis of the Space Center was explained. "When something is brought to you by the Kansas Highway Patrol, and they assure you it's a legitimate story," said Max Ary, the center's director, "you tend to believe them."

The most unbelievable claims are surely those pertaining to abductions by space aliens. Sharon Sandusky, Ross's codirector on the film about UFO believers and researchers, said, "There is a belief that most abductees suffer from posttraumatic stress disorder, like rape victims and war survivors. They are ordinary, credible people who happen to be troubled by a singular event in their lives. According to a recent Roper poll, at least 3.75 million people in this country believe that they've experienced abductions. And many more claim to have seen UFOs. Statistics show that these 'percipients' cut across all socioeconomic strata, with as many men as women."

Vaccinations
Preschoolers in Need

"Nobody is against children, but the reality is, children don't vote. They are second-class citizens and we are putting a Band-Aid on a hemorrhage." — *Dr. Janet Squires, director of the pediatric division of the University of Texas Southwestern Medical School*

Poor access to health care, barriers set up by crowded clinics, and the skyrocketing cost of vaccines have left more than 50% of preschoolers in large cities without immunization against preventable childhood diseases. Between 1989 and 1992, 54,000 cases of measles broke out nationwide, causing 100 deaths and thousands of hospitalizations. Cases of whooping cough, mumps, and rubella have soared, and measles — well on its way to being wiped out in 1987 — increased fivefold, all of which makes vaccinations for toddlers urgent, says the Children's Defense Fund.

But the toddlers are not getting them. A major problem is the cost of vaccines, especially for poor families. With only three companies producing them, there is a shortage, which has caused prices to rise. From 1981 to 1991, the price of a single dose of diphtheria, tetanus, and whooping cough vaccine rose from 33 cents to $9.97, according to the Defense Fund.

The cost of a shot of measles, mumps, or German measles vaccine increased from $9.32 to $25.29 over the same period. When the costs of the doctor, clinic visit, and administrative expenses are added, a round of shots can soar to more than $200 a child, strapping even middle-class parents whose insurance doesn't cover it. According to the Defense Fund, 70% of public health centers surveyed in 1991 suffered a shortage of vaccines. Immunization experts say that as a result, clinics set up barriers to keep down the lines.

Vitamins

In today's health-conscious environment, you'd think the vast majority of Americans would take advantage of the new findings about nutrition, particularly the evidence that taking the right vitamins is linked with immunity to various diseases and with longevity. Surprisingly, only about 21% of Americans take vitamins.

According to the National Health Interview Survey in the *American Almanac — 1992-1993*, the following percentages of demographic groups of Americans take vitamins:

Males	31.2%
Females	41.3%
Whites	38.5%
Blacks	21.5%
Hispanics	28.7%

Generally, the most educated and prosperous Americans take the most vitamins. Ironically, they are probably the group needing them least. Undernourished individuals in poor households, the group using vitamins the least, are those most likely to need nutritional supplements. Some 44% of households with incomes of more then $40,000 use vitamins compared to 27% of those with incomes of less than $7,000.

Top-Selling Vitamins: Most Americans who use vitamins prefer the pharmaceutical companies to mix and match the various kinds they take, hence "multivitamins" are the biggest sellers. This table lists the most popular vitamins and their annual sales, according to the Council for Responsible Nutrition.

Multivitamins	$1.2 billion
Vitamin C	$350 million
Vitamin E	$275 million
B Complex	$260 million

Voice of America
Tuning in to America

Since 1942 the world has tuned in. In some places, such as Nazi Germany, Communist Eastern Europe, and remote villages in Asia, the VOA gave listeners the only media accounts of the troubles in their own nation.

Today it is still on the air, bolstered by powerful satellite transmissions. To 100 million listeners around the globe, it is their window on America. A 1993 budget of $355 million to open the portal is allotted by the U.S. Information Agency, under whose auspices VOA operates. Broadcasting in 49 languages, the agency beams its powerful signal primarily to central Asia, the Middle East, Europe, Africa, and Central and South America. The full-time employees number 3,074, 662 of whom are foreign nationals whose language skills create the homey, credible voice that has made the VOA a welcome companion around the world.

Unlike its sister frequency, Radio Free Europe, the VOA is not concerned with official U.S. positions on international matters, so its journalists can express their own political positions. Their goal is primarily to spread American goodwill and cultural understanding. Broadcasts carry both news and tales of life in the U.S. Recent programs featured stories about a 90-year-old woman who celebrated her birthday by skydiving and a New England couple setting out to buy a home. Some broadcasts target younger listeners by airing American pop music. Fully half the programs are English lessons.

The VOA makes a regular practice of changing its priorities as world situations change. In Europe, for example, with communism no longer a threat,

During World War II, the VOA informed millions around the globe.

one of the most popular programs in the new democratic republics is "Democracy in Action," a series that not only gives examples of the Western style of governing but offers advice to potential entrepreneurs about success, Western style. Starting a business is a popular theme.

The last major stronghold of communism, China, is of special interest. Recently the China branch of the VOA has expanded to 12 hours daily, with programs in Mandarin, the most common Chinese dialect. Events in Asia are covered in depth due to the Hong Kong office's having expanded its research branch.

War Dead

Warfare Now 200 Times "Safer"

The odds that American military personnel will die in combat have been reduced two hundred–fold over the last 130 years. In the Civil War (1861–65), 1 in 16 soldiers died; in World War II (1941–45), 1 in 55 died. By the time of the Korean conflict (1950–53), the fatality ratio had dropped to 1 in 170.

The dominant reason for this reduction is the introduction of the helicopter, which made it possible to move the wounded from the battlefields to nearby hospitals quickly. In the Vietnam conflict (1964–73), 1 in 184 who served died, and by the time of Operation Desert Storm, fatalities dropped to 1 in 3,156. The dramatic drop in fatalities in Desert Storm is generally attributed to the limited ground war made possible by the devastating U.S. air strikes before the ground action was begun.

This list represents the number of war dead in U.S. military history, according to the Department of Defense.

World War II	291,557
Civil War*	140,414
World War I	53,402
Vietnam War	47,382
Korea	33,629
Revolutionary War	4,435
War of 1812	2,260
Mexican War	1,733
Spanish-American War	385

This includes only Union casualties; Confederate deaths are estimated at about the same number, although accurate figures were not often kept by the Confederacy.

Though all other wars pale by comparison with America's losses in World War II, our nation lost relatively few military personnel compared to other combatants. The next list represents the approximate number of war dead in the military during all of World War II, according to *World Military and Social Expenditures.*

Soviet Union	7.5 million
Germany	4.75 million
Japan	1.5 million

China	1.35 million
Poland	600,000
United States	291,557
Yugoslavia	400,000
Hungary	400,000
Britain	350,000
Romania	340,000
Austria	280,000
Czechoslovakia	250,000
France	200,000
Italy	150,000
Belgium	110,000
Netherlands	6,000

The figures below, compiled in *World Military and Social Expenditures*, show America's civilian fatalities in World War II compared to those of other nations.

Soviet Union	7.5 million
Poland	6.0 million
Germany	1.47 million
Yugoslavia	1 million
China	800,000
Japan	500,000
Hungary	450,000
France	450,000
Romania	300,000
Netherlands	200,000
Austria	125,000
Britain	100,000
Belgium	90,000

The Vietnam Veterans Memorial preserves the names of the 58,000 members of the armed forces who died in the war. Photo, courtesy the Washington DC Convention and Visitors Bureau.

Italy	70,000
Czechoslovakia	30,000
United States	0

Weekends
What We Live For

Only about half the world breaks on Saturday and Sunday; outside the Western world, the idea has yet to catch on universally.

Henry Ford had a brilliant idea, the weekend. Not so coincidentally, sales of his early cars soared as America took to the road to enjoy two days off every week! Photos, courtesy Henry Ford Museum, Dearborn, Mich.

Henry Ford and the Jews: In 1908, the first five-day work week came to America when a spinning mill in New England arranged its hours to accommodate its Jewish workers, who observed the Sabbath on Saturday. Unionism, which was on the rise in America, had many Jewish leaders, particularly in the garment industries of the manufacturing centers of the North. Hard-goods manufacturers soon followed suit. Ironically, Henry Ford, an alleged anti-Semite and staunch anti-unionist, was the first industrial baron to launch a five-day week, in 1926, when he closed his plants on Saturday. His motives were, however, less than altruistic. At that time the automobile was no less a recreational item than a mode of transportation, and Ford believed the practice would be a boon to the leisure industry.

Ford got his way. America took to the weekend — and to the automobile — with a vengeance. The list below, compiled by the American Automobile Association, reveals how we travel on our weekend jaunts. The average cost of a weekend for a family of two adults and two children is about $200.

Type of Stay	% of Travelers
Hotels	54%
Friends or relatives	22%
Campgrounds	17%
Vacation homes	7%

Below is a selected list of popular weekend pastimes, compiled from sources that include "Sports Poll" (conducted by *Sports Illustrated*), the National Recreation Survey (conducted by the Census Bureau), a Harris poll, and a Gallup poll. (The figures do not add up to 100% because many individuals reported several activities.)

Spectator outings	76%
Visit zoos and fairs	50%
Flower gardening	47%
Driving for pleasure	43%
Photography	35%
Sightseeing	34%
Fishing	34%
Boating	28%
Running/jogging	26%
Camping	24%
Team sports	24%
Tennis	17%
Golfing	13%
Skiing	9%

Whales on the Beach

Most whaling ended in 1986 because of an international agreement aimed at preserving the endangered species. America and Japan are allowed limited catches. In the U.S., catches are permitted only by Inuit

Members of the Coast Guard help Humphrey the whale leave San Francisco Bay. Photo, courtesy U.S. Coast Guard.

and Eskimo tribes, which depend on whales for their survival.

However, a substantial number of whales get "caught" by absolutely natural means. According to the Smithsonian Institution, approximately 600 whales and porpoises were stranded on American shores in 1990, most in the spring, with March being the peak month

The Case of Humphrey: The most famous stranded whale in American history is Humphrey, a humpback whale who refused to leave San Francisco Bay after becoming a celebrity during the summer of 1989. Rather than being beached, Humphrey swam freely for 12 days as far north in the bay as Richmond and south to Palo Alto. It was estimated that over one weekend, Humphrey drew crowds larger than those drawn by the San Francisco Giants and Oakland Athletics. Undaunted by numerous attempts to lead him back into open water, Humphrey eventually received an official escort from the Coast Guard. Though never ashore and still officially a whale without a country, Humphrey is the first alien sea creature known to get a free lunch from the government when the Coast Guard threw Humphrey 1,100 pounds of aromatic mackerel as it led him by his nose to the Pacific.

Millions of whales are swimming freely in the world's oceans, but some whale species, such as the blue whale, are on the edge of extinction. This list represents the estimated populations of various whale species at the beginning of the century and today.

	1900	1993
Sperm	2,500,000	1,950,000
Fin	500,000	140,000
Blue	250,000	500
Sei	250,000	50,000
Humpback	120,000	10,000
Right	100,000	4,000

Want a free horse? The federal government will gladly give you a wild one like one of these, which roam free on public land.

Clearly, whales are endangered; nevertheless, three countries are threatening to defy the ban on whaling: Japan, Norway, and Russia.

Wild Horses
Descendants of Early Europeans

Some wandered from the herd; others were sent out to pasture and never came back. The descendants of the more than 40,000 horses and burros brought to America 500 years ago, primarily by the Spanish, have returned to the wild. In many parts of the West, they live as their ancestors did before they became domesticated in Asia Minor 5,000 years ago.

The Bureau of Land Management maintains an adoption program for these animals and has placed more than 100,000 of them with individuals since the program began. Recently, the BLM has instituted stricter adoption policies to prevent the commercial exploitation of adopted equines.

This list shows the last count in the states where the most horses roam free on public lands, according to the Public Land Statistics, Department of the Interior.

Nevada	30,798
Wyoming	4,115
Oregon	1,891
Utah	1,884
California	1,745
Colorado	605
Idaho	354
Arizona	225
Montana	128

Wild burros in the U.S. are most numerous in Arizona, where they number 2,075; California has 1,333 and Nevada, 1,269.

Wolf Dogs
Family Pets or Killers?

Wolves love their offspring, hunt in packs, are very territorial, and have a long and honorable history, but handling them singly — for example, in a home with children — can have dire results. Dogs that are bred with wolves are no exception. These "wolf dogs," as they are now called, are the latest fad in pets for adventurous animal lovers.

The Case of Mr. Ed: Carol Stegall, an intensive care nurse and air force reserve lieutenant from Chicago, found a strange, wild-looking dog running along a street on Thanksgiving Day, 1991. Thinking he was just another dog, she fed him a hot dog, "and that was okay," she said. "But when I tried to grab his collar, he bit me. It was just a warning. And he did allow me to follow him back to his yard. He opened the latch with his paw. I saw how he was able to escape." She later learned that Mr. Ed, a wolf–Alaskan malamute cross, a man-made hybrid, had spent most of his one-plus years on a chain.

No one knows for sure how many wolf dogs there are in the U.S., but estimates range between 300,000 and 1 million; they sell for between $100 and $6,000. The U.S. Wolf Hybrid Association in Covington, Pa., lists 50,000, which represents twelve generations of the hybrids; however, most wolf dogs do not get registered. Intensely social animals, wolf dogs have two behavioral exceptions: many are almost impossible to housebreak, particularly first-generation crosses, and many are vicious. At least seven children in the U.S. have been killed by wolf dogs.

Most humane societies will not accept a known wolf dog, and with good reason. In 1986, the Humane Society in Washington, D.C., paid a $450,000 settlement to the family of a 4-year-old boy who was killed just hours after a wolf hybrid was placed in a Florida home. Eight states have banned the hybrids, although there is no test to prove whether an animal has any wolf blood. In Illinois, an odd fiction is maintained: they are legal as long as the owner represents them as dogs. Call one a wolf and it's as illegal as a pet lion.

Women and Drug Crimes
More Women Go to Jail

The percentage of women inmates is greater than that of men inmates jailed for drug crimes, according to a study of inmates in 424 of the nation's 3,316 jails, which held 37,383 women; 1 in 3 women were held on drug charges compared with 1 in 4 men. Ten years ago, about 1 in 8 women inmates were held on drug charges.

Overall, drug crimes accounted for almost half of the 137% increase in the number of women jailed during the last decade, according to a Justice Department study. Women who were convicted were almost twice as likely as men to have used serious drugs daily in the month before their offense. About 1 in 4 of the women committed her crime to get money for drugs.

According to the study, in the 1980s women were the fastest-growing segment of the U.S. jail population.

Women Drivers
Fatalities Growing

"We don't know why this is happening and we don't know how to prevent it. We just wanted to raise some warning flags." — *Mike Brownlee, Centers for Disease Control*

The number of women in fatal automobile accidents is on the rise — up almost 30% since 1982, when 10,675 died, compared to 13,693 in 1990. The number of women found to have alcohol in their blood after a crash, however, has decreased, from 2,783 in 1982 to 2,635 in 1990. Even so, Brownlee, an associate administrator for traffic safety programs at the agency, could not confirm reports that more women are driving drunk.

The study also indicated that men are four times more likely than women to be the driver in a fatal automobile accident and that the number of male drivers involved in fatal crashes remains virtually unchanged between 1982 and 1990.

Women in the Military
Army Proving Big Lure

They may still be barred from engaging in direct combat, but in the Gulf War nearly 30,000 women showed that they could fly helicopters, direct artillery fire, drive trucks, and run prisoner-of-war camps.

What branch of service attracts the most females? They are almost equally drawn to the army and the air force, according to Defense Department figures. A total of 83,681 were enlisted in the army in 1992, and 73,341 in the air force. The navy attracted 56,970, while the Marines drew 9,305.

The list below represents the percentages of officers and enlisted personnel in the various branches of the armed services.

	Officers	Enlisted
Air force	13.4%	14.9%
Army	11.8%	11.3%
Navy	10.9%	9.8%
Marines	3.5%	4.8%

Women-owned Businesses
Move Over, Fortune 500

Looking for work? The nation's 5.4 million businesses owned by women are the ones with the most jobs, according to a report by the National Foundation for Women Business Owners.

Today, women-owned businesses have as many employees as the Fortune 500 companies, the mainstay of employment for U.S. workers. Women manage and own 28% of U.S. businesses, according to the foundation, and employ 11.7 million. The Fortune 500 companies, however, lost about a quarter of a million jobs in 1992, while women-owned companies added 350,000, and these trends appear to be continuing.

The report also indicated that 9% of women-owned firms have annual sales of more than $1 million, compared with 14% of all businesses, and more than 40% of their businesses have been established for more than twelve years.

This list shows the breakdown of the various categories of firms owned by women, according to the foundation's report, and compares them to all firms.

	Women-owned	All Firms
Agriculture, mining, construction	6.2%	7.1%
Wholesale	5.4%	5.0%
Transportation, communication, utilities	4.0%	7.1%
Retail	28.0%	18.8%
Professional services	20.4%	17.3%
Manufacturing	11.8%	25.2%
Finance, insurance, real estate	5.6%	9.3%
Business services	18.7%	10.2%

Women in Politics
Gain in State Legislatures

Twenty women have been, or currently are, presidents or prime ministers of their countries — Golda Meir of Israel, Margaret Thatcher of Great Britain, Gro Harlem Brundtland of Norway, and Mary Robinson of Ireland, to name a few. Will an American follow suit in the foreseeable future?

Things are looking up for women in state legislatures across the nation, often the stepping stone to higher office. In 1993, women held 20.2% of the seats in state legislatures, up from 18.4% in 1992, according to the Center for the American Woman and Politics. The increase is the biggest since 1981 and continues the trend of gains made every year since 1969.

Overall, women won 332 state senate seats and 1,171 state house seats, more than 50% of the open seat races, and a dominant number of redistricting races. Some 60% of women state legislators are Democrats, 38.5% are Republicans. Women made the biggest strides in the Western states and the least in the South, where holdouts with the "belle mentality" may think politics is a dirty subject.

This table lists the states with the most and least women legislators by percentage, adapted from the Center for the American Woman and Politics and Rutgers University data.

Most Women

Washington	38.1%
Arizona	35.6%
Colorado	34.0%
New Hampshire	34.0%
Vermont	33.9%
Idaho	31.4%
Maine	31.2%
Kansas	28.5%
Nevada	27.0%
Oregon	26.7%

Fewest Women

Kentucky	4.3%
Alabama	5.7%
Louisiana	6.3%
Oklahoma	9.4%
Arkansas	9.6%
Pennsylvania	9.9%
Mississippi	10.9%
Virginia	11.4%
Tennessee	12.1%
So. Carolina	12.4%

Working Parents

"Flex-time," Their Godsend

For working mothers, it's about time — time for job, time for husband, time for housework, and time for family. Most working moms find the day is too short to accommodate all their responsibilities.

A survey conducted by the Families and Work Institute found that 33% of employees with children worry about the care their child receives while they are working; 25% with children under 12 have child care problems two to three times in three months. Such studies underscore the growing lament of working mothers and have forced an increasing number of companies to create programs to help their workers merge job and family responsibilities.

The solution for many companies is to offer part-time or "flex-time" (flexible hours) for workers — both male and female. In the last ten years, the number of such companies in the U.S. increased from 600 to more than 6,000; among them is Aetna Life & Casualty, in Hartford, Conn., which says it saves $2 million a year through a program benefiting high-performing women for a period of time after they have a child.

Part-time schedules are offered by 87.7% of the companies that have parenting programs, but there are drawbacks for employees who choose them: often they must cover a larger portion of their medical and dental benefits. Flex-time — in which an employee might work the usual number of hours but not adhere to a five-day, 9-to-5 schedule — does not usually have this drawback. Flex-time began to grow in acceptance in the 1980s and is now the fourth most popular program, with 77.1% of the companies that have parenting programs offering it.

This list shows the breakdown by percentage of the various programs offered by companies that have special programs for parents, compiled by the Families and Work Institute.

Part-time	87.7%
Employee assistance	85.6%
Personal days	77.4%
Flexible time	77.1%
Leaves of absence	70.4%
Child care resource and referral	54.6%
Spouse job assistance	51.9%
Dependent care aid plans	49.5%
Job sharing	47.9%
Flexible place	35.1%

Worries Aplenty
What Keeps America Up at Night?

Nuclear disasters, Japanese corporate takeovers, the Russians, high interest rates, AIDS, unemployment?

Today there is a new set of problems on the national agenda of things people worry about, according to a study commissioned by the Kaiser Family Foundation and Commonwealth Edison. The economy led the parade of worries, with 50% of respondents indicating it was their chief nightmare. Health care was second, with 25%; however, a majority said they were satisfied with it and 26%

were dissatisfied, a doubling since 1987.

According to a poll conducted by Louis Harris and Associates, here is what keeps America up at night, or at least what individuals named as the issues most likely to influence their vote just before the 1992 election.

	% named
The economy	50%
Health care	25%
Taxes	11%
Jobs	8%
Education	7%
Foreign policy	5%
Abortion	4%

Wrongful Convictions
Innocents in Prison Abound

Celebrated cases of wrongful conviction for a crime make it appear that such cases are unusual. Not so. "It's endemic," says Dennis Cogan, the cochair of the National Association of Criminal Lawyers for the Convicted Innocent. Cogan has written a study on the issue with Michael Radelet, a sociology professor at the University of Florida.

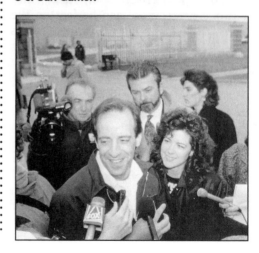

Before and after. Above, David Dowaliby is in prison in Joliet, Ill., serving a 45-year sentence. Below, he shows his jubilation moments after he was released 43 years early. Photographs © J. Carl Ganter.

Scouring newspapers, death penalty literature, libraries, and newsletters, Cogan and Radelet found 420 cases since 1900 in which 23 innocent people were executed. They also reported that since 1970, 46 persons on Death Row were eventually released, having been found innocent. The study said that most of those wrongfully convicted were poor and could not afford a defense attorney; half were black or Hispanic. The authors also concluded that the prisoners were convicted on "shoddy evidence," "unreliable testimony," and even coerced confessions.

The Case of David Dowaliby's Nose: Before an election, politically ambitious prosecutors can be fast on the trigger when it comes to filing charges in a high-profile case. Prosecutor Richard M. Daley, now mayor of Chicago, was no exception. When young Jaclyn Dowaliby disappeared, her parents showed police a broken window they maintained an intruder had smashed. No, said the police; it was Jaclyn's parents, David and Cynthia, who smashed the window — from the *inside*. Soon after, Daley charged the grieving parents with the murder. Several days later, a state forensic analysis proved that the window had, in fact, been broken from the outside, and the centerpiece of the police theory was destroyed, but Daley proceeded with the state's case.

A judge found the evidence against Cynthia insufficient and dropped the case against her, but her husband (who was charged based on the same evidence) had a "new" problem, his prominent nose. A witness claimed to have seen someone with such a nose near the spot where Jaclyn's body was dumped. Though the witness was far away and viewed the scene in the pitch black of the night, Dowaliby was convicted and sentenced to 45 years. The flimsy evidence was reported in a book by David Protess and Rob Warden, *Gone in the Night*. Shortly after its publication the public outcry was intense; Dowaliby was exonerated and released from prison.

American Highs

Below are some of the most encouraging numbers that have been culled from the data on the previous pages.

- In 1945, the average farm's net worth was $12,502. In 1991, it rose to $326,251.

- College enrollments continue to soar among the young, with a record 62% of high school graduates enrolled.

- In 1992, an average 1991 income tax refund check of $1,000 went out to 86 million Americans.

- The average annual profit from small stocks that mutual funds invested in between 1926 and 1992 was 17.6%.

- The federal government reserves 3% of the total U.S. land area for national parks — 354 areas covering about 76 million acres.

- The assets of all U.S. pension funds have increased fourfold in the last decade to total a staggering $2 trillion.

- Average SAT scores among American students have increased for the first time in seven years.

- The total outstanding stock in 1965 was valued at $713 billion; today, the value approaches $5 trillion.

- Deaths on the nation's highways are declining precipitously. In 1992, there were less than 40,000, the lowest in 30 years.

- The odds that American military personnel will die in combat have been reduced two hundredfold in the last 130 years.

- The nation's 5.4 million businesses owned by women employ as many individuals as the Fortune 500 companies.

American Lows

Below are some of the most discouraging numbers that have been culled from the data on the previous pages.

- On U.S. air carriers, 125,000 passengers are annually bumped due to overbooking.

- Nationwide, almost half of the women deserving child support payments do not get their due: 24% receive none, and 23.8% receive only partial payments.

- One third of today's recent college graduates hold jobs that do not require college degrees.

- The courts are overloaded — approximately 100 million cases are on file in the state courts alone, close to one for every household.

- The average young couple earns $19,783 but spends $21,401.

- Among America's 65 million senior citizens, 12% suffer from depression and 3% are considered pathologically depressed.

- If the burden of paying off the national debt were shared equally, each household would have to contribute about $40,000.

- The cost of health care has quadrupled since 1980, whereas the costs of all other goods and services have increased an average of 65%.

- 91% of us lie regularly.

- Since 1986, the average American made virtually no gain in net worth after inflation is factored in; 80% have actually suffered losses in net worth.

- About 36 million Americans are trapped in poverty — 40% are children, 11% are elderly.

- As many as 2 million teenagers carry guns, knives, clubs, or razors.

- The murder rate on television programs has risen 27% since last year — viewers will see one murder every 78 minutes.